I0027878

Anonymus

Agricultural statistics of Ireland 1897

Anonymus

Agricultural statistics of Ireland 1897

ISBN/EAN: 9783742811004

Manufactured in Europe, USA, Canada, Australia, Japa

Cover: Foto ©Suzi / pixelio.de

Manufactured and distributed by brebook publishing software
(www.brebook.com)

Anonymus

Agricultural statistics of Ireland 1897

AGRICULTURAL STATISTICS

OF

IRELAND,

WITH

DETAILED REPORT ON AGRICULTURE,

FOR THE YEAR

1897.

DIVISION OF LAND; ACREAGE UNDER CROPS; NUMBER AND SIZE OF HOLDINGS; NUMBER OF OCCUPIERS OF LAND; WOODS AND PLANTATIONS; RATES OF PRODUCE; NUMBER, AGES, &c., OF LIVE STOCK; NUMBER OF BOARS KEPT FOR BREEDING PURPOSES; DAIRY INDUSTRIES; DISEASES OF ANIMALS; EXPORTS AND IMPORTS OF LIVE STOCK; HONEY PRODUCED; NUMBER OF SCUTCHING MILLS; NUMBER OF CORN MILLS; SILOS AND ENSILAGE; FORESTRY OPERATIONS; WAGES OF AGRICULTURAL LABOURERS; THE WEATHER.

Presented to Parliament by Command of Her Majesty.

DUBLIN:
PRINTED FOR HER MAJESTY'S STATIONERY OFFICE,
BY ALEXANDER THOM & CO. (LIMITED).

And to be purchased, either directly or through any Bookseller, from
Hodges, Figgis, and Co. (Limited), 104, Grafton-street, Dublin; or
Eyre and Spottiswoode, East Harding-street, Fleet-street, E.C., and
32, Abingdon-street, Westminster, S.W.; or
John Menzies and Co., 12, Hanover-street, Edinburgh, and 90, West Nile-street, Glasgow.

1898.

CONTENTS.

DETAILED TABLES.

Tillage, Meadow and Clover, &c.:

Live Stock:

APPENDIX.

AGRICULTURAL STATISTICS OF IRELAND,

FOR THE YEAR 1897.

TO HIS EXCELLENCY GEORGE HENRY, EARL CADOGAN, K.G.,

&c., &c., &c.,

LORD LIEUTENANT-GENERAL AND GENERAL GOVERNOR OF IRELAND.

MAY IT PLEASE YOUR EXCELLENCY,

I have the honour to submit to your Excellency the following Report and detailed Tables concerning Agriculture in Ireland for the year 1897.

A review of the detailed Tables confirms the observations I made when presenting the General Abstracts in August, 1897, and the Produce Returns in February last.

DIVISION OF LAND, TILLAGE, &c.

The acreage under Crops, Grass, Fallow, Woods and Plantations, and Bog, Waste, Water, &c., in 1896 and 1897, was as follows:—

—	1896.	1897.	Increase or Decrease between 1896 and 1897.	
			Increase.	Decrease.
	Acres.	Acres.	Acres.	Acres.
Under Crops, including Meadow and Clover,	4,843,320	4,745,106	—	98,214
" Grass, or Pasture,	10,333,527	10,462,310	128,783	—
" Fallow,	18,283	19,978	1,695	—
" Woods and Plantations,	307,407	307,441	34	—
" Bog, Waste, Water, &c.,*	4,830,910	4,798,612	—	32,298
Total,†	20,333,344	20,333,344	—	—

The area under Crops in 1897, compared with 1896, shows a decrease of 98,214 acres—there being a decrease of 71,932 acres in tillage, of 17,948 acres in the area under hay from permanent pasture or grass not broken up in rotation, and of 8,339 acres in the extent under hay from clover, sainfoin, and grasses under rotation. There is an increase of 128,783 acres in the area under grass not for hay; an increase of 1,695 acres of Fallow land; and of 34 acres under Woods and Plantations; and a decrease of 32,298 acres under Bog, Waste, Water, &c.

Of the 4,798,612 acres given as under "Bog, Waste, Water, &c.," in 1897, 1,147,181 acres were enumerated as "Turf Bog," 430,077 acres as "Marsh," 2,264,130 acres as "Barren Mountain Land," and 957,274 acres as "Water, Roads, Fences, &c." Compared with 1896, "Bog and Marsh" appears to have decreased by 34,160 acres, and "Barren Mountain Land" to have increased by 8,843 acres.

The area and proportionate extent of each crop in 1896 and 1897, with the increase or decrease in the latter year, are given in the following Table (I.), from which it appears that, compared with 1896, there was, last year, a net decrease of 12,940 acres, or 0·9 per cent. in cereals, as an increase of 9,216 acres in wheat was accompanied by a decrease of 18,463 acres in oats, 2,528 acres in barley, 893 acres in bere and rye, and 272 acres in beans and pease.

In green crops there was a net decrease of 32,278 acres, or 2·8 per cent., as potatoes decreased by 28,449 acres, cabbage by 3,601 acres, vetches and rape by 369 acres, and carrots, parsnips, and "other green crops" by 700 acres, while the only increases were 475 acres in turnips and 348 acres in mangel wurzel and beet root.

Flax shows a decrease of 26,716 acres, or 37·0 per cent., and meadow and clover a decrease of 26,288 acres, or 1·2 per cent.

In 1897, 29·7 acres in every 100 under crops were under cereals, 23·5 under green crops, 0·9 under flax, and 45·9 under meadow and clover.

Varieties of Potatoes.

It will be observed from Table 14, page 70, that of the 677,218 acres planted with potatoes, 73·6 per cent. were under "Champions," 7·7 per cent. under Flounders, 4·7 per cent. under Irish Whites, 3·3 per cent. under Magnum Bonums, 2·6 per cent. under Sutton's Abundance, 1·8 per cent. under Skerry Blues, 1·0 per cent. under Beauties of Bute, and 5·7 per cent. under all other varieties. The percentage under Champions, although still very large, has declined gradually during the last six years.

Table 16 points out the best potato-growing districts in Ireland, and the varieties which appear to thrive best in particular counties.

Extent under Crops.

Of the total extent under crops in 1897, 85·0 per cent., or over five-sixths, were under three crops—corn (24·8 per cent.), potatoes (14·3), and meadow and clover (45·9).

(TABLE I.)—The Acreage under Crops in 1896 and 1897, and the Increase or Decrease in the latter year :—

Crops.	1896.	1897.	Increase in 1897.		Decrease in 1897.	
			Extent.	Per Centage.	Extent.	Per Centage.
	Acres.	Acres.	Acres.		Acres.	
Wheat,	38,019	47,335	9,316	24·5	—	—
Oats,	1,193,581	1,175,118	—	—	18,463	1·5
Barley,	173,039	170,504	—	—	2,535	1·5
Bere and Rye,	14,093	13,206	—	—	887	6·3
Beans and Peas,	2,090	1,817	—	—	273	13·1
TOTAL EXTENT under CEREAL CROPS,	1,420,870	1,407,960	—	—	12,910	0·9
Potatoes,	705,366	677,218	—	—	28,148	4·0
Turnips,	308,471	308,964	493	0·2	—	—
Mangel Wurzel and Beet Root,	31,301	31,649	348	1·1	—	—
Cabbage,	44,198	40,597	—	—	3,601	8·1
Vetches and Rape,	10,516	9,546	—	—	970	9·2
Carrots, Parsnips, and other Green Crops,	24,776	24,076	—	—	700	2·8
TOTAL EXTENT under GREEN CROPS,	1,147,723	1,118,437	—	—	29,286	2·6
Flax,	72,253	43,537	—	—	28,716	39·7
TOTAL under TILLAGE,	2,640,796	2,569,864	—	—	71,932	2·7
Meadow and Clover :—						
Clover, Sainfoin, and Grasses under Rotation,	655,071	637,128	—	—	17,943	2·7
Permanent Pasture or Grass not broken up in Rotation,	1,547,165	1,539,014	—	—	8,151	0·5
TOTAL EXTENT under CROPS,	4,843,032	4,745,006	—	—	98,026	2·0

The Proportionate Area under each Crop in 1896 and 1897 :—

Crops.	Proportion per cent. 1896.	Proportion per cent. 1897.	Crops.	Proportion per cent. 1896.	Proportion per cent. 1897.
Wheat,	0·8	1·0	Cabbage,	0·9	0·9
Oats,	24·6	24·8	Vetches and Rape,	0·2	0·2
Barley,	3·6	3·6	Carrots, Parsnips, and other Green Crops,	0·5	0·5
Bere and Rye,	0·3	0·3			
Beans and Peas,	—	—	UNDER GREEN CROPS,	23·7	23·6
UNDER CEREAL CROPS,	29·3	29·7	Flax,	1·5	0·9
Potatoes,	14·5	14·3	Meadow and Clover,	45·3	45·9
Turnips,	6·4	6·5			
Mangel Wurzel and Beet Root,	1·1	1·1	TOTAL,	100·0	100·0

Tables showing the extent of land under crops in 1897 by Counties and Provinces, and by Poor Law Unions, and from 1888 to 1897 by Counties and Provinces, are given at pages 38, 42, and 50, respectively.

The extent of land under grass in 1897 (*exclusive of that under meadow and clover for hay*) was 10,463,310 acres, or 51·3 in every 100 of the entire country: in 1896 the extent was 10,333,327 acres or 50·8 per cent. Of the 10,463,310 acres under grass, not for hay, last year 614,361 were under clover, sainfoin and grasses under rotation, and 9,847,949 under permanent pasture or grass not broken up in rotation. The relative proportions under grass (pasture) in each Province were—in Leinster 56·5 per cent. in 1897, and 55·7 per cent. in 1896; Munster 55·1 per cent. in 1897, and 54·9 per cent. in 1896; Connaught 50·2 per cent. in 1897, and 49·5 per cent. in 1896; and Ulster 44·0 per cent. in 1897, and 42·8 in 1896. Grazing Land, 1896 and 1897.

Thus, in 1897 there was an increase of pasture land in Leinster of 0·8 per cent. of the total area of the province, in Munster of 0·2 per cent., in Connaught of 0·7 per cent., and in Ulster of 1·2 per cent.

Of the counties—Clare, Kilkenny, Limerick, Meath, and Westmeath had each 60 acres or upwards in every 100 of their entire area under grass (pasture) in 1897; Fermanagh, Kildare, Leitrim, Roscommon, Tipperary, and Wexford had above 55 and under 60 acres; Carlow, Cavan, Cork, Dublin, Galway, Longford, Monaghan, Queen's, Sligo, and Waterford, had from 50 to 55 acres; Antrim, Armagh, Down, Kerry, King's, Louth, Mayo, Tyrone, and Wicklow had above 40 and under 50 acres; and Donegal and Londonderry had over 30 and under 40 acres in every 100 acres under grass in 1897. Only 34·0 per cent. of the total area of Donegal was enumerated in 1897 as under grass. Meath shows the highest percentage, 70·9. Grazing Land in 1897.

The area of each County and Province, and the extent and percentage under grass in 1897, are given at page 34.

As already stated, the land under grass (pasture) in 1897 formed a little more than half of the total area (20,333,344 statute acres) of the country. It will be observed from the succeeding Table (Table II.) that the area under grass in 1897 is slightly in excess of the average for the preceding ten years, and also somewhat more than the extent for the year 1896, the proportion of the total area having increased from 50·8 per cent. in 1896, to 51·3 in 1897. Division of land, 1887–1897.

In Cereal Crops a continuous decrease is shown for all the years covered by the Table, except 1888 and 1892, in each of which there was a slight increase as compared with the extent for the year immediately preceding. The average area under cereals in the ten years 1887–96 was 1,500,413 acres, and the extent in 1897 was 1,407,880 acres, being a decline of 92,533 acres or 6·2 per cent.

The average area under Green Crops in the ten years was 1,188,020 acres, and in 1897 the area was 1,115,447 acres, being 72,573 acres or 6·1 per cent. under the average. The extent under Green Crops in 1896 was 1,147,728 acres.

The area under Flax, after having risen from 67,487 acres in 1893 to 101,081 acres in 1894, fell to 95,203 acres in 1895, to 72,253 acres in 1896, and to 46,587 acres in 1897, which extent shows a decrease of 48,041 acres, or 51·3 per cent., as compared with the average for the ten years 1887–96.

There were 2,209,424 acres under Meadow and Clover in 1896, and 2,176,142 acres in 1897; the average extent for the ten years 1887–96 was 2,169,626 acres, the yearly extent varying from 2,059,529 acres in 1891 to 2,231,980 acres in 1886.

The extent of Fallow or uncropped arable land in 1897 was 19,975 acres, being an increase of 1,695 acres as compared with the preceding year, and 2,037 acres over the average extent for the ten years 1887–96.

The area returned under "Bog, Waste, Barren Mountain, Water, &c." in 1897 was 4,798,812 acres, being 32,298 acres less than the corresponding extent for the preceding year, and 69,713 acres below the average for the ten years 1887–96.

Division of Land.

TABLE II.—The Extent of Land in Statute Acres, and the proportional Area, under Cereal Crops, Green Crops, Flax, Meadow and Clover, Grass, Woods and Plantations, Fallow, Bog, Waste, Water, &c., in each Year from 1887 to 1897, with averages for the ten years, 1887-96; also the Number of Holdings exceeding 1 acre.

Years.	Number of Holdings exceeding 1 Acre.	Cereal Crops.	Green Crops.	Flax.	Meadow and Clover.	Grass (Pasture).	All Land in use for Agriculture.	Woods and Plantations.	Fallow.	Bog, Waste, Marsh, Water, Roads, &c.
		Acres.	Acres.	Acres.	Acres.	Acres.	Acres.	Acres.	Acres.	Acres.
1887,	[illegible]	[illegible]	[illegible]	[illegible]	[illegible]	[illegible]	[illegible]	[illegible]	[illegible]	[illegible]
1888,	[illegible]	[illegible]	[illegible]	[illegible]	[illegible]	[illegible]	[illegible]	[illegible]	[illegible]	[illegible]
1889,	[illegible]	[illegible]	[illegible]	[illegible]	[illegible]	[illegible]	[illegible]	[illegible]	[illegible]	[illegible]
1890,	[illegible]	[illegible]	[illegible]	[illegible]	[illegible]	[illegible]	[illegible]	[illegible]	[illegible]	[illegible]
1891,	[illegible]	[illegible]	[illegible]	[illegible]	[illegible]	[illegible]	[illegible]	[illegible]	[illegible]	[illegible]
1892,	[illegible]	[illegible]	[illegible]	[illegible]	[illegible]	[illegible]	[illegible]	[illegible]	[illegible]	[illegible]
1893,	[illegible]	[illegible]	[illegible]	[illegible]	[illegible]	[illegible]	[illegible]	[illegible]	[illegible]	[illegible]
1894,	[illegible]	[illegible]	[illegible]	[illegible]	[illegible]	[illegible]	[illegible]	[illegible]	[illegible]	[illegible]
1895,	[illegible]	[illegible]	[illegible]	[illegible]	[illegible]	[illegible]	[illegible]	[illegible]	[illegible]	[illegible]
1896,	[illegible]	[illegible]	[illegible]	[illegible]	[illegible]	[illegible]	[illegible]	[illegible]	[illegible]	[illegible]
Average 1887-96,	515,611	1,380,418	[illegible]	[illegible]	[illegible]	10,188,679	[illegible]	[illegible]	17,066	[illegible]
1897,	[illegible]	[illegible]	[illegible]	[illegible]	2,178,169	[illegible]	[illegible]	[illegible]	[illegible]	[illegible]

Years.	—	Cereal Crops.	Green Crops.	Flax.	Meadow and Clover.	Grass (Pasture).	All Land in use for Agriculture.	Woods and Plantations.	Fallow.	Bog, Waste, Marsh, Water, Roads, &c.
		Percentage per Cent. of Total Area.								
1887,	-	7·7	[illegible]	[illegible]	[illegible]	[illegible]	[illegible]	1·6	0·1	[illegible]
1888,	-	7·7	[illegible]	[illegible]	[illegible]	[illegible]	[illegible]	[illegible]	0·1	[illegible]
1889,	-	7·6	[illegible]	[illegible]	[illegible]	[illegible]	[illegible]	[illegible]	[illegible]	[illegible]
1890,	-	7·4	[illegible]	[illegible]	[illegible]	[illegible]	[illegible]	[illegible]	0·1	[illegible]
1891,	-	[illegible]	[illegible]	[illegible]	[illegible]	[illegible]	[illegible]	[illegible]	[illegible]	[illegible]
1892,	-	7·6	[illegible]	[illegible]	[illegible]	[illegible]	[illegible]	[illegible]	0·1	[illegible]
1893,	-	[illegible]	[illegible]	[illegible]	[illegible]	[illegible]	[illegible]	[illegible]	0·1	[illegible]
1894,	-	[illegible]	[illegible]	[illegible]	[illegible]	[illegible]	[illegible]	[illegible]	0·1	[illegible]
1895,	-	[illegible]	[illegible]	[illegible]	[illegible]	[illegible]	[illegible]	[illegible]	0·1	[illegible]
1896,	-	[illegible]	[illegible]	[illegible]	[illegible]	[illegible]	[illegible]	[illegible]	0·1	[illegible]
Average 1887-96,	-	[illegible]	[illegible]	[illegible]	[illegible]	[illegible]	[illegible]	[illegible]	[illegible]	[illegible]
1897,	-	[illegible]	[illegible]	[illegible]	[illegible]	[illegible]	[illegible]	[illegible]	0·1	[illegible]

Turf Bog.

Tables showing the extent and the proportionate area under Crops, Grass, Fallow, Woods and Plantations, Turf Bog, Marsh, Barren Mountain Land, and Water, Roads, Fences, &c., in 1897, by counties and provinces, will be found at page 24. From these it appears that there are three counties with upwards of 100,000 acres under "Turf Bog," viz.:—Mayo, with 214,585 acres, or 16·2 per cent. of its entire area; Galway, 146,890 acres, or 9·6 per cent.; and Donegal, 120,043 acres, or 10·1 per cent. No "Turf Bog" is returned for Dublin, and of the other counties the following are those having the smallest areas under that heading, viz.:—Carlow, 737 acres, or 0·3 per cent. of its entire area; Louth, 782 acres, or 0·4 per cent.; Wexford, 1,321 acres, or 0·2 per cent.; Down, 1,771 acres, or 0·3 per cent.; Waterford, 2,510 acres, or 0·5 per cent.; Kilkenny, 2,723 acres, or 0·5 per cent.; and Wicklow, 3,904 acres, or 0·8 per cent. In the province of Connaught, 484,042 acres, being 11·4 per cent. of its entire area, are returned as under "Turf Bog," including 69,685 acres, or 11·9 per cent. of the County of Roscommon, in addition to the large extent in Mayo and Galway as mentioned above.

Marsh.

In Mayo, 66,011 acres, or 5·1 per cent. of the area of the county are under Marsh; in Cork, 65,950 acres, or 3·6 per cent.; in Galway, 55,090 acres, or 3·6 per cent.; in Kerry, 42,354 acres, or 3·6 per cent., and in Donegal, 38,558 acres, or 3·2 per cent. The counties with the smallest area under "Marsh" are, Dublin with 505 acres, or 0·2 per cent. of its entire area; Louth, 1,611 acres, or 0·8 per cent.; Monaghan, 1,940 acres, or 0·6 per cent.; Fermanagh, 1,998 acres, or 0·5 per cent.; and Meath, 2,019 acres, or 0·4 per cent.

The following statement shows in a concise manner the extent of Meadow and Clover and Pasture, respectively, in Ireland during the 11 years, 1887–97, and the average extents for the 10 years, 1887–96:— Meadow and Clover and Pasture.

Year.	Meadow and Clover.	Pasture.	Total Grass Land.
	Acres.	Acres.	Acres.
1887, . . .	2,143,818	10,049,507	12,193,325
1888, . . .	2,221,980	9,935,097	12,157,077
1889, . . .	2,167,522	9,978,797	12,146,319
1890, . . .	2,093,634	10,212,256	12,305,890
1891, . . .	2,049,519	10,516,664	12,566,183
1892, . . .	2,142,810	10,253,824	12,396,634
1893, . . .	2,157,113	10,321,107	12,479,380
1894, . . .	2,180,598	10,214,096	12,394,694
1895, . . .	2,194,476	10,280,424	12,474,900
1896, . . .	2,205,524	10,329,327	12,534,851
Average, 1887–96, . .	2,159,626	10,186,679	12,346,305
1897, . . .	2,176,142	10,462,310	12,638,452

It will be observed that the total area of grass lands has increased from 12,193,325 acres in 1887 to 12,638,452 acres in 1897, being an increase of 445,127 acres or 3·7 per cent. However, it will be seen farther on in this Report that cattle and sheep, although not as numerous as in some of the intervening years, have increased since 1887 in a much greater ratio than the pasture lands, showing that the latter are more

NUMBER OF HOLDINGS AND NUMBER OF OCCUPIERS.

According to the returns for 1897, the number of separate holdings was 576,975, being 1,311 more than in the previous year. The holdings which *decreased* in number were—those "above 1 and not exceeding 5 acres" by 191; those "above 5 and not exceeding 15 acres" by 262; and those "above 200 and not exceeding 500 acres" by 52. The holdings which *increased* in number were those not exceeding 1 acre by 1,882; those "above 15 and not exceeding 30 acres" by 97; those "above 30 and not exceeding 50 acres" by 76; those "above 50 and not exceeding 100 acres" by 211; those "above 100 and not exceeding 200 acres" by 44, and those "above 500 acres" by 13.

Size of Holdings.	Number in 1896.	Number in 1897.	Increase or Decrease in 1897.	
			Increase.	Decrease.
Not exceeding 1 Acre,	60,[illegible]7	62,159	1,882	–
Above 1 and not exceeding 5 Acres,	65,221	65,030	–	191
" 5 " 15 "	164,253	163,[illegible]61	–	262
" 15 " 30 "	133,311	133,308	97	–
" 30 " 50 "	74,005	74,081	76	–
" 50 " 100 "	57,243	57,451	211	–
" 100 " 200 "	22,967	23,011	44	–
" 200 " 500 "	8,397	8,345	–	52
Above 500 Acres,	1,350	1,363	13	–
Total,	575,664	576,975	1,311	–

A table showing the number of holdings, by classes, for each Poor Law Union, in 1897, will be found on pp. 35 and 36.

The number of separate holdings in each county and province, in 1896 and 1897, is given by classes in Table III. on the opposite page.

As in many instances landholders occupy more than one farm, and as, in other cases, farms extend into two or more townlands—*the portion in each townland being enumerated and classified as a separate holding*—it has been considered desirable, with the view of ascertaining the number of *Occupiers*, and of classifying them according to the total extent of land held by each, to obtain a Return of the number of persons having more than one farm or holding. Each Enumerator is, therefore, required to furnish the name of every landholder residing in his district who has two or more farms, or whose farm extends into two or more townlands, together with the area of each portion, and the locality in which it is situated. The number of actual occupiers in 1897 thus arrived at is given in Table IV., page 12, by counties and provinces. On comparing the results in this Table with the figures given in Table III., it appears that in 1897 there were 576,975 holdings in the hands of 533,514 occupiers.

The number of separate holdings and the number of occupiers in each Province in 1896 and 1897, respectively, were :—

Provinces.	Number of Separate Holdings.		Number of Occupiers.	
	1896.	1897.	1896.	1897.
Leinster,	134,384	133,318	111,[illegible]	112,7[illegible]
Munster,	129,885	124,910	117,170	117,175
Ulster,	200,045	200,0[illegible]	1[illegible],257	157,963
Connaught,	112,649	112,691	116,650	115,684
Total,	575,664	576,975	533,048	533,514

Number and size of Holdings, 1896 and 1897.

TABLE III.—The number of Holdings, by classes, for each County and Province, in 1896 and 1897, and the increase or decrease in the latter year:—

Counties	Year	Not exceeding 1 acre*	Above 1	Above 5	Above 15	Above 30	Above 50	Above 100	Above 200	Above 500	Total
Antrim,	1896	[illegible]	[illegible]	[illegible]	[illegible]	[illegible]	[illegible]	[illegible]	[illegible]	[illegible]	[illegible]
	1897	[illegible]	[illegible]	[illegible]	[illegible]	[illegible]	[illegible]	[illegible]	[illegible]	[illegible]	[illegible]
Armagh,	1896	[illegible]	[illegible]	[illegible]	[illegible]	[illegible]	[illegible]	[illegible]	[illegible]	[illegible]	[illegible]
	1897	[illegible]	[illegible]	[illegible]	[illegible]	[illegible]	[illegible]	[illegible]	[illegible]	[illegible]	[illegible]
Carlow,	1896	[illegible]	[illegible]	[illegible]	[illegible]	[illegible]	[illegible]	[illegible]	[illegible]	[illegible]	[illegible]
	1897	[illegible]	[illegible]	[illegible]	[illegible]	[illegible]	[illegible]	[illegible]	[illegible]	[illegible]	[illegible]
Cavan,	1896	[illegible]	[illegible]	[illegible]	[illegible]	[illegible]	[illegible]	[illegible]	[illegible]	[illegible]	[illegible]
	1897	[illegible]	[illegible]	[illegible]	[illegible]	[illegible]	[illegible]	[illegible]	[illegible]	[illegible]	[illegible]
Clare,	1896	[illegible]	[illegible]	[illegible]	[illegible]	[illegible]	[illegible]	[illegible]	[illegible]	[illegible]	[illegible]
	1897	[illegible]	[illegible]	[illegible]	[illegible]	[illegible]	[illegible]	[illegible]	[illegible]	[illegible]	[illegible]
Cork,	1896	[illegible]	[illegible]	[illegible]	[illegible]	[illegible]	[illegible]	[illegible]	[illegible]	[illegible]	[illegible]
	1897	[illegible]	[illegible]	[illegible]	[illegible]	[illegible]	[illegible]	[illegible]	[illegible]	[illegible]	[illegible]
Donegal,	1896	[illegible]	[illegible]	[illegible]	[illegible]	[illegible]	[illegible]	[illegible]	[illegible]	[illegible]	[illegible]
	1897	[illegible]	[illegible]	[illegible]	[illegible]	[illegible]	[illegible]	[illegible]	[illegible]	[illegible]	[illegible]
Down,	1896	[illegible]	[illegible]	[illegible]	[illegible]	[illegible]	[illegible]	[illegible]	[illegible]	[illegible]	[illegible]
	1897	[illegible]	[illegible]	[illegible]	[illegible]	[illegible]	[illegible]	[illegible]	[illegible]	[illegible]	[illegible]
Dublin,	1896	[illegible]	[illegible]	[illegible]	[illegible]	[illegible]	[illegible]	[illegible]	[illegible]	[illegible]	[illegible]
	1897	[illegible]	[illegible]	[illegible]	[illegible]	[illegible]	[illegible]	[illegible]	[illegible]	[illegible]	[illegible]
Fermanagh,	1896	[illegible]	[illegible]	[illegible]	[illegible]	[illegible]	[illegible]	[illegible]	[illegible]	[illegible]	[illegible]
	1897	[illegible]	[illegible]	[illegible]	[illegible]	[illegible]	[illegible]	[illegible]	[illegible]	[illegible]	[illegible]
Galway,	1896	[illegible]	[illegible]	[illegible]	[illegible]	[illegible]	[illegible]	[illegible]	[illegible]	[illegible]	[illegible]
	1897	[illegible]	[illegible]	[illegible]	[illegible]	[illegible]	[illegible]	[illegible]	[illegible]	[illegible]	[illegible]
Kerry,	1896	[illegible]	[illegible]	[illegible]	[illegible]	[illegible]	[illegible]	[illegible]	[illegible]	[illegible]	[illegible]
	1897	[illegible]	[illegible]	[illegible]	[illegible]	[illegible]	[illegible]	[illegible]	[illegible]	[illegible]	[illegible]
Kildare,	1896	[illegible]	[illegible]	[illegible]	[illegible]	[illegible]	[illegible]	[illegible]	[illegible]	[illegible]	[illegible]
	1897	[illegible]	[illegible]	[illegible]	[illegible]	[illegible]	[illegible]	[illegible]	[illegible]	[illegible]	[illegible]
Kilkenny,	1896	[illegible]	[illegible]	[illegible]	[illegible]	[illegible]	[illegible]	[illegible]	[illegible]	[illegible]	[illegible]
	1897	[illegible]	[illegible]	[illegible]	[illegible]	[illegible]	[illegible]	[illegible]	[illegible]	[illegible]	[illegible]
King's,	1896	[illegible]	[illegible]	[illegible]	[illegible]	[illegible]	[illegible]	[illegible]	[illegible]	[illegible]	[illegible]
	1897	[illegible]	[illegible]	[illegible]	[illegible]	[illegible]	[illegible]	[illegible]	[illegible]	[illegible]	[illegible]
Leitrim,	1896	[illegible]	[illegible]	[illegible]	[illegible]	[illegible]	[illegible]	[illegible]	[illegible]	[illegible]	[illegible]
	1897	[illegible]	[illegible]	[illegible]	[illegible]	[illegible]	[illegible]	[illegible]	[illegible]	[illegible]	[illegible]
Limerick,	1896	[illegible]	[illegible]	[illegible]	[illegible]	[illegible]	[illegible]	[illegible]	[illegible]	[illegible]	[illegible]
	1897	[illegible]	[illegible]	[illegible]	[illegible]	[illegible]	[illegible]	[illegible]	[illegible]	[illegible]	[illegible]
Londonderry,	1896	[illegible]	[illegible]	[illegible]	[illegible]	[illegible]	[illegible]	[illegible]	[illegible]	[illegible]	[illegible]
	1897	[illegible]	[illegible]	[illegible]	[illegible]	[illegible]	[illegible]	[illegible]	[illegible]	[illegible]	[illegible]
Longford,	1896	[illegible]	[illegible]	[illegible]	[illegible]	[illegible]	[illegible]	[illegible]	[illegible]	[illegible]	[illegible]
	1897	[illegible]	[illegible]	[illegible]	[illegible]	[illegible]	[illegible]	[illegible]	[illegible]	[illegible]	[illegible]
Louth & Drogheda Co. of Town,	1896	[illegible]	[illegible]	[illegible]	[illegible]	[illegible]	[illegible]	[illegible]	[illegible]	[illegible]	[illegible]
	1897	[illegible]	[illegible]	[illegible]	[illegible]	[illegible]	[illegible]	[illegible]	[illegible]	[illegible]	[illegible]
Mayo,	1896	[illegible]	[illegible]	[illegible]	[illegible]	[illegible]	[illegible]	[illegible]	[illegible]	[illegible]	[illegible]
	1897	[illegible]	[illegible]	[illegible]	[illegible]	[illegible]	[illegible]	[illegible]	[illegible]	[illegible]	[illegible]
Meath,	1896	[illegible]	[illegible]	[illegible]	[illegible]	[illegible]	[illegible]	[illegible]	[illegible]	[illegible]	[illegible]
	1897	[illegible]	[illegible]	[illegible]	[illegible]	[illegible]	[illegible]	[illegible]	[illegible]	[illegible]	[illegible]
Monaghan,	1896	[illegible]	[illegible]	[illegible]	[illegible]	[illegible]	[illegible]	[illegible]	[illegible]	[illegible]	[illegible]
	1897	[illegible]	[illegible]	[illegible]	[illegible]	[illegible]	[illegible]	[illegible]	[illegible]	[illegible]	[illegible]
Queen's,	1896	[illegible]	[illegible]	[illegible]	[illegible]	[illegible]	[illegible]	[illegible]	[illegible]	[illegible]	[illegible]
	1897	[illegible]	[illegible]	[illegible]	[illegible]	[illegible]	[illegible]	[illegible]	[illegible]	[illegible]	[illegible]
Roscommon,	1896	[illegible]	[illegible]	[illegible]	[illegible]	[illegible]	[illegible]	[illegible]	[illegible]	[illegible]	[illegible]
	1897	[illegible]	[illegible]	[illegible]	[illegible]	[illegible]	[illegible]	[illegible]	[illegible]	[illegible]	[illegible]
Sligo,	1896	[illegible]	[illegible]	[illegible]	[illegible]	[illegible]	[illegible]	[illegible]	[illegible]	[illegible]	[illegible]
	1897	[illegible]	[illegible]	[illegible]	[illegible]	[illegible]	[illegible]	[illegible]	[illegible]	[illegible]	[illegible]
Tipperary,	1896	[illegible]	[illegible]	[illegible]	[illegible]	[illegible]	[illegible]	[illegible]	[illegible]	[illegible]	[illegible]
	1897	[illegible]	[illegible]	[illegible]	[illegible]	[illegible]	[illegible]	[illegible]	[illegible]	[illegible]	[illegible]
Tyrone,	1896	[illegible]	[illegible]	[illegible]	[illegible]	[illegible]	[illegible]	[illegible]	[illegible]	[illegible]	[illegible]
	1897	[illegible]	[illegible]	[illegible]	[illegible]	[illegible]	[illegible]	[illegible]	[illegible]	[illegible]	[illegible]
Waterford,	1896	[illegible]	[illegible]	[illegible]	[illegible]	[illegible]	[illegible]	[illegible]	[illegible]	[illegible]	[illegible]
	1897	[illegible]	[illegible]	[illegible]	[illegible]	[illegible]	[illegible]	[illegible]	[illegible]	[illegible]	[illegible]
Westmeath,	1896	[illegible]	[illegible]	[illegible]	[illegible]	[illegible]	[illegible]	[illegible]	[illegible]	[illegible]	[illegible]
	1897	[illegible]	[illegible]	[illegible]	[illegible]	[illegible]	[illegible]	[illegible]	[illegible]	[illegible]	[illegible]
Wexford,	1896	[illegible]	[illegible]	[illegible]	[illegible]	[illegible]	[illegible]	[illegible]	[illegible]	[illegible]	[illegible]
	1897	[illegible]	[illegible]	[illegible]	[illegible]	[illegible]	[illegible]	[illegible]	[illegible]	[illegible]	[illegible]
Wicklow,	1896	[illegible]	[illegible]	[illegible]	[illegible]	[illegible]	[illegible]	[illegible]	[illegible]	[illegible]	[illegible]
	1897	[illegible]	[illegible]	[illegible]	[illegible]	[illegible]	[illegible]	[illegible]	[illegible]	[illegible]	[illegible]

SUMMARY OF IRELAND.

Provinces	Year										
Leinster,	1896	[illegible]	[illegible]	[illegible]	[illegible]	[illegible]	[illegible]	[illegible]	[illegible]	[illegible]	[illegible]
	1897	[illegible]	[illegible]	[illegible]	[illegible]	[illegible]	[illegible]	[illegible]	[illegible]	[illegible]	[illegible]
Munster,	1896	[illegible]	[illegible]	[illegible]	[illegible]	[illegible]	[illegible]	[illegible]	[illegible]	[illegible]	[illegible]
	1897	[illegible]	[illegible]	[illegible]	[illegible]	[illegible]	[illegible]	[illegible]	[illegible]	[illegible]	[illegible]
Ulster,	1896	[illegible]	[illegible]	[illegible]	[illegible]	[illegible]	[illegible]	[illegible]	[illegible]	[illegible]	[illegible]
	1897	[illegible]	[illegible]	[illegible]	[illegible]	[illegible]	[illegible]	[illegible]	[illegible]	[illegible]	[illegible]
Connaught,	1896	[illegible]	[illegible]	[illegible]	[illegible]	[illegible]	[illegible]	[illegible]	[illegible]	[illegible]	[illegible]
	1897	[illegible]	[illegible]	[illegible]	[illegible]	[illegible]	[illegible]	[illegible]	[illegible]	[illegible]	[illegible]
Total of Ireland,	1896	[illegible]	[illegible]	[illegible]	[illegible]	[illegible]	[illegible]	[illegible]	[illegible]	[illegible]	[illegible]
	1897	[illegible]	[illegible]	[illegible]	[illegible]	[illegible]	[illegible]	[illegible]	[illegible]	[illegible]	[illegible]
Increase or Decrease in 1897,		Increase. [illegible]	Decrease. [illegible]	Decrease. [illegible]	Increase. [illegible]	Increase. [illegible]	Increase. [illegible]	Increase. [illegible]	Decrease. [illegible]	Increase. [illegible]	Increase. [illegible]

* [illegible]

Number of Occupiers in each County and Province in 1897.

TABLE IV.—Return of the number of Occupiers resident in each County and Province in 1897, classified according to the *total extent* of land held, without reference to the Townland, Poor Law Union, County, or Province in which the portions of land are situated:—

Counties.	Number of Occupiers holding Land									
	Not exceeding 1 Acre.	Above 1 and not exceeding 5 Acres.	Above 5 and not exceeding 15 Acres.	Above 15 and not exceeding 30 Acres.	Above 30 and not exceeding 50 Acres.	Above 50 and not exceeding 100 Acres.	Above 100 and not exceeding 200 Acres.	Above 200 and not exceeding 500 Acres.	Above 500 Acres.	Total.
Antrim,	[illegible]	[illegible]	[illegible]	[illegible]	[illegible]	[illegible]	[illegible]	[illegible]	[illegible]	[illegible]
Armagh,	[illegible]	[illegible]	[illegible]	[illegible]	[illegible]	[illegible]	[illegible]	[illegible]	[illegible]	[illegible]
Carlow,	[illegible]	[illegible]	[illegible]	[illegible]	[illegible]	[illegible]	[illegible]	[illegible]	[illegible]	[illegible]
Cavan,	[illegible]	[illegible]	[illegible]	[illegible]	[illegible]	[illegible]	[illegible]	[illegible]	[illegible]	[illegible]
Clare,	[illegible]	[illegible]	[illegible]	[illegible]	[illegible]	[illegible]	[illegible]	[illegible]	[illegible]	[illegible]
Cork,	[illegible]	[illegible]	[illegible]	[illegible]	[illegible]	[illegible]	[illegible]	[illegible]	[illegible]	[illegible]
Donegal,	[illegible]	[illegible]	[illegible]	[illegible]	[illegible]	[illegible]	[illegible]	[illegible]	[illegible]	[illegible]
Down,	[illegible]	[illegible]	[illegible]	[illegible]	[illegible]	[illegible]	[illegible]	[illegible]	[illegible]	[illegible]
Dublin,	[illegible]	[illegible]	[illegible]	[illegible]	[illegible]	[illegible]	[illegible]	[illegible]	[illegible]	[illegible]
Fermanagh,	[illegible]	[illegible]	[illegible]	[illegible]	[illegible]	[illegible]	[illegible]	[illegible]	[illegible]	[illegible]
Galway,	[illegible]	[illegible]	[illegible]	[illegible]	[illegible]	[illegible]	[illegible]	[illegible]	[illegible]	[illegible]
Kerry,	[illegible]	[illegible]	[illegible]	[illegible]	[illegible]	[illegible]	[illegible]	[illegible]	[illegible]	[illegible]
Kildare,	[illegible]	[illegible]	[illegible]	[illegible]	[illegible]	[illegible]	[illegible]	[illegible]	[illegible]	[illegible]
Kilkenny,	[illegible]	[illegible]	[illegible]	[illegible]	[illegible]	[illegible]	[illegible]	[illegible]	[illegible]	[illegible]
King's,	[illegible]	[illegible]	[illegible]	[illegible]	[illegible]	[illegible]	[illegible]	[illegible]	[illegible]	[illegible]
Leitrim,	[illegible]	[illegible]	[illegible]	[illegible]	[illegible]	[illegible]	[illegible]	[illegible]	[illegible]	[illegible]
Limerick,	[illegible]	[illegible]	[illegible]	[illegible]	[illegible]	[illegible]	[illegible]	[illegible]	[illegible]	[illegible]
Londonderry,	[illegible]	[illegible]	[illegible]	[illegible]	[illegible]	[illegible]	[illegible]	[illegible]	[illegible]	[illegible]
Longford,	[illegible]	[illegible]	[illegible]	[illegible]	[illegible]	[illegible]	[illegible]	[illegible]	[illegible]	[illegible]
Louth and Drogheda, Co. of Town,	[illegible]	[illegible]	[illegible]	[illegible]	[illegible]	[illegible]	[illegible]	[illegible]	[illegible]	[illegible]
Mayo,	[illegible]	[illegible]	[illegible]	[illegible]	[illegible]	[illegible]	[illegible]	[illegible]	[illegible]	[illegible]
Meath,	[illegible]	[illegible]	[illegible]	[illegible]	[illegible]	[illegible]	[illegible]	[illegible]	[illegible]	[illegible]
Monaghan,	[illegible]	[illegible]	[illegible]	[illegible]	[illegible]	[illegible]	[illegible]	[illegible]	[illegible]	[illegible]
Queen's,	[illegible]	[illegible]	[illegible]	[illegible]	[illegible]	[illegible]	[illegible]	[illegible]	[illegible]	[illegible]
Roscommon,	[illegible]	[illegible]	[illegible]	[illegible]	[illegible]	[illegible]	[illegible]	[illegible]	[illegible]	[illegible]
Sligo,	[illegible]	[illegible]	[illegible]	[illegible]	[illegible]	[illegible]	[illegible]	[illegible]	[illegible]	[illegible]
Tipperary,	[illegible]	[illegible]	[illegible]	[illegible]	[illegible]	[illegible]	[illegible]	[illegible]	[illegible]	[illegible]
Tyrone,	[illegible]	[illegible]	[illegible]	[illegible]	[illegible]	[illegible]	[illegible]	[illegible]	[illegible]	[illegible]
Waterford,	[illegible]	[illegible]	[illegible]	[illegible]	[illegible]	[illegible]	[illegible]	[illegible]	[illegible]	[illegible]
Westmeath,	[illegible]	[illegible]	[illegible]	[illegible]	[illegible]	[illegible]	[illegible]	[illegible]	[illegible]	[illegible]
Wexford,	[illegible]	[illegible]	[illegible]	[illegible]	[illegible]	[illegible]	[illegible]	[illegible]	[illegible]	[illegible]
Wicklow,	[illegible]	[illegible]	[illegible]	[illegible]	[illegible]	[illegible]	[illegible]	[illegible]	[illegible]	[illegible]
SUMMARY OF IRELAND.										
Provinces.										
Leinster,	[illegible]	[illegible]	[illegible]	[illegible]	[illegible]	[illegible]	[illegible]	[illegible]	[illegible]	[illegible]
Munster,	[illegible]	[illegible]	[illegible]	[illegible]	[illegible]	[illegible]	[illegible]	[illegible]	[illegible]	[illegible]
Ulster,	[illegible]	[illegible]	[illegible]	[illegible]	[illegible]	[illegible]	[illegible]	[illegible]	[illegible]	[illegible]
Connaught,	[illegible]	[illegible]	[illegible]	[illegible]	[illegible]	[illegible]	[illegible]	[illegible]	[illegible]	[illegible]
Total of Ireland,	[illegible]	[illegible]	[illegible]	[illegible]	[illegible]	[illegible]	[illegible]	[illegible]	[illegible]	[illegible]

Number of Occupiers of Land, 1891 to 1897.

The following statement shows the number of occupiers of land in each year from 1891 to 1897, by Provinces:—

Provinces.	Number of Occupiers in the Year						
	1891.	1892.	1893.	1894.	1895.	1896.	1897.
Leinster,	109,860	108,475	109,916	110,163	111,573	111,856	112,723
Munster,	116,383	114,306	115,160	116,094	116,786	117,170	117,173
Ulster,	168,125	159,020	167,616	168,308	167,947	168,357	167,983
Connaught,	111,037	115,374	114,633	115,684	115,576	116,080	115,664
IRELAND,	505,610	503,370	507,384	510,134	531,673	533,043	533,916

Increase or decrease in Holdings by Classes between 1841 and 1897.

As will be seen from Table V. on the opposite page, the number of holdings "above 1 and not exceeding 5 acres" diminished greatly between 1841 and 1897. In Leinster the decrease was 64·8 per cent.; in Munster 80·6; in Ulster 79·8; in Connaught 87·5; and in all Ireland 80·0 per cent.

In the same period holdings "above 5 and not exceeding 15 acres" also diminished in number; the decrease in all Ireland was 38·7 per cent.; it was—in Leinster 44·8 per cent.; in

Holdings "above 30 acres" increased 118·9 per cent. in Leinster; 343·5 in Munster; 361·0 in Ulster; 439·0 in Connaught; and 238·1 per cent. in all Ireland.

The total number of holdings "above 1 acre" decreased between 1841 and 1897 by 22·6 per cent. in Leinster; 32·0 per cent. in Munster; 23·9 in Ulster; and 25·8 in Connaught.

The total number of holdings in Ireland "above 1 acre" was 691,202 in 1841; 570,338 in 1851; 568,484 in 1861; 544,143 in 1871; 526,746 in 1881; 517,012 in 1891; and 514,786 in 1897, showing a decrease of 176,416 or 25·5 per cent. in the period between 1841 and 1897.

TABLE V.—The number of Holdings above 1 acre in each Province in 1841, 1851, 1861, 1871, 1881, 1891, and 1897, according to the classification used by the Census Commissioners of 1841 (in which "above 30 acres" was the maximum): the increase or decrease in the numbers in each class, and the difference per cent., between 1841 and 1897 :— Number of Holdings in 1841, 1851, 1861, 1871, 1881, 1891, and 1897.

Size of Holdings.		Leinster.	Munster.	Ulster.	Connaught.	Total.
		Number.	Number.	Number.	Number.	Number.
Above 1 and not exceeding 5 Acres,	1841,	50,110	57,587	102,379	100,254	310,436
	1851,	15,711	16,800	39,709	15,863	88,083
	1861,	13,845	13,136	38,438	19,437	85,469
	1871,	11,489	12,799	34,837	10,854	74,809
	1881,	15,804	11,096	31,971	18,200	67,071
	1891,	12,034	11,307	31,837	18,934	63,464
	1897,	17,638	11,349	30,404	18,539	62,039
		Decrease.	Decrease.	Decrease.	Decrease.	Decrease.
Decrease in number between 1841 and 1897,		32,472	46,608	61,611	87,715	248,404
Rate per cent.,		64·6	80·4	79·6	87·5	80·0
Above 5 and not exceeding 15 Acres,	1841,	46,039	61,722	99,833	43,405	252,799
	1851,	33,056	51,346	63,174	49,356	191,854
	1861,	29,916	31,580	82,463	50,404	183,931
	1871,	27,378	20,409	73,647	50,051	171,383
	1881,	26,045	19,767	66,568	48,888	164,046
	1891,	25,651	19,264	64,140	46,760	155,667
	1897,	25,411	18,153	62,694	44,697	152,044
		Decrease.	Decrease.	Decrease.	Increase.	Decrease.
Increase or Decrease in number between 1841 and 1897,		20,628	43,651	36,131	1,293	97,136
Rate per cent.,		44·8	69·0	35·9	2·7	38·7
Above 15 and not exceeding 30 Acres,	1841,	20,658	17,511	25,219	5,634	79,342
	1851,	26,006	25,848	57,631	32,769	141,311
	1861,	24,276	25,605	57,440	33,380	141,251
	1871,	23,443	25,681	54,678	33,702	138,647
	1881,	22,623	25,080	54,377	32,913	134,793
	1891,	22,248	21,898	53,422	33,494	133,047
	1897,	21,999	24,089	53,567	33,666	133,366
		Increase.	Increase.	Increase.	Increase.	Increase.
Increase or Decrease in number between 1841 and 1897,		1,339	5,339	28,348	27,962	53,966
Rate per cent.,		6·3	13·9	112·4	478·4	68·0
Above 30 Acres,	1841,	17,943	16,866	9,642	3,893	48,625
	1851,	35,098	48,074	37,013	20,107	149,090
	1861,	38,374	44,832	38,454	24,169	157,833
	1871,	38,651	56,188	41,071	22,878	158,803
	1881,	38,475	56,161	42,510	21,709	158,834
	1891,	39,188	56,518	44,087	22,397	162,910
	1897,	38,982	57,079	44,505	23,513	164,384
		Increase.	Increase.	Increase.	Increase.	Increase.
Increase in number between 1841 and 1897,		21,343	40,473	34,863	19,181	115,759
Rate per cent.,		118·9	345·8	361·0	439·0	238·1
TOTAL, ABOVE 1 ACRE,	1841,	134,760	163,866	233,494	158,842	691,202
	1851,	122,871	139,494	210,349	116,634	570,338
	1861,	116,973	118,525	207,435	125,943	568,484
	1871,	111,676	114,765	194,528	121,965	544,112
	1881,	108,950	112,014	188,070	118,700	526,743
	1891,	105,311	111,347	183,939	116,424	517,012
	1897,	104,330	111,516	183,363	116,276	514,786
		Decrease.	Decrease.	Decrease.	Decrease.	Decrease.
Decrease in number between 1841 and 1897,		30,430	52,350	54,131	39,167	176,416
Rate per cent.,		22·6	32·0	23·9	24·3	25·5

WOODS AND PLANTATIONS.

Woods and Plantations.

In addition to the information regarding the total area under Woods and Plantations, returns were obtained in 1897, showing the proportion of the area entered under this heading occupied by each of the various kinds of trees. According to these Returns 44,862 acres of the total area (307,441 statute acres) under Woods and Plantations last year, were under Larch, 35,004 under Fir, 14,725 under Spruce, 2,788 under Pine, 26,804 under Oak, 6,383 under Ash, 10,084 under Beech, 2,696 under Sycamore, 3,249 under Elm, 3,645 under Other Trees, and 154,301 were returned as under Mixed Trees. The area under Woods and Plantations in Leinster was 93,837 acres, in Munster 103,927 acres, in Ulster 58,092 acres, and in Connaught 51,585 acres.

PRODUCE OF THE CROPS.

Mode of collecting the Returns of Produce.

The Tables relating to the *produce* of the crops have been carefully compiled from information obtained by members of the Royal Irish Constabulary and of the Metropolitan Police from practical farmers and other persons qualified to form an opinion as to the yield in that *Poor Law Electoral Division* for which they were requested to afford the information. The names and residences of the parties so co-operating and assisting are stated by the Enumerators on the Returns.

The Weather.

The Weather being a potent factor in influencing the produce of the crops, both as to quantity and quality, the following particulars, and those given on pages 97–131, are inserted by the kind permission of the Editor of the Dublin Journal of Medical Science: they have been derived from Returns of Meteorological Observations taken in Dublin City during the years 1877–97, by J. W. Moore, Esq., M.D., F.R.C.P.I., F.R. MET. SOC.; and published in the Journal during the years 1897–98. The Tables on pages 132–134 also, are founded on Dr. Moore's observations:—

The mean Atmospherical Pressure has been obtained from daily readings of the barometer at 9 A.M. and 9 P.M. corrected and reduced to 32° Fahrenheit at the mean sea level. The Mean Temperature values have been deduced from the maximal and minimal readings of the thermometer in the shade. The Rainfall is that measured daily at 9 A.M. A rainy day is one on which at least ·005 inch of rain falls within the twenty-four hours from 9 A.M. to 9 A.M.

The *Mean Height of the Barometer* during the year 1897 was 29·911 inches. The highest observed reading was 30·664 inches at 9 P.M. on November 30th. The lowest observed reading was 28·740 inches, at 11 P.M. on December 29th. The extreme range of atmospherical pressure was 1·914 inches compared with 2·427 inches in 1896.

The *Mean Temperature* of the year, deduced from the arithmetical mean of the maximal and minimal readings of the thermometer in the shade was 50·6°. The highest reading was 70·8° on August 4th; the lowest reading was 25·0 on January 17th. The average mean temperature for the years 1877–96 calculated in the same way was 49·7°. The mean temperature deduced from the daily readings of the dry bulb thermometer at 9 A.M. and 9 P.M. was 49·6°.

Rain fell on 211 days, including snow or sleet on 14 days, and hail on 20 days. The average annual number of rainy days in the years 1877–96 was 196·9. The total rainfall measured 26·344 inches compared with an average of 27·643 inches in the twenty years 1877–96. During the first half of 1897 (January to June, inclusive) the rainfall was 13·050 inches on 113 days; during the second half (July to December, inclusive) 13·294 inches fell on 98 days.

As regards the *Direction of the Wind*, 730 observations were made during the year, with this result—N., 31; N.E., 44; E., 109; S.E., 76; S., 78; S.W., 109; W., 169; N.W., 91; Calms, 23.

In Green Crops, potatoes show a decrease of 1,202,384 tons, or 44·5 per cent.; turnips a decrease of 649,174 tons, or 13·6 per cent.; mangel wurzel and beet-root a decrease of 31,516 tons, or 4·0 per cent.; and cabbage a decrease of 103,715 tons, or 22·8 per cent. Total produce in 1896 and 1897.

Flax shows a decrease of 483,913 stones of 14 lbs., or 29·3 per cent. (following a decrease of 304,173 stones, or 15·6 per cent. in 1896, as compared with 1895, and a decrease of 1,490,281 stones, or 43·3 per cent. in 1895 as compared with 1894, and an increase of 980,112 stones, or 39·8 per cent., in 1894, as compared with 1893); hay from clover, sainfoin, and grasses under rotation, an increase of 108,881 tons, or 8·2 per cent.; and hay from permanent pasture or grass not broken up in rotation, an increase of 247,781 tons, or 7·3 per cent.; the entire hay crop showing an increase of 356,462 tons, or 7·5 per cent.

The yield per acre of Cereal Crops in 1897 compared with that of 1896 shows an increase in bere from 12·3 cwts. to 12·7 cwts.; and in beans from 16·3 cwts. to 16·5 cwts.; while there was a decrease in wheat from 16·8 cwts. to 15·4 cwts.; in oats from 14·2 cwts. to 13·5 cwts.; in barley from 16·2 cwts. to 15·2 cwts.; in rye from 12·7 cwts. to 10·8 cwts.; and in peas from 13·6 cwts. to 12·7 cwts. In other crops—potatoes show a decrease from 3·8 tons to 2·2 tons; turnips decreased from 15·5 tons to 13·6 tons; mangel wurzel and beet-root from 14·4 tons to 13·7 tons; and cabbage from 10·3 tons to 8·7 tons. Hay from clover, sainfoin, and grasses under rotation shows an increase from 2·0 tons to 2·3 tons; and the yield of hay from permanent pasture or grass not broken up in rotation, an increase from 2·2 tons to 2·4 tons. Estimated average produce per acre in 1896 and 1897.

The yield per acre of flax was 25·6 stones against 22·8 stones in 1896, and 20·5 stones in 1895, when the yield was lower than in any year since 1871 with the exception of 1887.

The *total produce* of the principal crops in 1896 and 1897, and the increase or decrease in the latter year, are given in the following Table (VI.); the *average produce* per statute acre in Table VII.; and in Table VIII. are given the total extent under each of the principal crops, the *estimated average* yield per statute acre, and the total produce for each year from 1887 to 1897 inclusive.

TABLE VI.—The *total produce* of the principal Crops in 1896 and 1897 and the increase or decrease in the latter year:— Produce of the Crops, 1896-97.

Crops.	Produce 1896.	Produce 1897.	Increase in 1897. Quantity.	Increase in 1897. Percentage.	Decrease in 1897. Quantity.	Decrease in 1897. Percentage.
Wheat, Cwts. of 112 lbs.,	638,870	725,031	86,316	13·5	—	—
Oats,	17,008,136	16,264,735	—	—	743,401	4·4
Barley,	3,143,580	2,587,137	—	—	555,443	17·7
Bere,	4,708	1,876	—	—	2,832	60·2
Rye,	174,873	141,583	—	—	33,290	18·9
Beans,	28,874	25,424	—	—	3,450	11·9
Peas,	4,341	5,603	1,262	29·1	—	—
Potatoes, in Tons,	2,701,000	1,498,616	—	—	1,202,384	44·5
Turnips,	4,782,759	4,133,585	—	—	649,174	13·6
Mangel Wurzel and Beet-Root,	782,572	751,056	—	—	31,516	4·0
Cabbage,	455,021	351,306	—	—	103,715	22·8
Flax, in Stones of 14 lbs.,	1,646,777	1,163,564	—	—	483,913	29·3
Hay, in Tons. Clover, Sainfoin, and Grasses under Rotation,	1,326,003	1,434,884	108,881	8·2	—	—
Hay, in Tons. Permanent Pasture or Grass not broken up in Rotation,	3,405,450	3,653,231	247,781	7·3	—	—

Average produce of Crops in 1896 and 1897.

TABLE VII.—The *estimated average produce* per statute acre of the principal crops in 1896 and 1897, and the *increase* or *decrease* in 1897 compared with 1896 :—

Crops.		Produce per Statute Acre. 1896.	Produce per Statute Acre. 1897.	Increase in 1897.	Decrease in 1897.
Wheat, in Cwts. of 112 lbs.,		16·8	15·4	—	1·4
Oats,		14·2	13·8	—	0·4
Barley,		16·3	13·3	—	3·0
Bere,		13·3	13·7	0·4	—
Rye,		12·7	10·8	—	1·9
Beans,		16·3	18·6	2·3	—
Pease,		13·6	12·7	—	0·9
Potatoes, in Tons,		3·6	2·2	—	1·4
Turnips,		15·5	13·4	—	2·1
Mangel Wurzel and Beet Root,		14·4	13·7	—	0·7
Cabbage,		10·3	8·7	—	1·6
Flax, in Stones of 14 lbs.,		22·8	25·6	2·8	—
Hay, in Tons	Clover, Sainfoin, and Grasses under Rotation,	3·0	3·3	0·3	—
	Permanent Pasture or Grass not broken up in Rotation,	2·2	2·4	0·2	—

Extent under Crops, produce, &c., 1887–97.

The further statement contained in Table VIII. gives a general view of the state of agriculture during the year 1897 as compared with the preceding ten years.

Tables showing the total produce of the Crops in 1897, by counties and provinces, will be found at page 40, and by poor law unions at page 46. The average rates by counties and provinces for each year from 1856 to 1897, are given at pages 55 to 59.

TABLE VIII.—The extent under each of the principal Crops—the average Yield per Statute Acre, and the total Produce for all Ireland, in each year from 1887 to 1897, inclusive, with the average for the ten years, 1887 to 1896.

Years.	Wheat.	Oats.	Barley.	Bere.	Rye.	Potatoes.	Turnips.	Mangel Wurzel and Beet Root.	Cabbage.	Flax.	Hay.
EXTENT UNDER CROPS IN STATUTE MEASURE.											
[illegible]	[illegible]	[illegible]	[illegible]	[illegible]	[illegible]	[illegible]	[illegible]	[illegible]	[illegible]	[illegible]	[illegible]
Average, 1887–96.	[illegible]	[illegible]	[illegible]	[illegible]	[illegible]	[illegible]	[illegible]	[illegible]	[illegible]	[illegible]	[illegible]
1897.	[illegible]	[illegible]	[illegible]	[illegible]	[illegible]	[illegible]	[illegible]	[illegible]	[illegible]	[illegible]	[illegible]
ESTIMATED AVERAGE PRODUCE PER STATUTE ACRE.											
[illegible]	[illegible]	[illegible]	[illegible]	[illegible]	[illegible]	[illegible]	[illegible]	[illegible]	[illegible]	[illegible]	[illegible]
Average, 1887–96.	[illegible]	[illegible]	[illegible]	[illegible]	[illegible]	[illegible]	[illegible]	[illegible]	[illegible]	[illegible]	[illegible]
1897.	[illegible]	[illegible]	[illegible]	[illegible]	[illegible]	[illegible]	[illegible]	[illegible]	[illegible]	[illegible]	[illegible]
TOTAL PRODUCE.											
[illegible]	[illegible]	[illegible]	[illegible]	[illegible]	[illegible]	[illegible]	[illegible]	[illegible]	[illegible]	[illegible]	[illegible]
Average, 1887–96.	[illegible]	[illegible]	[illegible]	[illegible]	[illegible]	[illegible]	[illegible]	[illegible]	[illegible]	[illegible]	[illegible]
1897.	[illegible]	[illegible]	[illegible]	[illegible]	[illegible]	[illegible]	[illegible]	[illegible]	[illegible]	[illegible]	[illegible]

One year old and upwards, .	2,432,365
Under one year, . .	1,648,346
Total No. of Sheep, .	4,080,711
One year old and upwards, .	163,913
Under one year, . .	[illegible]

Number of Live Stock. The number of Sheep in 1897, was 4,157,906, being 77,195, or 1·9 per cent. more than the number for the previous year, and 39,080, or 0·9 per cent. more than the average for the ten years 1887-96; the "one year old and upwards" increased by 34,223, or 1·4 per cent., as compared with the number in 1896, and those "under one year" by 42,970, or 2·6 per cent.

Pigs were returned as 1,327,430 in 1897, showing a *decrease* of 77,186, or 5·5 per cent., as compared with the previous year. The "one year old and upwards" *decreased* by 13,907, or 8·6 per cent., and those "under one year" by 63,229, or 5·1 per cent.

Comparing the number of pigs returned in 1897 with the average for the ten years 1887-96, we find a *decrease* of 24,679, or 1·8 per cent.

The number of goats in 1897 was 300,080, being 7,350 *less* than in 1896, and 13,003, or 4·2 per cent., *under* the average for the ten years 1887-96.

Poultry. Poultry numbered 17,777,248 in 1897, being 219,678 more than in 1896, and 2,176,346, or 14·0 per cent., over the average for the ten years 1887-96. Of the 17,777,248 poultry in 1897, 1,065,774 were turkeys; 2,072,702 geese; 2,976,019 ducks, and 11,662,753 ordinary fowl.

Compared with 1896, turkeys *decreased* by 24,888, and geese by 69,844, but ducks *increased* by 3,553, and ordinary fowl by 880,607.

Number of Live Stock, 1887 to 1897.

TABLE X.—The Number of Live Stock in Ireland, in each year from 1887 to 1897 inclusive, with the average numbers for the ten years 1887-96:—

Years.	Horses and Mules.	Asses.	Cattle.	Sheep.	Pigs.	Goats.	Poultry.
1887, . .	587,234	192,612	4,157,404	3,377,876	1,408,466	271,129	14,460,943
1888, . .	595,348	198,181	4,099,193	3,526,660	1,377,628	288,670	14,[illegible]
1889, . .	601,102	200,336	4,094,174	3,760,167	1,[illegible],670	293,733	14,[illegible]
1890, . .	614,644	213,018	4,240,318	4,323,345	1,570,364	337,114	15,[illegible]
1891, . .	631,479	216,240	4,449,311	4,722,613	1,367,715	338,337	15,[illegible]
1892, . .	633,373	217,684	4,431,153	4,837,777	1,113,479	328,736	15,334,[illegible]
1893, . .	613,129	218,729	4,464,857	4,421,433	1,152,417	323,173	16,[illegible]
1894, . .	633,030	224,013	4,[illegible]	[illegible]	1,[illegible]	316,[illegible]	16,[illegible]
1895, . .	640,117	226,168	4,256,032	3,913,449	1,338,164	304,[illegible]	16,[illegible]
1896, . .	639,175	228,[illegible]	4,408,133	4,080,711	1,404,[illegible]	308,145	17,[illegible]
Average 1887-96, .	637,336	218,618	4,310,870	4,118,836	1,352,329	313,[illegible]	15,[illegible]
1897, . .	639,488	230,253	4,464,874	4,157,906	1,327,430	300,080	17,777,248

Number of Live Stock, 1887 to 1897.

TABLE XI.—The proportion per cent. of Horses, Cattle, Sheep, and Pigs in Ireland at each Age, for the years 1887 to 1897, inclusive, and averages for the ten years 1887-96.

Years.	Horses.			Cattle.			Sheep.		Pigs.	
	Percentage at each age.			Percentage at each age.			Percentage at each age.		Percentage at each age.	
	Two Years old and upwards.	One Year old and under Two.	Under One Year.	Two Years old and upwards.	One Year old and under Two.	Under One Year.	One Year old and upwards.	Under One Year.	One Year old and upwards.	Under One Year.
1887, .	73·6	13·9	11·7	55·7	20·5	23·8	60·5	39·5	13·7	87·3
1888, .	74·4	13·1	12·5	55·3	21·5	23·2	59·6	40·4	12·2	87·8
1889, .	74·4	13·4	12·2	55·5	21·2	23·3	59·5	40·5	12·2	87·8
1890, .	72·2	13·7	13·0	54·7	21·3	24·1	58·7	41·3	12·1	87·9
1891, .	72·2	14·6	13·2	54·1	22·0	23·9	59·0	41·0	11·7	88·3
1892, .	71·1	15·5	13·4	55·1	23·4	21·5	59·7	40·3	13·0	87·0
1893, .	71·2	15·9	12·9	56·9	21·7	21·4	60·5	39·5	12·1	87·9
1894, .	71·7	15·9	12·4	57·3	20·8	21·9	60·7	39·3	11·3	88·7
1895, .	73·0	15·1	11·9	55·7	20·9	23·4	60·0	40·0	11·7	88·3
1896, .	73·8	14·5	11·7	55·1	21·7	23·2	59·6	40·4	11·7	88·3
Average 1887-96,	72·1	14·6	12·3	55·7	21·4	22·9	59·8	40·2	12·0	88·0
1897, .	75·7	13·7	10·6	54·6	21·6	23·6	59·3	40·7	11·3	88·7

MILCH COWS.

The following statement (Table XII.) shows the number of Milch Cows in Ireland in each year from 1854—the first year in which Milch Cows were separately enumerated—to 1897. The average number for the first five years of the period was 1,579,831, and for the last five years 1,437,498, being a decline of 142,333 or 9·0 per cent. The highest number in any one year was 1,690,359 in 1859, and the lowest 1,348,886 in 1864. The number for last year was 1,434,925, being 5,707 under the average for the preceding five years, but 5,130 over the number for 1896. Milch Cows.

Years.	No. of Milch Cows.	Years.	No. of Milch Cows.	Years.	No. of Milch Cows.	Years.	No. of Milch Cows.
1854, .	1,517,673	1865, .	1,387,448	1876, .	1,532,971	1887, .	1,394,138
1855, .	1,561,596	1866, .	1,483,616	1877, .	1,522,811	1888, .	1,384,771
1856, .	1,579,379	1867, .	1,521,033	1878, .	1,481,315	1889, .	1,383,781
1857, .	1,603,330	1868, .	1,476,339	1879, .	1,464,918	1890, .	1,400,857
1858, .	1,633,400	1869, .	1,506,838	1880, .	1,398,047	1891, .	1,413,368
1859, .	1,690,359	1870, .	1,359,034	1881, .	1,382,019	1892, .	1,431,089
1860, .	1,626,433	1871, .	1,349,603	1882, .	1,339,006	1893, .	1,441,399
1861, .	1,643,148	1872, .	1,561,784	1883, .	1,402,364	1894, .	1,447,441
1862, .	1,499,835	1873, .	1,578,130	1884, .	1,356,486	1895, .	1,433,988
1863, .	1,396,931	1874, .	1,491,375	1885, .	1,417,422	1896, .	1,429,795
1864, .	1,348,886	1875, .	1,380,369	1886, .	1,418,444	1897, .	1,434,925

BOARS KEPT FOR BREEDING PURPOSES.

In connexion with the Agricultural Statistics for 1897, a return of the number of Boars kept for breeding purposes in his District was obtained from each Enumerator, and the information thus arrived at will be found set forth by Provinces and Counties, in Table 17, pages 74-75. The total number of Boars returned is 1,924, of which 42 were imported, and 1,882 bred in Ireland. The number of each of the principal descriptions is shown in the Table, from which it will be observed that more than one-half (971) of the total were White Pigs of the Large, Middle, or Small Yorkshire varieties. Boars.

DAIRY INDUSTRIES.

As the increase during recent years in the number of Dairy Factories appeared to render it desirable that some particulars should be obtained regarding what is now an important Agricultural Industry, information on several points connected with the subject was collected through the medium of the Enumerators in each of the last seven years. Statistics were also had respecting the number of Milk Separators used in private establishments. Dairy Industries.

The Table on the next page shows, *inter alia*, that the number of Factories from which statistics were obtained in 1897 was 324, being an increase of 45 as compared with the number returned in 1896, and that the number of hands permanently employed amounted to 2,692, or 487 more than the number for 1896. Of the 324 factories, 132 were owned by individual proprietors, 107 were the property of Joint Stock Companies, and 85 belonged to Co-operative Farmers. In the 324 Factories there were 668 milk separators, of which 568, or 85·0 per cent., were worked by steam-power. Nearly four-fifths of the total number of Factories were in Munster, the number for that province being 250; in Leinster there were 47, in Ulster 21, and in Connaught 6. The quantity of Butter returned as produced during the year ended 30th September, 1897, was 294,105 cwts. (against 274,592 cwts. in the preceding year), and of Cheese 500 cwts., and the number of lbs. of Condensed Milk 20,980,505.

DISEASES OF ANIMALS.

The following information has been derived from Returns compiled in pursuance of the provisions of the 50th section of the Diseases of Animals Act, 1894, for the year ended the 31st December, 1897.

No outbreaks of Pleuro-Pneumonia have occurred during the last five years. The numbers for the four previous years were 86 for 1892, 189 for 1891, 95 for 1890, and 108 for 1889.

Ireland continues to be free from Foot-and-Mouth Disease. No case has occurred since the year 1884.

As regards Swine Fever, during the year 1897, 3,800 suspected outbreaks were reported. The existence of disease was confirmed in 491 of these cases by the Veterinary Officers of the Privy Council Department, who examined the internal organs of the dead or slaughtered swine. There were 5,864 outbreaks in the preceding year. In the year 1895 the number was 8,045; in 1894 it was 7,619, and in 1893, 506.

Only one outbreak of Glanders was reported during the year.

There were no outbreaks of Anthrax during either of the last two years. There were 4 in 1895, 5 in 1894, 22 in 1893, 8 in 1892, 29 in 1891, 17 in 1890, and 21 in 1889.

The Returns show that 497 cases of Rabies were reported in 1897, as compared with 687 in 1896, 771 in 1895, 779 in 1894, 424 in 1893, 446 in 1892, 470 in 1891, and 353 in 1890.

EXPORTS AND IMPORTS OF LIVE STOCK.

With the view of giving a more accurate idea of the number of live stock produced in Ireland, the statement (Table XIV.) on page 22 has been compiled from Statistical Returns prepared under the "Diseases of Animals Act, 1894," by the Veterinary Department of the Privy Council.

Viewing the number of animals exported to Great Britain in relation to those enumerated, it is found that the cattle exported bear a relation of 16·7 per cent. to those enumerated in 1897, as compared with 15·3 per cent. in 1896; sheep 19·3 per cent. as compared with 18·1 per cent. in 1896; and pigs 59·4 per cent. as compared with 48·6 per cent. in 1896.

From the same Returns it appears that the number of horses exported to Great Britain in 1897 amounted to 38,422, equal to 6·3 per cent. of those enumerated.

It also appears that during the same period there were imported into Ireland, 5,298 horses, 493 cattle (including 29 calves), and 28,194 sheep, and that 57 pigs were imported.

[Table XIV.

TABLE XIV.—Number of Cattle, Sheep, and Swine, exported from Ireland to Great Britain during each of the twenty-three years, 1875–97:—

Years.	Cattle.						Sheep.			Swine.			Years.
	Oxen, Bulls, and Cows.												
	Fat Cattle.	Store Cattle for Fattening or breeding purposes.	Other Cattle.	Total.	Calves.	Total.	Sheep.	Lambs.	Total.	Fat Swine.	Store Swine.	Total.	
1875.	[illegible]	[illegible]	[illegible]	[illegible]	[illegible]	[illegible]	[illegible]	[illegible]	[illegible]	[illegible]	[illegible]	[illegible]	1875.
1876.	[illegible]	[illegible]	[illegible]	[illegible]	[illegible]	[illegible]	[illegible]	[illegible]	[illegible]	[illegible]	[illegible]	[illegible]	1876.
1877.	[illegible]	[illegible]	[illegible]	[illegible]	[illegible]	[illegible]	[illegible]	[illegible]	[illegible]	[illegible]	[illegible]	[illegible]	1877.
1878.	[illegible]	[illegible]	[illegible]	[illegible]	[illegible]	[illegible]	[illegible]	[illegible]	[illegible]	[illegible]	[illegible]	[illegible]	1878.
1879.	[illegible]	[illegible]	[illegible]	[illegible]	[illegible]	[illegible]	[illegible]	[illegible]	[illegible]	[illegible]	[illegible]	[illegible]	1879.
1880.	[illegible]	[illegible]	[illegible]	[illegible]	[illegible]	[illegible]	[illegible]	[illegible]	[illegible]	[illegible]	[illegible]	[illegible]	1880.
1881.	[illegible]	[illegible]	[illegible]	[illegible]	[illegible]	[illegible]	[illegible]	[illegible]	[illegible]	[illegible]	[illegible]	[illegible]	1881.
1882.	[illegible]	[illegible]	[illegible]	[illegible]	[illegible]	[illegible]	[illegible]	[illegible]	[illegible]	[illegible]	[illegible]	[illegible]	1882.
1883.	[illegible]	[illegible]	[illegible]	[illegible]	[illegible]	[illegible]	[illegible]	[illegible]	[illegible]	[illegible]	[illegible]	[illegible]	1883.
1884.	[illegible]	[illegible]	[illegible]	[illegible]	[illegible]	[illegible]	[illegible]	[illegible]	[illegible]	[illegible]	[illegible]	[illegible]	1884.
1885.	[illegible]	[illegible]	[illegible]	[illegible]	[illegible]	[illegible]	[illegible]	[illegible]	[illegible]	[illegible]	[illegible]	[illegible]	1885.
1886.	[illegible]	[illegible]	[illegible]	[illegible]	[illegible]	[illegible]	[illegible]	[illegible]	[illegible]	[illegible]	[illegible]	[illegible]	1886.
1887.	[illegible]	[illegible]	[illegible]	[illegible]	[illegible]	[illegible]	[illegible]	[illegible]	[illegible]	[illegible]	[illegible]	[illegible]	1887.
1888.	[illegible]	[illegible]	[illegible]	[illegible]	[illegible]	[illegible]	[illegible]	[illegible]	[illegible]	[illegible]	[illegible]	[illegible]	1888.
1889.	[illegible]	[illegible]	[illegible]	[illegible]	[illegible]	[illegible]	[illegible]	[illegible]	[illegible]	[illegible]	[illegible]	[illegible]	1889.
1890.	[illegible]	[illegible]	[illegible]	[illegible]	[illegible]	[illegible]	[illegible]	[illegible]	[illegible]	[illegible]	[illegible]	[illegible]	1890.
1891.	[illegible]	[illegible]	[illegible]	[illegible]	[illegible]	[illegible]	[illegible]	[illegible]	[illegible]	[illegible]	[illegible]	[illegible]	1891.
1892.	[illegible]	[illegible]	[illegible]	[illegible]	[illegible]	[illegible]	[illegible]	[illegible]	[illegible]	[illegible]	[illegible]	[illegible]	1892.
1893.	[illegible]	[illegible]	[illegible]	[illegible]	[illegible]	[illegible]	[illegible]	[illegible]	[illegible]	[illegible]	[illegible]	[illegible]	1893.
1894.	[illegible]	[illegible]	[illegible]	[illegible]	[illegible]	[illegible]	[illegible]	[illegible]	[illegible]	[illegible]	[illegible]	[illegible]	1894.
1895.	[illegible]	[illegible]	[illegible]	[illegible]	[illegible]	[illegible]	[illegible]	[illegible]	[illegible]	[illegible]	[illegible]	[illegible]	1895.
1896.	[illegible]	[illegible]	[illegible]	[illegible]	[illegible]	[illegible]	[illegible]	[illegible]	[illegible]	[illegible]	[illegible]	[illegible]	1896.
1897.	[illegible]	[illegible]	[illegible]	[illegible]	[illegible]	[illegible]	[illegible]	[illegible]	[illegible]	[illegible]	[illegible]	[illegible]	1897.

HONEY PRODUCED IN 1896.

The inquiries made in the preceding eleven years relative to the extent to which bee-keeping is followed in Ireland, and the degree of success attained in this special branch of rural economy, were repeated last year with reference to the season of 1896.

According to the Returns received there would appear to have been an increase of 15·4 per cent. in the quantity of honey produced in 1896, as compared with the preceding year, the returns for which showed an increase of 1·4 per cent. as compared with the quantity in 1894.

The quantity of honey produced, according to the Returns, was 274,809 lbs.; of this, 78,392 lbs. were produced in the province of Leinster; 102,965 lbs. in Munster; 57,449 lbs. in Ulster; and 40,903 lbs. in Connaught. Of the 274,809 lbs., 164,459 lbs. were produced "in Hives having Movable Combs," and 110,350 lbs. "in other Hives." It was stated that 128,596 lbs. was "Run Honey," and 146,216 lbs. "Section Honey."

The number of stocks brought through the winter of 1896–97 amounted to 16,505; of which 7,761 were in hives having movable combs, and 8,743 in other hives.

According to the returns collected there were 3,982 lbs. of wax manufactured in 1896; of which 2,092 lbs. were from hives having movable combs, and 1,810 lbs. from other hives.

The Returns received in 1896 gave the number of swarms at work during the season of 1895 as 14,300; the quantity of honey as 238,171 lbs.; the number of stocks brought through the winter of 1895–96 as 17,026; and the quantity of wax manufactured in 1895 as 4,048 lbs.

The following Table shows the quantity of Honey returned as produced in Ireland during each of the eleven years, 1886–96. It will be observed, that the quantity produced in 1896, although greater than that for any of the five years, 1891–5, was somewhat below the average for the ten years 1886–95.

TABLE XV.—Showing for each of the Eleven Years 1886–96 the Quantity of HONEY Produced in Ireland, distinguishing the quantity Produced in Hives having Movable Combs from that Produced in other Hives and RUN HONEY from SECTION HONEY; with the average annual quantity for the Ten Years 1886–95:—

YEARS.	HONEY PRODUCED, IN LBS.						
	In Hives having Movable Combs			In other Hives.			GENERAL TOTAL.
	Run.	Section.	Total.	Run.	Section.	Total.	
1886, . .	57,809	74,333	128,941	143,132	59,094	204,226	331,167
1887, . .	77,897	134,257	212,154	188,951	58,181	247,153	459,306
1888, . .	65,768	83,683	148,441	137,301	42,350	179,651	328,092
1889, . .	74,948	143,564	218,508	192,104	63,976	256,080	474,588
1890, . .	47,953	86,130	134,083	115,509	42,429	158,038	292,116
1891, . .	43,067	91,501	134,568	82,608	30,604	112,913	247,481
1892, . .	34,707	69,629	104,336	66,730	27,388	93,121	178,457
1893, . .	40,900	91,413	132,313	81,694	34,386	116,080	248,393
1894, . .	42,181	87,644	129,825	70,150	34,863	105,013	234,838
1895, . .	43,710	95,041	138,751	71,311	28,104	99,415	238,171
Average 1886–95, .	61,378	98,033	159,011	111,189	46,474	156,763	300,374
1896, . .	43,964	119,185	164,459	81,329	29,031	110,350	274,309

SCUTCHING MILLS.

The number of Mills for scutching Flax in Ireland in 1897 was 918, being a decrease of 15 compared with the number for 1896, and a decrease of 152 since the year 1888. Of the 918 Mills, 907 were in Ulster, 4 in Connaught, 5 in Leinster, and 2 in Munster. There were 398 Mills with from 1 to 4 stocks; 283 having 5 or 6; 207 with from 7 to 12; 20 having from 13 to 18, and 2 having above 18 stocks; 741 were worked by water power; 123 by steam; 53 by water and steam; and one by horse power. The total number of Stocks in Ireland in 1897 amounted to 5,489, and of this number 5,387 were in Mills situated in Ulster. Scutching Mills, 1897.

The following is the number of Scutching Mills, in each year, from 1888 to 1897, inclusive, by Provinces:— Scutching Mills, 1888 to 1897.

PROVINCES.	1888.	1889.	1890.	1891.	1892.	1893.	1894.	1895.	1896.	1897.
Leinster, . .	8	7	7	7	4	6	8	7	7	6
Munster, . .	4	4	5	6	8	4	4	5	3	3
Ulster, . .	1,056	1,043	1,045	993	971	954	945	933	917	907
Connaught, . .	2	3	2	2	4	6	5	6	5	4
IRELAND, .	1,070	1,053	1,059	1,008	983	970	959	951	933	918

Scutching Mills, 1897.

TABLE XVI.—Number of SCUTCHING MILLS in 1897, by COUNTIES and PROVINCES, classified according to the number of Stocks in each Mill, and the Power used in working them; with the Total Number of Stocks in each County:—

Provinces and Counties in which there were Scutching Mills.	Power Employed.					Total No. of Mills.	Classification of Mills.					Total No. of Stocks.
	Water.	Steam.	Water and Steam.	Horse.	Wind.		Having 1, 2, 3 or 4 Stocks.	Having 5 or 6 Stocks.	Having above 6 and not exceeding 12 Stocks.	Having above 12 and not exceeding 18 Stocks.	Having above 18 Stocks.	
LEINSTER:												
Louth & Drogheda, Co. of Town.	2	1	.	.	.	3	.	.	3	.	.	30
Meath, . .	2	.	.	.	.	2	.	1	1	.	.	14
Total, . .	4	1	.	.	.	5	.	1	4	.	.	44
MUNSTER:												
Cork, . . .	2	.	.	.	.	2	.	2	.	.	.	11
ULSTER:												
Antrim, . .	113	16	6	.	.	135	63	52	18	3	.	736
Armagh, . .	51	16	7	.	.	74	8	30	29	5	2	610
Cavan, . .	31	7	.	.	.	38	7	17	13	1	.	353
Donegal, . .	130	1	3	.	.	134	106	18	10	.	.	547
Down, . .	78	34	21	.	.	133	76	13	33	11	.	1,022
Fermanagh, .	19	3	1	.	.	23	10	7	3	3	.	138
Londonderry, .	134	15	2	.	.	151	80	50	20	1	.	784
Monaghan, . .	53	14	4	.	.	71	33	23	11	4	.	500
Tyrone, . .	117	19	10	1	.	147	77	40	29	1	.	764
Total, . .	733	130	53	1	.	907	398	250	200	28	2	4,587
CONNAUGHT:												
Leitrim, . .	1	.	.	.	.	1	.	.	1	.	.	8
Mayo, . .	.	1	.	.	.	1	.	.	1	.	.	11
Roscommon, .	1	1	.	.	.	2	.	.	1	1	.	28
Total, . .	2	2	.	.	.	4	.	.	3	1	.	47
TOTAL OF IRELAND,	741	133	53	1	.	916	398	253	207	29	2	4,689

CORN MILLS.

Corn Mills.

As in the six preceding years, returns were obtained in 1897 showing the number of Corn Mills in Ireland, with details as to the power used, the kind of corn chiefly ground, and the average quantity ground per week when the mills are at work. The results are given, by provinces and counties, in the following table, from which it appears that the total number of mills returned is 1,434 (a decrease of 40 as compared with the number for 1896) of which 1,251 were worked by water, 90 by steam, 23 by wind, and 70 by water and steam; and that wheat was the chief kind of corn ground in 209 mills, oats in 950, and Indian corn in 246. In 209 of the 1,434 mills the average quantity ground per week, when the mills are at work, exceeds 500 cwts. Corn Mills

TABLE XVII.—Number of CORN MILLS in 1897, by COUNTIES and PROVINCES, classified according to the Power used, the kind of Corn chiefly ground, and the average Quantity (in cwts.) ground per week when the Mills are at work.

Counties and Provinces.	Total No. of Mills.	Description of Power Used. — Water.	Steam.	Wind.	Water and Steam.	Kind of Corn chiefly Ground. — Wheat.	Oats.	Indian Corn.	[illegible]	Average Quantity Ground per Week when at Work. — Under 20 cwts.	20 and under 50 cwts.	50 and under 100 cwts.	100 and under 200 cwts.	200 and under 500 cwts.	500 cwts. and upwards.
		Number of Mills.				Number of Mills.				Number of Mills.					
LEINSTER:															
Carlow,	[illegible]	[illegible]	[illegible]	[illegible]	[illegible]	[illegible]	[illegible]	[illegible]	[illegible]	[illegible]	[illegible]	[illegible]	[illegible]	[illegible]	[illegible]
Dublin,	[illegible]	[illegible]	[illegible]	[illegible]	[illegible]	[illegible]	[illegible]	[illegible]	[illegible]	[illegible]	[illegible]	[illegible]	[illegible]	[illegible]	[illegible]
Kildare,	[illegible]	[illegible]	[illegible]	[illegible]	[illegible]	[illegible]	[illegible]	[illegible]	[illegible]	[illegible]	[illegible]	[illegible]	[illegible]	[illegible]	[illegible]
Kilkenny,	[illegible]	[illegible]	[illegible]	[illegible]	[illegible]	[illegible]	[illegible]	[illegible]	[illegible]	[illegible]	[illegible]	[illegible]	[illegible]	[illegible]	[illegible]
King's,	[illegible]	[illegible]	[illegible]	[illegible]	[illegible]	[illegible]	[illegible]	[illegible]	[illegible]	[illegible]	[illegible]	[illegible]	[illegible]	[illegible]	[illegible]
Longford,	[illegible]	[illegible]	[illegible]	[illegible]	[illegible]	[illegible]	[illegible]	[illegible]	[illegible]	[illegible]	[illegible]	[illegible]	[illegible]	[illegible]	[illegible]
Louth and Drogheda, County of Town,	[illegible]	[illegible]	[illegible]	[illegible]	[illegible]	[illegible]	[illegible]	[illegible]	[illegible]	[illegible]	[illegible]	[illegible]	[illegible]	[illegible]	[illegible]
Meath,	[illegible]	[illegible]	[illegible]	[illegible]	[illegible]	[illegible]	[illegible]	[illegible]	[illegible]	[illegible]	[illegible]	[illegible]	[illegible]	[illegible]	[illegible]
Queen's,	[illegible]	[illegible]	[illegible]	[illegible]	[illegible]	[illegible]	[illegible]	[illegible]	[illegible]	[illegible]	[illegible]	[illegible]	[illegible]	[illegible]	[illegible]
Westmeath,	[illegible]	[illegible]	[illegible]	[illegible]	[illegible]	[illegible]	[illegible]	[illegible]	[illegible]	[illegible]	[illegible]	[illegible]	[illegible]	[illegible]	[illegible]
Wexford,	[illegible]	[illegible]	[illegible]	[illegible]	[illegible]	[illegible]	[illegible]	[illegible]	[illegible]	[illegible]	[illegible]	[illegible]	[illegible]	[illegible]	[illegible]
Wicklow,	[illegible]	[illegible]	[illegible]	[illegible]	[illegible]	[illegible]	[illegible]	[illegible]	[illegible]	[illegible]	[illegible]	[illegible]	[illegible]	[illegible]	[illegible]
Total,	[illegible]	[illegible]	[illegible]	[illegible]	[illegible]	[illegible]	[illegible]	[illegible]	[illegible]	[illegible]	[illegible]	[illegible]	[illegible]	[illegible]	[illegible]
MUNSTER:															
Clare,	[illegible]	[illegible]	[illegible]	[illegible]	[illegible]	[illegible]	[illegible]	[illegible]	[illegible]	[illegible]	[illegible]	[illegible]	[illegible]	[illegible]	[illegible]
Cork,	[illegible]	[illegible]	[illegible]	[illegible]	[illegible]	[illegible]	[illegible]	[illegible]	[illegible]	[illegible]	[illegible]	[illegible]	[illegible]	[illegible]	[illegible]
Kerry,	[illegible]	[illegible]	[illegible]	[illegible]	[illegible]	[illegible]	[illegible]	[illegible]	[illegible]	[illegible]	[illegible]	[illegible]	[illegible]	[illegible]	[illegible]
Limerick,	[illegible]	[illegible]	[illegible]	[illegible]	[illegible]	[illegible]	[illegible]	[illegible]	[illegible]	[illegible]	[illegible]	[illegible]	[illegible]	[illegible]	[illegible]
Tipperary,	[illegible]	[illegible]	[illegible]	[illegible]	[illegible]	[illegible]	[illegible]	[illegible]	[illegible]	[illegible]	[illegible]	[illegible]	[illegible]	[illegible]	[illegible]
Waterford,	[illegible]	[illegible]	[illegible]	[illegible]	[illegible]	[illegible]	[illegible]	[illegible]	[illegible]	[illegible]	[illegible]	[illegible]	[illegible]	[illegible]	[illegible]
Total,	[illegible]	[illegible]	[illegible]	[illegible]	[illegible]	[illegible]	[illegible]	[illegible]	[illegible]	[illegible]	[illegible]	[illegible]	[illegible]	[illegible]	[illegible]
ULSTER:															
Antrim,	[illegible]	[illegible]	[illegible]	[illegible]	[illegible]	[illegible]	[illegible]	[illegible]	[illegible]	[illegible]	[illegible]	[illegible]	[illegible]	[illegible]	[illegible]
Armagh,	[illegible]	[illegible]	[illegible]	[illegible]	[illegible]	[illegible]	[illegible]	[illegible]	[illegible]	[illegible]	[illegible]	[illegible]	[illegible]	[illegible]	[illegible]
Cavan,	[illegible]	[illegible]	[illegible]	[illegible]	[illegible]	[illegible]	[illegible]	[illegible]	[illegible]	[illegible]	[illegible]	[illegible]	[illegible]	[illegible]	[illegible]
Donegal,	[illegible]	[illegible]	[illegible]	[illegible]	[illegible]	[illegible]	[illegible]	[illegible]	[illegible]	[illegible]	[illegible]	[illegible]	[illegible]	[illegible]	[illegible]
Down,	[illegible]	[illegible]	[illegible]	[illegible]	[illegible]	[illegible]	[illegible]	[illegible]	[illegible]	[illegible]	[illegible]	[illegible]	[illegible]	[illegible]	[illegible]
Fermanagh,	[illegible]	[illegible]	[illegible]	[illegible]	[illegible]	[illegible]	[illegible]	[illegible]	[illegible]	[illegible]	[illegible]	[illegible]	[illegible]	[illegible]	[illegible]
Londonderry,	[illegible]	[illegible]	[illegible]	[illegible]	[illegible]	[illegible]	[illegible]	[illegible]	[illegible]	[illegible]	[illegible]	[illegible]	[illegible]	[illegible]	[illegible]
Monaghan,	[illegible]	[illegible]	[illegible]	[illegible]	[illegible]	[illegible]	[illegible]	[illegible]	[illegible]	[illegible]	[illegible]	[illegible]	[illegible]	[illegible]	[illegible]
Tyrone,	[illegible]	[illegible]	[illegible]	[illegible]	[illegible]	[illegible]	[illegible]	[illegible]	[illegible]	[illegible]	[illegible]	[illegible]	[illegible]	[illegible]	[illegible]
Total,	[illegible]	[illegible]	[illegible]	[illegible]	[illegible]	[illegible]	[illegible]	[illegible]	[illegible]	[illegible]	[illegible]	[illegible]	[illegible]	[illegible]	[illegible]
CONNAUGHT:															
Galway,	[illegible]	[illegible]	[illegible]	[illegible]	[illegible]	[illegible]	[illegible]	[illegible]	[illegible]	[illegible]	[illegible]	[illegible]	[illegible]	[illegible]	[illegible]
Leitrim,	[illegible]	[illegible]	[illegible]	[illegible]	[illegible]	[illegible]	[illegible]	[illegible]	[illegible]	[illegible]	[illegible]	[illegible]	[illegible]	[illegible]	[illegible]
Mayo,	[illegible]	[illegible]	[illegible]	[illegible]	[illegible]	[illegible]	[illegible]	[illegible]	[illegible]	[illegible]	[illegible]	[illegible]	[illegible]	[illegible]	[illegible]
Roscommon,	[illegible]	[illegible]	[illegible]	[illegible]	[illegible]	[illegible]	[illegible]	[illegible]	[illegible]	[illegible]	[illegible]	[illegible]	[illegible]	[illegible]	[illegible]
Sligo,	[illegible]	[illegible]	[illegible]	[illegible]	[illegible]	[illegible]	[illegible]	[illegible]	[illegible]	[illegible]	[illegible]	[illegible]	[illegible]	[illegible]	[illegible]
Total,	[illegible]	[illegible]	[illegible]	[illegible]	[illegible]	[illegible]	[illegible]	[illegible]	[illegible]	[illegible]	[illegible]	[illegible]	[illegible]	[illegible]	[illegible]
TOTAL OF IRELAND,	[illegible]	[illegible]	[illegible]	[illegible]	[illegible]	[illegible]	[illegible]	[illegible]	[illegible]	[illegible]	[illegible]	[illegible]	[illegible]	[illegible]	[illegible]

SILOS AND ENSILAGE.

Following the course adopted in the ten previous years relative to Ensilage, I communicated with those Landed Proprietors and Landholders, throughout the country, reported to me as having Silos or otherwise making Ensilage, requesting them to favour me with certain details regarding the methods followed and the results obtained in the year 1897. I received replies to 139 out of 194 circulars issued by me, and I beg to express my obligations to my correspondents for the valuable and interesting information afforded. It will be found set forth in the Appendix, pp. 76 to 95. Many of the replies stated that no ensilage was made during the season of 1897, owing to the weather being so favourable for the saving of hay.

The following Table (XVIII.) shows, by Counties and Provinces, for the years 1896 and 1897, the number of Silos or Stacks mentioned in the communications received from the persons who forwarded replies to the circular above referred to:—

Counties.	Number in 1896.	Number in 1897.	Counties.	Number in 1896.	Number in 1897.
Antrim,	6	10	Mayo,	5	3
Armagh,	–	–	Meath,	20	12
Carlow,	2	3	Monaghan,	–	3
Cavan,	2	3	Queen's,	6	3
Clare,	4	4	Roscommon,	7	10
Cork,	–	7	Sligo,	2	3
Donegal,	5	8	Tipperary,	12	11
Down,	6	1	Tyrone,	2	1
Dublin,	2	8	Waterford,	1	–
Fermanagh,	6	2	Westmeath,	7	14
Galway,	5	6	Wexford,	2	1
Kerry,	1	1	Wicklow,	3	5
Kildare,	4	1			
Kilkenny,	5	5	PROVINCES.		
King's,	13	9	Leinster,	80	83
Leitrim,	3	3	Munster,	23	26
Limerick,	5	3	Ulster,	38	27
Londonderry,	11	5	Connaught,	24	21
Longford,	–	2			
Louth,	6	–	TOTAL OF IRELAND,	165	158

FORESTRY OPERATIONS.

The inquiries into Forestry Operations instituted in 1890, and continued in the six following years, were repeated in 1897. The details are set forth in the GENERAL ABSTRACT of FORESTRY OPERATIONS in IRELAND during the year ended 30th June, 1897. The subjects dealt with in the Abstract are—I. Planting—The area planted during the year ended 30th June, 1897, the total number of trees planted in that period, and the number of each description; II. Felling—The area cleared and the number of trees of each description felled; III. Ages of trees felled; IV. Disposal of timber. The inquiry did not extend to the planting or felling of isolated trees.

It appears that during the period 1851–97 there were some slight fluctuations in the acreage, and that comparing 1897 with 1851 there has been an increase of about 0·5 per cent., the extent under woods and plantations in 1851 being 304,906 statute acres, and in last year 307,441 acres.

During the year ended 30th June, 1897, 1,164 acres were planted with trees, being 64 acres more than the extent planted in the preceding year.

In connection with this subject it may be here mentioned that from the passing of the Act 29 and 30 Vic., cap. 40, to the 31st March, 1897, 130 loans for £29,750 were sanctioned for planting for shelter, and of this number five, amounting to £1,790, were sanctioned in the last year of that period.

The number of trees felled both for clearance and for thinning plantations amounted to 1,209,283. The area returned as cleared is 1,102 acres.

Of the 1,209,283 trees felled, 873,040 were used for "propping," which appears to have been the chief purpose to which the timber of almost all descriptions was applied. The numbers applied to the principal specified uses comprise also:—13,100 trees for sleepers, 39,354 for paling, 157,123 for fuel, 20,050 for furniture and building purposes, 1,966 for carts, wagons, &c., and 5,702 for clog soles.

WAGES OF AGRICULTURAL LABOURERS IN 1897.

Enquiries were made as to the Wages paid per day to Agricultural Labourers in 1897, and the information received from the District Inspectors of the Royal Irish Constabulary with reference to their respective districts is shown in the following Table (XIK.) and notes appended thereto.

1.—PROVINCE OF LEINSTER.

Counties and Constabulary Districts.	Summer.								Winter.							
	Men.		Boys.		Women.		Girls.		Men.		Boys.		Women.		Girls.	
	From	To	From	To	From	To	From	To	From	To	From	To	From	To	From	To
	s. d.	s. d.	s. d.	s. d.	s. d.	s. d.	s. d.	s. d.	s. d.	s. d.	s. d.	s. d.	s. d.	s. d.	s. d.	s. d.
CARLOW COUNTY.																
[illegible] (a)	[illegible]	[illegible]	[illegible]	[illegible]	[illegible]	[illegible]	[illegible]	[illegible]	[illegible]	[illegible]	[illegible]	[illegible]	[illegible]	[illegible]	[illegible]	[illegible]
[illegible] (b)	[illegible]	[illegible]	[illegible]	[illegible]	[illegible]	[illegible]	[illegible]	[illegible]	[illegible]	[illegible]	[illegible]	[illegible]	[illegible]	[illegible]	[illegible]	[illegible]
DUBLIN COUNTY.																
[illegible]	[illegible]	[illegible]	[illegible]	[illegible]	[illegible]	[illegible]	[illegible]	[illegible]	[illegible]	[illegible]	[illegible]	[illegible]	[illegible]	[illegible]	[illegible]	[illegible]
[illegible]	[illegible]	[illegible]	[illegible]	[illegible]	[illegible]	[illegible]	[illegible]	[illegible]	[illegible]	[illegible]	[illegible]	[illegible]	[illegible]	[illegible]	[illegible]	[illegible]
[illegible]	[illegible]	[illegible]	[illegible]	[illegible]	[illegible]	[illegible]	[illegible]	[illegible]	[illegible]	[illegible]	[illegible]	[illegible]	[illegible]	[illegible]	[illegible]	[illegible]
[illegible]	[illegible]	[illegible]	[illegible]	[illegible]	[illegible]	[illegible]	[illegible]	[illegible]	[illegible]	[illegible]	[illegible]	[illegible]	[illegible]	[illegible]	[illegible]	[illegible]
KILDARE COUNTY.																
[illegible]	[illegible]	[illegible]	[illegible]	[illegible]	[illegible]	[illegible]	[illegible]	[illegible]	[illegible]	[illegible]	[illegible]	[illegible]	[illegible]	[illegible]	[illegible]	[illegible]
[illegible]	[illegible]	[illegible]	[illegible]	[illegible]	[illegible]	[illegible]	[illegible]	[illegible]	[illegible]	[illegible]	[illegible]	[illegible]	[illegible]	[illegible]	[illegible]	[illegible]
[illegible] (c)	[illegible]	[illegible]	[illegible]	[illegible]	[illegible]	[illegible]	[illegible]	[illegible]	[illegible]	[illegible]	[illegible]	[illegible]	[illegible]	[illegible]	[illegible]	[illegible]
[illegible]	[illegible]	[illegible]	[illegible]	[illegible]	[illegible]	[illegible]	[illegible]	[illegible]	[illegible]	[illegible]	[illegible]	[illegible]	[illegible]	[illegible]	[illegible]	[illegible]
KILKENNY COUNTY.																
[illegible]	[illegible]	[illegible]	[illegible]	[illegible]	[illegible]	[illegible]	[illegible]	[illegible]	[illegible]	[illegible]	[illegible]	[illegible]	[illegible]	[illegible]	[illegible]	[illegible]
[illegible]	[illegible]	[illegible]	[illegible]	[illegible]	[illegible]	[illegible]	[illegible]	[illegible]	[illegible]	[illegible]	[illegible]	[illegible]	[illegible]	[illegible]	[illegible]	[illegible]
[illegible] (d)	[illegible]	[illegible]	[illegible]	[illegible]	[illegible]	[illegible]	[illegible]	-	[illegible]	[illegible]	[illegible]	[illegible]	[illegible]	[illegible]	[illegible]	[illegible]
[illegible]	[illegible]	[illegible]	[illegible]	[illegible]	[illegible]	[illegible]	[illegible]	[illegible]	[illegible]	[illegible]	[illegible]	[illegible]	[illegible]	[illegible]	[illegible]	[illegible]
[illegible] (f)	[illegible]	[illegible]	[illegible]	[illegible]	[illegible]	[illegible]	[illegible]	[illegible]	[illegible]	[illegible]	[illegible]	[illegible]	[illegible]	[illegible]	[illegible]	[illegible]
[illegible] (g)	[illegible]	[illegible]	[illegible]	[illegible]	[illegible]	[illegible]	[illegible]	[illegible]	[illegible]	[illegible]	[illegible]	[illegible]	[illegible]	[illegible]	[illegible]	[illegible]
KING'S COUNTY.																
[illegible] (h)	[illegible]	[illegible]	[illegible]	[illegible]	[illegible]	[illegible]	[illegible]	[illegible]	[illegible]	[illegible]	[illegible]	[illegible]	-	-	-	-
[illegible]	[illegible]	[illegible]	[illegible]	[illegible]	[illegible]	[illegible]	[illegible]	[illegible]	[illegible]	[illegible]	[illegible]	[illegible]	[illegible]	[illegible]	[illegible]	[illegible]
[illegible]	[illegible]	[illegible]	[illegible]	[illegible]	[illegible]	[illegible]	[illegible]	[illegible]	[illegible]	[illegible]	[illegible]	[illegible]	[illegible]	[illegible]	[illegible]	[illegible]
[illegible]	[illegible]	[illegible]	[illegible]	[illegible]	[illegible]	[illegible]	[illegible]	[illegible]	[illegible]	[illegible]	[illegible]	[illegible]	[illegible]	[illegible]	[illegible]	[illegible]
[illegible]	[illegible]	[illegible]	[illegible]	[illegible]	[illegible]	[illegible]	[illegible]	[illegible]	[illegible]	[illegible]	[illegible]	[illegible]	[illegible]	[illegible]	[illegible]	[illegible]
LONGFORD COUNTY.																
[illegible]	[illegible]	[illegible]	[illegible]	[illegible]	[illegible]	[illegible]	[illegible]	[illegible]	[illegible]	[illegible]	[illegible]	[illegible]	[illegible]	[illegible]	[illegible]	[illegible]
[illegible]	[illegible]	[illegible]	[illegible]	[illegible]	[illegible]	[illegible]	[illegible]	[illegible]	[illegible]	[illegible]	[illegible]	[illegible]	[illegible]	[illegible]	[illegible]	[illegible]
[illegible]	[illegible]	[illegible]	[illegible]	[illegible]	[illegible]	[illegible]	[illegible]	[illegible]	[illegible]	[illegible]	[illegible]	[illegible]	[illegible]	[illegible]	[illegible]	[illegible]
LOUTH COUNTY.																
[illegible]	[illegible]	[illegible]	[illegible]	[illegible]	[illegible]	[illegible]	[illegible]	[illegible]	[illegible]	[illegible]	[illegible]	[illegible]	[illegible]	[illegible]	[illegible]	[illegible]
[illegible]	[illegible]	[illegible]	[illegible]	[illegible]	[illegible]	[illegible]	[illegible]	[illegible]	[illegible]	[illegible]	[illegible]	[illegible]	[illegible]	[illegible]	[illegible]	[illegible]
[illegible] (j)	[illegible]	[illegible]	[illegible]	[illegible]	[illegible]	[illegible]	[illegible]	[illegible]	[illegible]	[illegible]	[illegible]	[illegible]	[illegible]	[illegible]	[illegible]	[illegible]
[illegible]	[illegible]	[illegible]	[illegible]	[illegible]	[illegible]	[illegible]	[illegible]	[illegible]	[illegible]	[illegible]	[illegible]	[illegible]	[illegible]	[illegible]	[illegible]	[illegible]

I.—PROVINCE OF LEINSTER—*continued*.

Counties and Constabulary Districts.	Summer.								Winter.							
	Men.		Boys.		Women.		Girls.		Men.		Boys.		Women.		Girls.	
	From	To	From	To	From	To	From	To	From	To	From	To	From	To	From	To
MEATH COUNTY.	s. d.	s. d.	s. d.	s. d.	s. d.	s. d.	s. d.	s. d.	s. d.	s. d.	s. d.	s. d.	s. d.	s. d.	s. d.	s. d.
Athboy,	[illegible]	[illegible]	[illegible]	[illegible]	[illegible]	[illegible]	[illegible]	[illegible]	[illegible]	[illegible]	[illegible]	[illegible]	-	-	-	-
Dunshaughlin,	[illegible]	[illegible]	[illegible]	[illegible]	[illegible]	[illegible]	[illegible]	[illegible]	[illegible]	[illegible]	[illegible]	[illegible]	[illegible]	[illegible]	[illegible]	[illegible]
Kells,	[illegible]	-	[illegible]	-	[illegible]	-	[illegible]	-	[illegible]	-	[illegible]	-	[illegible]	-	[illegible]	-
Navan,	[illegible]	[illegible]	[illegible]	[illegible]	[illegible]	[illegible]	[illegible]	[illegible]	[illegible]	[illegible]	[illegible]	[illegible]	[illegible]	[illegible]	[illegible]	[illegible]
Slane,	[illegible]	[illegible]	[illegible]	[illegible]	[illegible]	[illegible]	[illegible]	[illegible]	[illegible]	[illegible]	[illegible]	[illegible]	[illegible]	[illegible]	[illegible]	[illegible]
Trim,	[illegible]	[illegible]	[illegible]	[illegible]	[illegible]	[illegible]	[illegible]	[illegible]	[illegible]	[illegible]	[illegible]	[illegible]	[illegible]	[illegible]	[illegible]	[illegible]
QUEEN'S COUNTY.																
Abbeyleix,	[illegible]	[illegible]	[illegible]	[illegible]	[illegible]	[illegible]	[illegible]	[illegible]	[illegible]	[illegible]	[illegible]	[illegible]	[illegible]	[illegible]	[illegible]	[illegible]
Ballybrittas (a),	[illegible]	[illegible]	[illegible]	[illegible]	[illegible]	[illegible]	[illegible]	[illegible]	[illegible]	[illegible]	[illegible]	[illegible]	[illegible]	[illegible]	[illegible]	[illegible]
Maryborough (b),	[illegible]	[illegible]	[illegible]	[illegible]	[illegible]	[illegible]	[illegible]	[illegible]	[illegible]	[illegible]	[illegible]	[illegible]	[illegible]	[illegible]	[illegible]	[illegible]
Mountrath,	[illegible]	[illegible]	[illegible]	[illegible]	[illegible]	[illegible]	[illegible]	[illegible]	[illegible]	[illegible]	[illegible]	[illegible]	[illegible]	[illegible]	[illegible]	[illegible]
WESTMEATH COUNTY.																
[illegible]	[illegible]	[illegible]	[illegible]	[illegible]	[illegible]	[illegible]	[illegible]	-	[illegible]	[illegible]	[illegible]	[illegible]	-	-	-	-
Castlepollard (c),	[illegible]	[illegible]	[illegible]	[illegible]	[illegible]	[illegible]	[illegible]	[illegible]	[illegible]	[illegible]	[illegible]	[illegible]	[illegible]	[illegible]	[illegible]	[illegible]
Delvin,	[illegible]	[illegible]	[illegible]	[illegible]	[illegible]	[illegible]	[illegible]	[illegible]	[illegible]	[illegible]	[illegible]	[illegible]	[illegible]	[illegible]	[illegible]	[illegible]
Kilbeggan,	[illegible]	[illegible]	[illegible]	[illegible]	[illegible]	[illegible]	[illegible]	[illegible]	[illegible]	[illegible]	[illegible]	[illegible]	[illegible]	[illegible]	[illegible]	[illegible]
Moate (d),	[illegible]	[illegible]	[illegible]	[illegible]	[illegible]	[illegible]	[illegible]	[illegible]	[illegible]	[illegible]	[illegible]	[illegible]	[illegible]	[illegible]	[illegible]	[illegible]
Mullingar,	[illegible]	[illegible]	[illegible]	[illegible]	[illegible]	[illegible]	[illegible]	[illegible]	[illegible]	[illegible]	[illegible]	[illegible]	[illegible]	[illegible]	[illegible]	[illegible]
WEXFORD COUNTY.																
Enniscorthy (e),	[illegible]	[illegible]	[illegible]	[illegible]	[illegible]	[illegible]	[illegible]	[illegible]	[illegible]	[illegible]	[illegible]	[illegible]	[illegible]	[illegible]	[illegible]	[illegible]
Gorey,	[illegible]	[illegible]	[illegible]	[illegible]	[illegible]	[illegible]	[illegible]	[illegible]	[illegible]	[illegible]	[illegible]	[illegible]	[illegible]	[illegible]	[illegible]	[illegible]
New Ross,	[illegible]	[illegible]	[illegible]	[illegible]	[illegible]	[illegible]	[illegible]	[illegible]	[illegible]	[illegible]	[illegible]	[illegible]	[illegible]	[illegible]	[illegible]	[illegible]
Taghmon (f),	[illegible]	[illegible]	[illegible]	[illegible]	[illegible]	[illegible]	[illegible]	[illegible]	[illegible]	[illegible]	[illegible]	[illegible]	[illegible]	[illegible]	[illegible]	[illegible]
Wexford (g),	[illegible]	[illegible]	[illegible]	[illegible]	[illegible]	[illegible]	[illegible]	[illegible]	[illegible]	[illegible]	[illegible]	[illegible]	[illegible]	[illegible]	[illegible]	-
WICKLOW COUNTY.																
Arklow,	[illegible]	[illegible]	[illegible]	[illegible]	[illegible]	[illegible]	[illegible]	[illegible]	[illegible]	[illegible]	[illegible]	[illegible]	[illegible]	[illegible]	[illegible]	[illegible]
Bray,	[illegible]	-	[illegible]	-	[illegible]	-	[illegible]	-	[illegible]	-	[illegible]	-	[illegible]	-	[illegible]	-
Rathdrum,	[illegible]	[illegible]	[illegible]	[illegible]	[illegible]	[illegible]	[illegible]	[illegible]	[illegible]	[illegible]	[illegible]	[illegible]	[illegible]	[illegible]	[illegible]	[illegible]
Wicklow (h),	[illegible]	[illegible]	[illegible]	[illegible]	[illegible]	[illegible]	[illegible]	[illegible]	[illegible]	[illegible]	[illegible]	[illegible]	[illegible]	[illegible]	[illegible]	[illegible]

II.—PROVINCE OF MUNSTER.

Counties and Constabulary Districts.	Summer Men From	Summer Men To	Summer Boys From	Summer Boys To	Summer Women From	Summer Women To	Summer Girls From	Summer Girls To	Winter Men From	Winter Men To	Winter Boys From	Winter Boys To	Winter Women From	Winter Women To	Winter Girls From	Winter Girls To
CLARE COUNTY.																
Ballyvaughan (i),	[illegible]	[illegible]	[illegible]	[illegible]	[illegible]	[illegible]	[illegible]	[illegible]	[illegible]	[illegible]	[illegible]	[illegible]	[illegible]	[illegible]	[illegible]	[illegible]
Corofin (j),	[illegible]	[illegible]	[illegible]	[illegible]	[illegible]	[illegible]	[illegible]	[illegible]	[illegible]	[illegible]	[illegible]	[illegible]	-	-	-	-
Ennis,	[illegible]	[illegible]	[illegible]	[illegible]	[illegible]	[illegible]	[illegible]	[illegible]	[illegible]	[illegible]	[illegible]	[illegible]	[illegible]	[illegible]	[illegible]	[illegible]
Ennistymon,	[illegible]	[illegible]	[illegible]	[illegible]	[illegible]	[illegible]	[illegible]	[illegible]	[illegible]	[illegible]	[illegible]	[illegible]	[illegible]	[illegible]	[illegible]	[illegible]
Killadysert (k),	[illegible]	[illegible]	[illegible]	[illegible]	[illegible]	[illegible]	[illegible]	[illegible]	[illegible]	[illegible]	[illegible]	[illegible]	[illegible]	[illegible]	[illegible]	[illegible]
Kilkee,	[illegible]	[illegible]	[illegible]	[illegible]	[illegible]	[illegible]	[illegible]	[illegible]	[illegible]	[illegible]	[illegible]	[illegible]	[illegible]	[illegible]	[illegible]	[illegible]
Kilrush (l),	[illegible]	[illegible]	[illegible]	[illegible]	[illegible]	[illegible]	[illegible]	[illegible]	[illegible]	[illegible]	[illegible]	[illegible]	[illegible]	[illegible]	[illegible]	[illegible]
[illegible] (m),	[illegible]	[illegible]	[illegible]	[illegible]	[illegible]	[illegible]	[illegible]	[illegible]	[illegible]	[illegible]	[illegible]	[illegible]	[illegible]	[illegible]	[illegible]	[illegible]
Tulla (n),	[illegible]	[illegible]	[illegible]	[illegible]	[illegible]	[illegible]	[illegible]	[illegible]	[illegible]	[illegible]	[illegible]	[illegible]	[illegible]	[illegible]	[illegible]	[illegible]

(a) [illegible]
(b) [illegible]
(c) [illegible]
(d) [illegible]
(e) [illegible]
(f) [illegible]
(g) [illegible]
(h) [illegible]
(i) [illegible]
(j) [illegible]
(k) [illegible]
(l) [illegible]
(m) [illegible]
(n) [illegible]

II.—PROVINCE OF MUNSTER—*continued.*

Counties and Constabulary Districts	Summer: Men From	Summer: Men To	Summer: Boys From	Summer: Boys To	Summer: Women From	Summer: Women To	Summer: Girls From	Summer: Girls To	Winter: Men From	Winter: Men To	Winter: Boys From	Winter: Boys To	Winter: Women From	Winter: Women To	Winter: Girls From	Winter: Girls To
	s. d.	s. d.	s. d.	s. d.	s. d.	s. d.	s. d.	s. d.	s. d.	s. d.	s. d.	s. d.	s. d.	s. d.	s. d.	s. d.
Cork County (E.R.)																
[illegible] (a),	[illegible]	[illegible]	[illegible]	[illegible]	[illegible]	[illegible]	[illegible]	[illegible]	[illegible]	[illegible]	[illegible]	[illegible]	[illegible]	[illegible]	[illegible]	[illegible]
Charleville,	[illegible]	[illegible]	[illegible]	[illegible]	[illegible]	[illegible]	[illegible]	[illegible]	[illegible]	[illegible]	[illegible]	[illegible]	[illegible]	[illegible]	[illegible]	[illegible]
Cork, North (b),	[illegible]	[illegible]	[illegible]	[illegible]	[illegible]	[illegible]	[illegible]	[illegible]	[illegible]	[illegible]	[illegible]	[illegible]	[illegible]	[illegible]	[illegible]	[illegible]
Cork, South,	[illegible]	[illegible]	[illegible]	[illegible]	[illegible]	[illegible]	[illegible]	[illegible]	[illegible]	[illegible]	[illegible]	[illegible]	[illegible]	[illegible]	[illegible]	[illegible]
Fermoy,	[illegible]	[illegible]	[illegible]	[illegible]	[illegible]	[illegible]	[illegible]	[illegible]	[illegible]	[illegible]	[illegible]	[illegible]	[illegible]	[illegible]	[illegible]	[illegible]
Kanturk (c),	[illegible]	[illegible]	[illegible]	[illegible]	[illegible]	[illegible]	[illegible]	[illegible]	[illegible]	[illegible]	[illegible]	[illegible]	[illegible]	[illegible]	[illegible]	[illegible]
Kinsale (d),	[illegible]	[illegible]	[illegible]	[illegible]	[illegible]	[illegible]	[illegible]	[illegible]	[illegible]	[illegible]	[illegible]	[illegible]	[illegible]	[illegible]	[illegible]	[illegible]
Mallow (e),	[illegible]	[illegible]	[illegible]	[illegible]	[illegible]	[illegible]	[illegible]	[illegible]	[illegible]	[illegible]	[illegible]	[illegible]	[illegible]	[illegible]	[illegible]	[illegible]
Middleton,	[illegible]	[illegible]	[illegible]	[illegible]	[illegible]	[illegible]	[illegible]	[illegible]	[illegible]	[illegible]	[illegible]	[illegible]	[illegible]	[illegible]	[illegible]	[illegible]
Mitchelstown,	[illegible]	[illegible]	[illegible]	[illegible]	[illegible]	[illegible]	[illegible]	[illegible]	[illegible]	[illegible]	[illegible]	[illegible]	[illegible]	[illegible]	[illegible]	[illegible]
[illegible],	[illegible]	[illegible]	[illegible]	[illegible]	[illegible]	[illegible]	[illegible]	[illegible]	[illegible]	[illegible]	[illegible]	[illegible]	[illegible]	[illegible]	[illegible]	[illegible]
Queenstown,	[illegible]	[illegible]	[illegible]	[illegible]	[illegible]	[illegible]	[illegible]	[illegible]	[illegible]	[illegible]	[illegible]	[illegible]	[illegible]	[illegible]	[illegible]	[illegible]
Youghal (f),	[illegible]	[illegible]	[illegible]	[illegible]	[illegible]	[illegible]	[illegible]	[illegible]	[illegible]	[illegible]	[illegible]	[illegible]	[illegible]	[illegible]	[illegible]	[illegible]
Youghal (g),	[illegible]	[illegible]	[illegible]	[illegible]	[illegible]	[illegible]	[illegible]	[illegible]	[illegible]	[illegible]	[illegible]	[illegible]	[illegible]	[illegible]	[illegible]	[illegible]
Cork County (W.R.)																
Bandon,	[illegible]	[illegible]	[illegible]	[illegible]	[illegible]	[illegible]	[illegible]	[illegible]	[illegible]	[illegible]	[illegible]	[illegible]	[illegible]	[illegible]	[illegible]	[illegible]
Bantry (h),	[illegible]	[illegible]	[illegible]	[illegible]	[illegible]	[illegible]	[illegible]	[illegible]	[illegible]	[illegible]	[illegible]	[illegible]	[illegible]	[illegible]	[illegible]	[illegible]
Castletown Bere,	[illegible]	[illegible]	[illegible]	[illegible]	[illegible]	[illegible]	[illegible]	[illegible]	[illegible]	[illegible]	[illegible]	[illegible]	[illegible]	[illegible]	[illegible]	[illegible]
Clonakilty (i),	[illegible]	[illegible]	[illegible]	[illegible]	[illegible]	[illegible]	[illegible]	[illegible]	[illegible]	[illegible]	[illegible]	[illegible]	[illegible]	[illegible]	[illegible]	[illegible]
Dunmanway (j),	[illegible]	[illegible]	[illegible]	[illegible]	[illegible]	[illegible]	[illegible]	[illegible]	[illegible]	[illegible]	[illegible]	[illegible]	[illegible]	[illegible]	[illegible]	[illegible]
Macroom (k),	[illegible]	[illegible]	[illegible]	[illegible]	[illegible]	[illegible]	[illegible]	[illegible]	[illegible]	[illegible]	[illegible]	[illegible]	[illegible]	[illegible]	[illegible]	[illegible]
Skibbereen (l),	[illegible]	[illegible]	[illegible]	[illegible]	[illegible]	[illegible]	[illegible]	[illegible]	[illegible]	[illegible]	[illegible]	[illegible]	[illegible]	[illegible]	[illegible]	[illegible]
[illegible] (m),	[illegible]	[illegible]	[illegible]	[illegible]	[illegible]	[illegible]	[illegible]	[illegible]	[illegible]	[illegible]	[illegible]	[illegible]	[illegible]	[illegible]	[illegible]	[illegible]
Skull (n),	[illegible]	[illegible]	[illegible]	[illegible]	[illegible]	[illegible]	[illegible]	[illegible]	[illegible]	[illegible]	[illegible]	[illegible]	[illegible]	[illegible]	[illegible]	[illegible]
Kerry County.																
Cahersiveen,	[illegible]	[illegible]	[illegible]	[illegible]	[illegible]	[illegible]	[illegible]	[illegible]	[illegible]	[illegible]	[illegible]	[illegible]	[illegible]	[illegible]	[illegible]	[illegible]
Castleisland,	[illegible]	[illegible]	[illegible]	[illegible]	[illegible]	[illegible]	[illegible]	[illegible]	[illegible]	[illegible]	[illegible]	[illegible]	[illegible]	[illegible]	[illegible]	[illegible]
Dingle,	[illegible]	[illegible]	[illegible]	[illegible]	[illegible]	[illegible]	[illegible]	[illegible]	[illegible]	[illegible]	[illegible]	[illegible]	[illegible]	[illegible]	[illegible]	[illegible]
Kenmare (o),	[illegible]	[illegible]	[illegible]	[illegible]	[illegible]	[illegible]	[illegible]	[illegible]	[illegible]	[illegible]	[illegible]	[illegible]	[illegible]	[illegible]	[illegible]	[illegible]
Killarney (a),	[illegible]	[illegible]	[illegible]	[illegible]	[illegible]	[illegible]	[illegible]	[illegible]	[illegible]	[illegible]	[illegible]	[illegible]	[illegible]	[illegible]	[illegible]	[illegible]
Killorglin,	[illegible]	[illegible]	[illegible]	[illegible]	[illegible]	[illegible]	[illegible]	[illegible]	[illegible]	[illegible]	[illegible]	[illegible]	[illegible]	[illegible]	[illegible]	[illegible]
Listowel,	[illegible]	[illegible]	[illegible]	[illegible]	[illegible]	[illegible]	[illegible]	[illegible]	[illegible]	[illegible]	[illegible]	[illegible]	[illegible]	[illegible]	[illegible]	[illegible]
Tralee,	[illegible]	[illegible]	[illegible]	[illegible]	[illegible]	[illegible]	[illegible]	[illegible]	[illegible]	[illegible]	[illegible]	[illegible]	[illegible]	[illegible]	[illegible]	[illegible]
Limerick County.																
Abbeyfeale,	[illegible]	[illegible]	[illegible]	[illegible]	[illegible]	[illegible]	[illegible]	[illegible]	[illegible]	[illegible]	[illegible]	[illegible]	[illegible]	[illegible]	[illegible]	[illegible]
Adare,	[illegible]	[illegible]	[illegible]	[illegible]	[illegible]	[illegible]	[illegible]	[illegible]	[illegible]	[illegible]	[illegible]	[illegible]	[illegible]	[illegible]	[illegible]	[illegible]
Bruff (p),	[illegible]	[illegible]	[illegible]	[illegible]	[illegible]	[illegible]	[illegible]	[illegible]	[illegible]	[illegible]	[illegible]	[illegible]	[illegible]	[illegible]	[illegible]	[illegible]
Kilmallock (r),	[illegible]	[illegible]	[illegible]	[illegible]	[illegible]	[illegible]	[illegible]	[illegible]	[illegible]	[illegible]	[illegible]	[illegible]	[illegible]	[illegible]	[illegible]	[illegible]
Limerick,	[illegible]	[illegible]	[illegible]	[illegible]	[illegible]	[illegible]	[illegible]	[illegible]	[illegible]	[illegible]	[illegible]	[illegible]	[illegible]	[illegible]	[illegible]	[illegible]
Newcastle (s),	[illegible]	[illegible]	[illegible]	[illegible]	[illegible]	[illegible]	[illegible]	[illegible]	[illegible]	[illegible]	[illegible]	[illegible]	[illegible]	[illegible]	[illegible]	[illegible]
New Pallas,	[illegible]	[illegible]	[illegible]	[illegible]	[illegible]	[illegible]	[illegible]	[illegible]	[illegible]	[illegible]	[illegible]	[illegible]	[illegible]	[illegible]	[illegible]	[illegible]
Rathkeale,	[illegible]	[illegible]	[illegible]	[illegible]	[illegible]	[illegible]	[illegible]	[illegible]	[illegible]	[illegible]	[illegible]	[illegible]	[illegible]	[illegible]	[illegible]	[illegible]

(a) With board. [illegible]

[illegible]

II.—PROVINCE OF MUNSTER—*continued.*

Counties and Constituent Unions.	Summer.								Winter.							
	Men.		Boys.		Women.		Girls.		Men.		Boys.		Women.		Girls.	
	From	To	From	To	From	To	From	To	From	To	From	To	From	To	From	To
	s. d.	s. d.	s. d.	s. d.	s. d.	s. d.	s. d.	s. d.	s. d.	s. d.	s. d.	s. d.	s. d.	s. d.	s. d.	s. d.
Tipperary Co., N.R.																
[illegible]	[illegible]	[illegible]	[illegible]	[illegible]	[illegible]	[illegible]	[illegible]	[illegible]	[illegible]	[illegible]	[illegible]	[illegible]	[illegible]	[illegible]	[illegible]	[illegible]
[illegible] (c),	[illegible]	[illegible]	[illegible]	[illegible]	[illegible]	[illegible]	[illegible]	[illegible]	[illegible]	[illegible]	[illegible]	[illegible]	[illegible]	[illegible]	[illegible]	[illegible]
[illegible]	[illegible]	[illegible]	[illegible]	[illegible]	[illegible]	[illegible]	[illegible]	[illegible]	[illegible]	[illegible]	[illegible]	[illegible]	[illegible]	[illegible]	[illegible]	[illegible]
[illegible]	[illegible]	[illegible]	[illegible]	[illegible]	[illegible]	[illegible]	[illegible]	[illegible]	[illegible]	[illegible]	[illegible]	[illegible]	[illegible]	[illegible]	[illegible]	[illegible]
[illegible]	[illegible]	[illegible]	[illegible]	[illegible]	[illegible]	[illegible]	[illegible]	[illegible]	[illegible]	[illegible]	[illegible]	[illegible]	[illegible]	[illegible]	[illegible]	[illegible]
Thurles,	[illegible]	[illegible]	[illegible]	[illegible]	[illegible]	[illegible]	[illegible]	[illegible]	[illegible]	[illegible]	[illegible]	[illegible]	[illegible]	[illegible]	[illegible]	[illegible]
Tipperary Co., S.R.																
Cahir (b),	[illegible]	[illegible]	[illegible]	[illegible]	[illegible]	[illegible]	[illegible]	[illegible]	[illegible]	[illegible]	[illegible]	[illegible]	[illegible]	[illegible]	[illegible]	[illegible]
[illegible] (d),	[illegible]	[illegible]	[illegible]	[illegible]	[illegible]	[illegible]	–	–	[illegible]	[illegible]	[illegible]	[illegible]	[illegible]	[illegible]	–	–
Carrick-on-Suir,	[illegible]	[illegible]	[illegible]	[illegible]	[illegible]	[illegible]	[illegible]	[illegible]	[illegible]	[illegible]	[illegible]	[illegible]	[illegible]	[illegible]	[illegible]	[illegible]
Cashel,	[illegible]	[illegible]	[illegible]	[illegible]	[illegible]	[illegible]	[illegible]	[illegible]	[illegible]	[illegible]	[illegible]	[illegible]	[illegible]	[illegible]	[illegible]	[illegible]
Clonmel,	[illegible]	[illegible]	[illegible]	[illegible]	[illegible]	[illegible]	[illegible]	[illegible]	[illegible]	[illegible]	[illegible]	[illegible]	[illegible]	[illegible]	[illegible]	[illegible]
[illegible] (d),	[illegible]	[illegible]	[illegible]	[illegible]	[illegible]	[illegible]	[illegible]	[illegible]	[illegible]	[illegible]	[illegible]	[illegible]	[illegible]	[illegible]	[illegible]	[illegible]
Tipperary (e),	[illegible]	[illegible]	[illegible]	[illegible]	[illegible]	[illegible]	[illegible]	[illegible]	[illegible]	[illegible]	[illegible]	[illegible]	[illegible]	[illegible]	[illegible]	[illegible]
Waterford Co.																
[illegible]	[illegible]	[illegible]	[illegible]	[illegible]	[illegible]	[illegible]	[illegible]	[illegible]	[illegible]	[illegible]	[illegible]	[illegible]	[illegible]	[illegible]	[illegible]	[illegible]
Dungarvan,	[illegible]	[illegible]	[illegible]	[illegible]	[illegible]	[illegible]	[illegible]	[illegible]	[illegible]	[illegible]	[illegible]	[illegible]	[illegible]	[illegible]	[illegible]	[illegible]
[illegible]	[illegible]	[illegible]	[illegible]	[illegible]	[illegible]	[illegible]	[illegible]	[illegible]	[illegible]	[illegible]	[illegible]	[illegible]	[illegible]	[illegible]	[illegible]	[illegible]
Waterford,	[illegible]	[illegible]	[illegible]	[illegible]	[illegible]	[illegible]	[illegible]	[illegible]	[illegible]	[illegible]	[illegible]	[illegible]	[illegible]	[illegible]	[illegible]	[illegible]

III.—PROVINCE OF ULSTER.

Counties and Constituent Unions.	Summer.								Winter.							
	Men.		Boys.		Women.		Girls.		Men.		Boys.		Women.		Girls.	
	From	To	From	To	From	To	From	To	From	To	From	To	From	To	From	To
Antrim County.																
Antrim,	[illegible]	[illegible]	[illegible]	[illegible]	[illegible]	[illegible]	[illegible]	[illegible]	[illegible]	[illegible]	[illegible]	[illegible]	[illegible]	[illegible]	[illegible]	[illegible]
[illegible]	[illegible]	[illegible]	[illegible]	[illegible]	[illegible]	[illegible]	[illegible]	[illegible]	[illegible]	[illegible]	[illegible]	[illegible]	[illegible]	[illegible]	[illegible]	[illegible]
[illegible] (f),	[illegible]	[illegible]	[illegible]	[illegible]	[illegible]	[illegible]	[illegible]	[illegible]	[illegible]	[illegible]	[illegible]	[illegible]	[illegible]	[illegible]	[illegible]	[illegible]
Belfast East,	[illegible]	[illegible]	[illegible]	[illegible]	[illegible]	[illegible]	[illegible]	[illegible]	[illegible]	[illegible]	[illegible]	[illegible]	[illegible]	[illegible]	[illegible]	[illegible]
Belfast North,	[illegible]	[illegible]	[illegible]	[illegible]	[illegible]	[illegible]	[illegible]	[illegible]	[illegible]	[illegible]	[illegible]	[illegible]	[illegible]	[illegible]	[illegible]	[illegible]
[illegible]	[illegible]	[illegible]	[illegible]	[illegible]	[illegible]	[illegible]	[illegible]	[illegible]	[illegible]	[illegible]	[illegible]	[illegible]	[illegible]	[illegible]	[illegible]	[illegible]
Belfast South (f),	[illegible]	–	–	–	[illegible]	–	–	–	[illegible]	–	–	–	[illegible]	–	–	–
Belfast West (h),	[illegible]	[illegible]	[illegible]	[illegible]	[illegible]	[illegible]	[illegible]	[illegible]	[illegible]	[illegible]	[illegible]	[illegible]	[illegible]	[illegible]	–	–
Larne,	[illegible]	[illegible]	[illegible]	[illegible]	[illegible]	[illegible]	[illegible]	[illegible]	[illegible]	[illegible]	[illegible]	[illegible]	[illegible]	[illegible]	[illegible]	[illegible]
Lisburn,	[illegible]	[illegible]	[illegible]	[illegible]	[illegible]	[illegible]	[illegible]	[illegible]	[illegible]	[illegible]	[illegible]	[illegible]	[illegible]	[illegible]	[illegible]	[illegible]
Armagh County.																
Armagh,	[illegible]	[illegible]	[illegible]	[illegible]	[illegible]	[illegible]	[illegible]	[illegible]	[illegible]	[illegible]	[illegible]	[illegible]	[illegible]	[illegible]	[illegible]	[illegible]
Lurgan (f),	[illegible]	[illegible]	[illegible]	[illegible]	[illegible]	[illegible]	[illegible]	[illegible]	[illegible]	[illegible]	[illegible]	[illegible]	[illegible]	[illegible]	[illegible]	[illegible]
Newry (f),	[illegible]	[illegible]	[illegible]	[illegible]	[illegible]	[illegible]	[illegible]	[illegible]	[illegible]	[illegible]	[illegible]	[illegible]	[illegible]	[illegible]	[illegible]	[illegible]
[illegible] (f),	[illegible]	[illegible]	[illegible]	[illegible]	[illegible]	[illegible]	[illegible]	[illegible]	[illegible]	[illegible]	[illegible]	[illegible]	[illegible]	[illegible]	[illegible]	[illegible]
Cavan County.																
[illegible] (k),	[illegible]	[illegible]	[illegible]	[illegible]	[illegible]	[illegible]	[illegible]	[illegible]	[illegible]	[illegible]	[illegible]	[illegible]	[illegible]	[illegible]	[illegible]	[illegible]
[illegible]	[illegible]	[illegible]	[illegible]	[illegible]	[illegible]	[illegible]	[illegible]	[illegible]	[illegible]	[illegible]	[illegible]	[illegible]	[illegible]	[illegible]	[illegible]	[illegible]
Cavan (m),	[illegible]	[illegible]	[illegible]	[illegible]	[illegible]	[illegible]	–	–	[illegible]	[illegible]	–	–	–	–	–	–
[illegible]	[illegible]	[illegible]	[illegible]	[illegible]	[illegible]	[illegible]	[illegible]	[illegible]	[illegible]	[illegible]	[illegible]	[illegible]	[illegible]	[illegible]	[illegible]	[illegible]
[illegible] (n),	[illegible]	[illegible]	[illegible]	[illegible]	[illegible]	[illegible]	[illegible]	[illegible]	[illegible]	[illegible]	[illegible]	[illegible]	[illegible]	[illegible]	[illegible]	[illegible]

(a) [illegible]
(b) [illegible]
(c) [illegible]
(d) [illegible]
(e) [illegible]
(f) [illegible]
(g) [illegible]
(h) [illegible]
(i) [illegible]
(k) [illegible]
(l) [illegible]
(m) [illegible]
(n) [illegible]

III.—PROVINCE OF ULSTER—continued.

Counties and Poor Law Unions	Summer								Winter							
	Men.		Boys.		Women.		Girls.		Men.		Boys.		Women.		Girls.	
	From	To	From	To	From	To	From	To	From	To	From	To	From	To	From	To
	s. d.	s. d.	s. d.	s. d.	s. d.	s. d.	s. d.	s. d.	s. d.	s. d.	s. d.	s. d.	s. d.	s. d.	s. d.	s. d.
[illegible] County.																
[illegible]	[illegible]	[illegible]	[illegible]	[illegible]	[illegible]	[illegible]		[illegible]	[illegible]	[illegible]	[illegible]	[illegible]	[illegible]	[illegible]	[illegible]	[illegible]
[illegible]	[illegible]	[illegible]	[illegible]	[illegible]	[illegible]	[illegible]	[illegible]	[illegible]	[illegible]	[illegible]	[illegible]	[illegible]	[illegible]	[illegible]	[illegible]	[illegible]
[illegible]	[illegible]	[illegible]	[illegible]	[illegible]	[illegible]	[illegible]	[illegible]	[illegible]	[illegible]	[illegible]	[illegible]	[illegible]	[illegible]	[illegible]	[illegible]	[illegible]
[illegible]	[illegible]	[illegible]	[illegible]	[illegible]	[illegible]	[illegible]	[illegible]	[illegible]	[illegible]	[illegible]	[illegible]	[illegible]	[illegible]	[illegible]	[illegible]	[illegible]
[illegible]	[illegible]	[illegible]	[illegible]	[illegible]	[illegible]	[illegible]	[illegible]	[illegible]	[illegible]	[illegible]	[illegible]	[illegible]	[illegible]	[illegible]	[illegible]	[illegible]
Letterkenny,	[illegible]	[illegible]	[illegible]	[illegible]	[illegible]	[illegible]	[illegible]	[illegible]	[illegible]	[illegible]	[illegible]	[illegible]	[illegible]	[illegible]	[illegible]	[illegible]
[illegible]	[illegible]	[illegible]	[illegible]	[illegible]	[illegible]	[illegible]	[illegible]	[illegible]	[illegible]	[illegible]	[illegible]	[illegible]	[illegible]	[illegible]	[illegible]	[illegible]
[illegible]	[illegible]	[illegible]	[illegible]	[illegible]	[illegible]	[illegible]	[illegible]	[illegible]	[illegible]	[illegible]	[illegible]	[illegible]	[illegible]	[illegible]	[illegible]	[illegible]
[illegible]	[illegible]	[illegible]	[illegible]	-	[illegible]	[illegible]	[illegible]	[illegible]	[illegible]	[illegible]	[illegible]	[illegible]	[illegible]	-	[illegible]	-
Down County.																
[illegible]	[illegible]	-	[illegible]	-	[illegible]	-	[illegible]	-	[illegible]	-	[illegible]	-	[illegible]	-	[illegible]	-
[illegible]	[illegible]	[illegible]	[illegible]	[illegible]	[illegible]	[illegible]	[illegible]	[illegible]	[illegible]	[illegible]	[illegible]	[illegible]	[illegible]	[illegible]	[illegible]	[illegible]
[illegible]	[illegible]	[illegible]	[illegible]	[illegible]	[illegible]	[illegible]	[illegible]	[illegible]	[illegible]	[illegible]	[illegible]	[illegible]	[illegible]	[illegible]	[illegible]	[illegible]
[illegible]	[illegible]	[illegible]	[illegible]	[illegible]	[illegible]	[illegible]	[illegible]	[illegible]	[illegible]	[illegible]	[illegible]	[illegible]	[illegible]	[illegible]	[illegible]	[illegible]
Fermanagh County.																
[illegible]	[illegible]	[illegible]	[illegible]	[illegible]	[illegible]	[illegible]	[illegible]	[illegible]	[illegible]	[illegible]	[illegible]	[illegible]	[illegible]	[illegible]	[illegible]	[illegible]
[illegible]	[illegible]	[illegible]	[illegible]	[illegible]	[illegible]	[illegible]	[illegible]	[illegible]	[illegible]	[illegible]	[illegible]	[illegible]	[illegible]	[illegible]	[illegible]	[illegible]
[illegible]	[illegible]	[illegible]	[illegible]	[illegible]	[illegible]	[illegible]	[illegible]	[illegible]	[illegible]	[illegible]	[illegible]	[illegible]	[illegible]	[illegible]	[illegible]	[illegible]
[illegible]	[illegible]	[illegible]	[illegible]	[illegible]	[illegible]	[illegible]	[illegible]	[illegible]	[illegible]	[illegible]	[illegible]	[illegible]	[illegible]	[illegible]	[illegible]	[illegible]
Londonderry Co.																
[illegible]	[illegible]	[illegible]	[illegible]	[illegible]	[illegible]	[illegible]	[illegible]	[illegible]	[illegible]	[illegible]	[illegible]	[illegible]	[illegible]	[illegible]	[illegible]	[illegible]
[illegible]	[illegible]	[illegible]	[illegible]	[illegible]	[illegible]	[illegible]	[illegible]	[illegible]	[illegible]	[illegible]	[illegible]	[illegible]	[illegible]	[illegible]	[illegible]	[illegible]
Londonderry,	[illegible]	[illegible]	[illegible]	[illegible]	[illegible]	[illegible]	[illegible]	[illegible]	[illegible]	[illegible]	[illegible]	[illegible]	[illegible]	[illegible]	[illegible]	[illegible]
[illegible]	[illegible]	[illegible]	[illegible]	[illegible]	[illegible]	[illegible]	[illegible]	[illegible]	[illegible]	[illegible]	[illegible]	[illegible]	[illegible]	[illegible]	[illegible]	[illegible]
Monaghan County.																
[illegible]	[illegible]	[illegible]	[illegible]	[illegible]	[illegible]	[illegible]	[illegible]	[illegible]	[illegible]	[illegible]	[illegible]	[illegible]	[illegible]	[illegible]	[illegible]	[illegible]
[illegible]	[illegible]	[illegible]	[illegible]	[illegible]	[illegible]	[illegible]	[illegible]	[illegible]	[illegible]	[illegible]	[illegible]	[illegible]	[illegible]	[illegible]	[illegible]	[illegible]
[illegible]	[illegible]	[illegible]	[illegible]	[illegible]	[illegible]	[illegible]	[illegible]	[illegible]	[illegible]	[illegible]	[illegible]	[illegible]	[illegible]	[illegible]	[illegible]	[illegible]
Tyrone County.																
[illegible]	[illegible]	[illegible]	[illegible]	[illegible]	[illegible]	[illegible]	[illegible]	[illegible]	[illegible]	[illegible]	[illegible]	[illegible]	[illegible]	[illegible]	[illegible]	[illegible]
[illegible]	[illegible]	[illegible]	[illegible]	[illegible]	[illegible]	[illegible]	[illegible]	[illegible]	[illegible]	[illegible]	[illegible]	[illegible]	[illegible]	[illegible]	[illegible]	[illegible]
[illegible]	[illegible]	[illegible]	[illegible]	[illegible]	[illegible]	[illegible]	[illegible]	[illegible]	[illegible]	[illegible]	[illegible]	[illegible]	[illegible]	[illegible]	[illegible]	[illegible]
[illegible]	[illegible]	[illegible]	[illegible]	[illegible]	[illegible]	[illegible]	[illegible]	[illegible]	[illegible]	[illegible]	[illegible]	[illegible]	[illegible]	[illegible]	[illegible]	[illegible]
[illegible]	[illegible]	[illegible]	[illegible]	[illegible]	[illegible]	[illegible]	[illegible]	[illegible]	[illegible]	[illegible]	[illegible]	[illegible]	[illegible]	[illegible]	[illegible]	[illegible]
[illegible]	[illegible]	[illegible]	[illegible]	[illegible]	[illegible]	[illegible]	[illegible]	[illegible]	[illegible]	[illegible]	[illegible]	[illegible]	[illegible]	[illegible]	[illegible]	[illegible]

[illegible]

IV.—PROVINCE OF CONNAUGHT.

Counties and Poor-Law Unions.	Summer.								Winter.							
	Men.		Boys.		Women.		Girls.		Men.		Boys.		Women.		Girls.	
	From	To	From	To	From	To	From	To	From	To	From	To	From	To	From	To
	s. d.	s. d.	s. d.	s. d.	s. d.	s. d.	s. d.	s. d.	s. d.	s. d.	s. d.	s. d.	s. d.	s. d.	s. d.	s. d.
GALWAY COUNTY.																
Athenry	[illegible]	[illegible]	[illegible]	[illegible]	[illegible]	[illegible]	[illegible]	[illegible]	[illegible]	[illegible]	[illegible]	[illegible]	[illegible]	[illegible]	[illegible]	[illegible]
Ballinasloe	[illegible]	[illegible]	[illegible]	[illegible]	[illegible]	[illegible]	[illegible]	[illegible]	[illegible]	[illegible]	[illegible]	[illegible]	[illegible]	[illegible]	[illegible]	[illegible]
Clifden	[illegible]	[illegible]	[illegible]	[illegible]	[illegible]	[illegible]	[illegible]	[illegible]	[illegible]	[illegible]	[illegible]	[illegible]	[illegible]	[illegible]	[illegible]	[illegible]
Glenamaddy	[illegible]	[illegible]	[illegible]	[illegible]	[illegible]	[illegible]	[illegible]	[illegible]	[illegible]	[illegible]	[illegible]	[illegible]	[illegible]	[illegible]	[illegible]	[illegible]
Dunmore	[illegible]	[illegible]	[illegible]	[illegible]	[illegible]	[illegible]	[illegible]	[illegible]	[illegible]	[illegible]	[illegible]	[illegible]	[illegible]	[illegible]	[illegible]	[illegible]
Galway	[illegible]	[illegible]	[illegible]	[illegible]	[illegible]	[illegible]	[illegible]	[illegible]	[illegible]	[illegible]	[illegible]	[illegible]	[illegible]	[illegible]	[illegible]	[illegible]
Gort	[illegible]	[illegible]	[illegible]	[illegible]	[illegible]	[illegible]	[illegible]	[illegible]	[illegible]	[illegible]	[illegible]	[illegible]	[illegible]	[illegible]	[illegible]	[illegible]
Loughrea	[illegible]	[illegible]	[illegible]	[illegible]	[illegible]	[illegible]	[illegible]	[illegible]	[illegible]	[illegible]	[illegible]	[illegible]	[illegible]	[illegible]	[illegible]	[illegible]
Mountbellew	[illegible]	[illegible]	[illegible]	[illegible]	[illegible]	[illegible]	[illegible]	[illegible]	[illegible]	[illegible]	[illegible]	[illegible]	[illegible]	[illegible]	[illegible]	[illegible]
Oughterard	[illegible]	[illegible]	[illegible]	[illegible]	[illegible]	[illegible]	[illegible]	[illegible]	[illegible]	[illegible]	[illegible]	[illegible]	[illegible]	[illegible]	[illegible]	[illegible]
Portumna	[illegible]	[illegible]	[illegible]	[illegible]	[illegible]	[illegible]	[illegible]	[illegible]	[illegible]	[illegible]	[illegible]	[illegible]	[illegible]	[illegible]	[illegible]	[illegible]
Roundstone	[illegible]	[illegible]	[illegible]	[illegible]	[illegible]	[illegible]	[illegible]	[illegible]	[illegible]	[illegible]	[illegible]	[illegible]	[illegible]	[illegible]	[illegible]	[illegible]
Spiddle	[illegible]	[illegible]	[illegible]	[illegible]	[illegible]	[illegible]	[illegible]	[illegible]	[illegible]	[illegible]	[illegible]	[illegible]	[illegible]	[illegible]	[illegible]	[illegible]
Tuam	[illegible]	[illegible]	[illegible]	[illegible]	[illegible]	[illegible]	[illegible]	[illegible]	[illegible]	[illegible]	[illegible]	[illegible]	[illegible]	[illegible]	[illegible]	[illegible]
Woodford	[illegible]	[illegible]	[illegible]	[illegible]	[illegible]	[illegible]	[illegible]	[illegible]	[illegible]	[illegible]	[illegible]	[illegible]	[illegible]	[illegible]	[illegible]	[illegible]
LEITRIM COUNTY.																
Ballinamore	[illegible]	[illegible]	[illegible]	[illegible]	[illegible]	[illegible]	[illegible]	[illegible]	[illegible]	[illegible]	[illegible]	[illegible]	[illegible]	[illegible]	[illegible]	[illegible]
Carrick-on-Shannon	[illegible]	[illegible]	[illegible]	[illegible]	[illegible]	[illegible]	[illegible]	[illegible]	[illegible]	[illegible]	[illegible]	[illegible]	[illegible]	[illegible]	[illegible]	[illegible]
Drumshanbo	[illegible]	[illegible]	[illegible]	[illegible]	[illegible]	[illegible]	[illegible]	[illegible]	[illegible]	[illegible]	[illegible]	[illegible]	[illegible]	[illegible]	[illegible]	[illegible]
Manorhamilton	[illegible]	[illegible]	[illegible]	[illegible]	[illegible]	[illegible]	[illegible]	[illegible]	[illegible]	[illegible]	[illegible]	[illegible]	[illegible]	[illegible]	[illegible]	[illegible]
Mohill	[illegible]	[illegible]	[illegible]	[illegible]	[illegible]	[illegible]	[illegible]	[illegible]	[illegible]	[illegible]	[illegible]	[illegible]	[illegible]	[illegible]	[illegible]	[illegible]
MAYO COUNTY.																
Ballaghaderreen	[illegible]	[illegible]	[illegible]	[illegible]	[illegible]	[illegible]	[illegible]	[illegible]	[illegible]	[illegible]	[illegible]	[illegible]	[illegible]	[illegible]	[illegible]	[illegible]
Ballina	[illegible]	[illegible]	[illegible]	[illegible]	[illegible]	[illegible]	[illegible]	[illegible]	[illegible]	[illegible]	[illegible]	[illegible]	[illegible]	[illegible]	[illegible]	[illegible]
Ballinrobe	[illegible]	[illegible]	[illegible]	[illegible]	[illegible]	[illegible]	[illegible]	[illegible]	[illegible]	[illegible]	[illegible]	[illegible]	[illegible]	[illegible]	[illegible]	[illegible]
Belmullet	[illegible]	[illegible]	[illegible]	[illegible]	[illegible]	[illegible]	[illegible]	[illegible]	[illegible]	[illegible]	[illegible]	[illegible]	[illegible]	[illegible]	[illegible]	[illegible]
Castlebar	[illegible]	[illegible]	[illegible]	[illegible]	[illegible]	[illegible]	[illegible]	[illegible]	[illegible]	[illegible]	[illegible]	[illegible]	[illegible]	[illegible]	[illegible]	[illegible]
Claremorris	[illegible]	[illegible]	[illegible]	[illegible]	[illegible]	[illegible]	[illegible]	[illegible]	[illegible]	[illegible]	[illegible]	[illegible]	[illegible]	[illegible]	[illegible]	[illegible]
Newport	[illegible]	[illegible]	[illegible]	[illegible]	[illegible]	[illegible]	[illegible]	[illegible]	[illegible]	[illegible]	[illegible]	[illegible]	[illegible]	[illegible]	[illegible]	[illegible]
Swinford	[illegible]	[illegible]	[illegible]	[illegible]	[illegible]	[illegible]	[illegible]	[illegible]	[illegible]	[illegible]	[illegible]	[illegible]	[illegible]	[illegible]	[illegible]	[illegible]
Westport	[illegible]	[illegible]	[illegible]	[illegible]	[illegible]	[illegible]	[illegible]	[illegible]	[illegible]	[illegible]	[illegible]	[illegible]	[illegible]	[illegible]	[illegible]	[illegible]
ROSCOMMON COUNTY.																
Athlone	[illegible]	[illegible]	[illegible]	[illegible]	[illegible]	[illegible]	[illegible]	[illegible]	[illegible]	[illegible]	[illegible]	[illegible]	[illegible]	[illegible]	[illegible]	[illegible]
Boyle	[illegible]	[illegible]	[illegible]	[illegible]	[illegible]	[illegible]	[illegible]	[illegible]	[illegible]	[illegible]	[illegible]	[illegible]	[illegible]	[illegible]	[illegible]	[illegible]
Castlerea	[illegible]	[illegible]	[illegible]	[illegible]	[illegible]	[illegible]	[illegible]	[illegible]	[illegible]	[illegible]	[illegible]	[illegible]	[illegible]	[illegible]	[illegible]	[illegible]
Roscommon	[illegible]	[illegible]	[illegible]	[illegible]	[illegible]	[illegible]	[illegible]	[illegible]	[illegible]	[illegible]	[illegible]	[illegible]	[illegible]	[illegible]	[illegible]	[illegible]
Strokestown	[illegible]	[illegible]	[illegible]	[illegible]	[illegible]	[illegible]	[illegible]	[illegible]	[illegible]	[illegible]	[illegible]	[illegible]	[illegible]	[illegible]	[illegible]	[illegible]
SLIGO COUNTY.																
Ballymote	[illegible]	[illegible]	[illegible]	[illegible]	[illegible]	[illegible]	[illegible]	[illegible]	[illegible]	[illegible]	[illegible]	[illegible]	[illegible]	[illegible]	[illegible]	[illegible]
Collooney	[illegible]	[illegible]	[illegible]	[illegible]	[illegible]	[illegible]	[illegible]	[illegible]	[illegible]	[illegible]	[illegible]	[illegible]	[illegible]	[illegible]	[illegible]	[illegible]
Easky	[illegible]	[illegible]	[illegible]	[illegible]	[illegible]	[illegible]	[illegible]	[illegible]	[illegible]	[illegible]	[illegible]	[illegible]	[illegible]	[illegible]	[illegible]	[illegible]
Sligo	[illegible]	[illegible]	[illegible]	[illegible]	[illegible]	[illegible]	[illegible]	[illegible]	[illegible]	[illegible]	[illegible]	[illegible]	[illegible]	[illegible]	[illegible]	[illegible]
Tobercurry	[illegible]	[illegible]	[illegible]	[illegible]	[illegible]	[illegible]	[illegible]	[illegible]	[illegible]	[illegible]	[illegible]	[illegible]	[illegible]	[illegible]	[illegible]	[illegible]

[illegible]

In conclusion I have to thank the occupiers and owners of land in general, and also the proprietors and managers of Scutching Mills, Corn Mills, and Dairy Factories, for their courtesy in supplying the information required for the various Returns to the Enumerators: and to add, as I do, with much pleasure, that the members of the Royal Irish Constabulary and the Metropolitan Police who acted as Enumerators discharged their duties as such with their usual efficiency.

I have the honour to remain

Your Excellency's faithful servant,

T. W. GRIMSHAW,

Registrar-General.

General Register Office,

Charlemont House, Dublin

19th May, 1898.

DETAILED TABLES.

TABLE I.—Showing, by Counties and Provinces, the Number of Holdings, their Size in Statute Acres, and the [illegible] of Land in the Year 18[illegible].

COUNTIES	[illegible]
[illegible]	[illegible]
PROVINCES	
[illegible]	[illegible]
Total of Ireland	[illegible]

[illegible]

TABLE 2.—Showing, by Poor Law Unions, the Number of Holdings, their Size in Statute Acres, and the Division of Land in the Year 1897—continued.

[illegible]

Table A—Showing, by Counties and Provinces, the Extent of Land

Counties.	[illegible]	[illegible]	[illegible]	[illegible]	[illegible]	[illegible]	[illegible]	[illegible]	[illegible]	[illegible]	[illegible]
	Corn, Beans, and Peas								Green Crops		
Antrim,	1,117	[illegible]	[illegible]	.	14	[illegible]	14	[illegible]	[illegible]	[illegible]	[illegible]
Armagh,	[illegible]	[illegible]	[illegible]	.	[illegible]	[illegible]	6	[illegible]	[illegible]	[illegible]	[illegible]
Carlow,	[illegible]	[illegible]	[illegible]		[illegible]	.	.	[illegible]	[illegible]	[illegible]	[illegible]
Cavan,	[illegible]	[illegible]	[illegible]	[illegible]	[illegible]	[illegible]	1	[illegible]	[illegible]	[illegible]	[illegible]
Clare,	[illegible]	[illegible]	[illegible]	[illegible]	[illegible]	[illegible]	.	[illegible]	[illegible]	[illegible]	[illegible]
Cork,	[illegible]	[illegible]	[illegible]	[illegible]	[illegible]	[illegible]	[illegible]	[illegible]	[illegible]	[illegible]	[illegible]
Donegal,	[illegible]	[illegible]	[illegible]	[illegible]	[illegible]	[illegible]	[illegible]	[illegible]	[illegible]	[illegible]	[illegible]
Down,	[illegible]	[illegible]	[illegible]	7	[illegible]	[illegible]	[illegible]	[illegible]	[illegible]	[illegible]	[illegible]
Dublin,	[illegible]	[illegible]	[illegible]	[illegible]	[illegible]	[illegible]	[illegible]	[illegible]	[illegible]	[illegible]	[illegible]
Fermanagh,	[illegible]	[illegible]	[illegible]	[illegible]	[illegible]	[illegible]	[illegible]	[illegible]	[illegible]	[illegible]	[illegible]
Galway,	[illegible]	[illegible]	[illegible]	[illegible]	[illegible]	[illegible]	[illegible]	[illegible]	[illegible]	[illegible]	[illegible]
Kerry,	[illegible]	[illegible]	[illegible]	[illegible]	[illegible]	[illegible]	.	[illegible]	[illegible]	[illegible]	[illegible]
Kildare,	[illegible]	[illegible]	[illegible]	[illegible]	[illegible]	.	[illegible]	[illegible]	[illegible]	[illegible]	[illegible]
Kilkenny,	[illegible]	[illegible]	[illegible]		[illegible]	.	[illegible]	[illegible]	[illegible]	[illegible]	[illegible]
King's,	[illegible]	[illegible]	[illegible]	[illegible]	[illegible]	.	.	[illegible]	[illegible]	[illegible]	[illegible]
Leitrim,	[illegible]	[illegible]	[illegible]	.	[illegible]	[illegible]	.	[illegible]	[illegible]	[illegible]	[illegible]
Limerick,	[illegible]	[illegible]	[illegible]	[illegible]	[illegible]	.	.	[illegible]	[illegible]	[illegible]	[illegible]
Londonderry,	[illegible]	[illegible]	[illegible]	[illegible]	[illegible]	[illegible]	[illegible]	[illegible]	[illegible]	[illegible]	[illegible]
Longford,	[illegible]	[illegible]	[illegible]	[illegible]	[illegible]	[illegible]	[illegible]	[illegible]	[illegible]	[illegible]	[illegible]
Louth and Drogheda County of Town	[illegible]	[illegible]	[illegible]	.	[illegible]	[illegible]	[illegible]	[illegible]	[illegible]	[illegible]	[illegible]
Mayo,	[illegible]	[illegible]	[illegible]	[illegible]	[illegible]	.	[illegible]	[illegible]	[illegible]	[illegible]	[illegible]
Meath,	[illegible]	[illegible]	[illegible]	[illegible]	[illegible]	[illegible]	[illegible]	[illegible]	[illegible]	[illegible]	[illegible]
Monaghan,	[illegible]	[illegible]	[illegible]	[illegible]	[illegible]	[illegible]	[illegible]	[illegible]	[illegible]	[illegible]	[illegible]
Queen's,	[illegible]	[illegible]	[illegible]	[illegible]	[illegible]	.	.	[illegible]	[illegible]	[illegible]	[illegible]
Roscommon,	[illegible]	[illegible]	[illegible]	[illegible]	[illegible]	.	.	[illegible]	[illegible]	[illegible]	[illegible]
Sligo,	[illegible]	[illegible]	[illegible]	[illegible]	[illegible]	.	.	[illegible]	[illegible]	[illegible]	[illegible]
Tipperary,	[illegible]	[illegible]	[illegible]	[illegible]	[illegible]	.	[illegible]	[illegible]	[illegible]	[illegible]	[illegible]
Tyrone,	[illegible]	[illegible]	[illegible]	[illegible]	[illegible]	[illegible]	[illegible]	[illegible]	[illegible]	[illegible]	[illegible]
Waterford,	[illegible]	[illegible]	[illegible]	.	[illegible]	[illegible]	.	[illegible]	[illegible]	[illegible]	[illegible]
Westmeath,	[illegible]	[illegible]	[illegible]	[illegible]	[illegible]	[illegible]	.	[illegible]	[illegible]	[illegible]	[illegible]
Wexford,	[illegible]	[illegible]	[illegible]	[illegible]	[illegible]	[illegible]	[illegible]	[illegible]	[illegible]	[illegible]	[illegible]
Wicklow,	[illegible]	[illegible]	[illegible]	.	[illegible]	.	.	[illegible]	[illegible]	[illegible]	[illegible]
Provinces.											
Leinster,	[illegible]	[illegible]	[illegible]	[illegible]	[illegible]	[illegible]	[illegible]	[illegible]	[illegible]	[illegible]	[illegible]
Munster,	[illegible]	[illegible]	[illegible]	[illegible]	[illegible]	[illegible]	[illegible]	[illegible]	[illegible]	[illegible]	[illegible]
Ulster,	[illegible]	[illegible]	[illegible]	[illegible]	[illegible]	[illegible]	[illegible]	[illegible]	[illegible]	[illegible]	[illegible]
Connaught,	[illegible]	[illegible]	[illegible]	[illegible]	[illegible]	[illegible]	[illegible]	[illegible]	[illegible]	[illegible]	[illegible]
Total,	[illegible]	[illegible]	[illegible]	[illegible]	[illegible]	[illegible]	[illegible]	[illegible]	[illegible]	[illegible]	[illegible]

[illegible] crops in the Year 1897; the Valuation in 1897; and the Population in 1891.

[illegible]	[illegible]	[illegible]	[illegible]	[illegible]	[illegible]	[illegible]	[illegible]	[illegible]	[illegible]	Valuation in 1897	Population in 1891	Counties.
Acres.	Acres.	Acres.	Acres.	Acres.	Acres.	Acres.	Acres.	Acres.	Acres.	£		
[illegible]	[illegible]	[illegible]	[illegible]	[illegible]	[illegible]	[illegible]	[illegible]	[illegible]	[illegible]	[illegible]	[illegible]	Antrim.
[illegible]	[illegible]	[illegible]	[illegible]	[illegible]	[illegible]	[illegible]	[illegible]	[illegible]	[illegible]	[illegible]	[illegible]	Armagh.
[illegible]	[illegible]	[illegible]	[illegible]	[illegible]	[illegible]	.	[illegible]	[illegible]	[illegible]	[illegible]	[illegible]	Carlow.
[illegible]	[illegible]	[illegible]	[illegible]	[illegible]	[illegible]	[illegible]	[illegible]	[illegible]	[illegible]	[illegible]	[illegible]	Cavan.
[illegible]	[illegible]	[illegible]	[illegible]	[illegible]	[illegible]	[illegible]	[illegible]	[illegible]	[illegible]	[illegible]	[illegible]	Clare.
[illegible]	[illegible]	[illegible]	[illegible]	[illegible]	[illegible]	[illegible]	[illegible]	[illegible]	[illegible]	[illegible]	[illegible]	Cork.
[illegible]	[illegible]	[illegible]	[illegible]	[illegible]	[illegible]	[illegible]	[illegible]	[illegible]	[illegible]	[illegible]	[illegible]	Donegal.
[illegible]	[illegible]	[illegible]	[illegible]	[illegible]	[illegible]	[illegible]	[illegible]	[illegible]	[illegible]	[illegible]	[illegible]	Down.
[illegible]	[illegible]	[illegible]	[illegible]	[illegible]	[illegible]	.	[illegible]	[illegible]	[illegible]	[illegible]	[illegible]	Dublin.
[illegible]	[illegible]	[illegible]	[illegible]	[illegible]	[illegible]	[illegible]	[illegible]	[illegible]	[illegible]	[illegible]	[illegible]	Fermanagh.
[illegible]	[illegible]	[illegible]	[illegible]	[illegible]	[illegible]	.	[illegible]	[illegible]	[illegible]	[illegible]	[illegible]	Galway.
[illegible]	[illegible]	[illegible]	[illegible]	[illegible]	[illegible]	[illegible]	[illegible]	[illegible]	[illegible]	[illegible]	[illegible]	Kerry.
[illegible]	[illegible]	[illegible]	[illegible]	[illegible]	[illegible]	.	[illegible]	[illegible]	[illegible]	[illegible]	[illegible]	Kildare.
[illegible]	[illegible]	[illegible]	[illegible]	[illegible]	[illegible]	.	[illegible]	[illegible]	[illegible]	[illegible]	[illegible]	Kilkenny.
[illegible]	[illegible]	[illegible]	[illegible]	[illegible]	[illegible]	.	[illegible]	[illegible]	[illegible]	[illegible]	[illegible]	King's.
[illegible]	[illegible]	[illegible]	.	[illegible]	[illegible]	[illegible]	[illegible]	[illegible]	[illegible]	[illegible]	[illegible]	Leitrim.
[illegible]	[illegible]	[illegible]	[illegible]	[illegible]	[illegible]	.	[illegible]	[illegible]	[illegible]	[illegible]	[illegible]	Limerick.
[illegible]	[illegible]	[illegible]	[illegible]	[illegible]	[illegible]	[illegible]	[illegible]	[illegible]	[illegible]	[illegible]	[illegible]	Londonderry.
[illegible]	[illegible]	[illegible]	[illegible]	[illegible]	[illegible]	[illegible]	[illegible]	[illegible]	[illegible]	[illegible]	[illegible]	Longford.
[illegible]	[illegible]	[illegible]	[illegible]	[illegible]	[illegible]	[illegible]	[illegible]	[illegible]	[illegible]	[illegible]	[illegible]	Louth & Drogheda, County of Town.
[illegible]	[illegible]	[illegible]	[illegible]	[illegible]	[illegible]	[illegible]	[illegible]	[illegible]	[illegible]	[illegible]	[illegible]	Mayo.
[illegible]	[illegible]	[illegible]	[illegible]	[illegible]	[illegible]	[illegible]	[illegible]	[illegible]	[illegible]	[illegible]	[illegible]	Meath.
[illegible]	[illegible]	[illegible]	[illegible]	[illegible]	[illegible]	[illegible]	[illegible]	[illegible]	[illegible]	[illegible]	[illegible]	Monaghan.
[illegible]	[illegible]	[illegible]	[illegible]	[illegible]	[illegible]	.	[illegible]	[illegible]	[illegible]	[illegible]	[illegible]	Queen's.
[illegible]	[illegible]	[illegible]	[illegible]	[illegible]	[illegible]	.	[illegible]	[illegible]	[illegible]	[illegible]	[illegible]	Roscommon.
[illegible]	[illegible]	[illegible]	[illegible]	[illegible]	[illegible]	[illegible]	[illegible]	[illegible]	[illegible]	[illegible]	[illegible]	Sligo.
[illegible]	[illegible]	[illegible]	[illegible]	[illegible]	[illegible]	.	[illegible]	[illegible]	[illegible]	[illegible]	[illegible]	Tipperary.
[illegible]	[illegible]	[illegible]	[illegible]	[illegible]	[illegible]	[illegible]	[illegible]	[illegible]	[illegible]	[illegible]	[illegible]	Tyrone.
[illegible]	[illegible]	[illegible]	[illegible]	[illegible]	[illegible]	.	[illegible]	[illegible]	[illegible]	[illegible]	[illegible]	Waterford.
[illegible]	[illegible]	[illegible]	[illegible]	[illegible]	[illegible]	.	[illegible]	[illegible]	[illegible]	[illegible]	[illegible]	Westmeath.
[illegible]	[illegible]	[illegible]	[illegible]	[illegible]	[illegible]	.	[illegible]	[illegible]	[illegible]	[illegible]	[illegible]	Wexford.
[illegible]	[illegible]	[illegible]	[illegible]	[illegible]	[illegible]	.	[illegible]	[illegible]	[illegible]	[illegible]	[illegible]	Wicklow.
												PROVINCES.
[illegible]	[illegible]	[illegible]	[illegible]	[illegible]	[illegible]	[illegible]	[illegible]	[illegible]	[illegible]	[illegible]	[illegible]	Leinster.
[illegible]	[illegible]	[illegible]	[illegible]	[illegible]	[illegible]	[illegible]	[illegible]	[illegible]	[illegible]	[illegible]	[illegible]	Munster.
[illegible]	[illegible]	[illegible]	[illegible]	[illegible]	[illegible]	[illegible]	[illegible]	[illegible]	[illegible]	[illegible]	[illegible]	Ulster.
[illegible]	[illegible]	[illegible]	[illegible]	[illegible]	[illegible]	[illegible]	[illegible]	[illegible]	[illegible]	[illegible]	[illegible]	Connaught.
[illegible]	[illegible]	[illegible]	[illegible]	[illegible]	[illegible]	[illegible]	[illegible]	[illegible]	[illegible]	*[illegible]	[illegible]	Total.

* The slight difference between the total Valuation by Counties and that by Unions is accounted for by the fact that the County and Union [illegible] [illegible] taken at the same period of the year; and also that the figures are taken to the nearest £ only.

Table 6—Showing, by Counties and Provinces, [illegible]

Counties.	Produce of — Corn, Beans, and Peas.						
	Wheat.	Oats.	Barley.	Bere.	Rye.	Beans.	Peas.
Antrim,	[illegible]	[illegible]	[illegible]	-	[illegible]	[illegible]	[illegible]
Armagh,	[illegible]	[illegible]	[illegible]	-	[illegible]	[illegible]	[illegible]
Carlow,	[illegible]	[illegible]	[illegible]	-	[illegible]	.	.
Cavan,	[illegible]	[illegible]	[illegible]	[illegible]	[illegible]	[illegible]	[illegible]
Clare,	[illegible]	[illegible]	[illegible]	[illegible]	[illegible]	[illegible]	.
Cork,	[illegible]	[illegible]	[illegible]	[illegible]	[illegible]	[illegible]	[illegible]
Donegal,	[illegible]	[illegible]	[illegible]	[illegible]	[illegible]	[illegible]	[illegible]
Down,	[illegible]	[illegible]	[illegible]	[illegible]	[illegible]	[illegible]	[illegible]
Dublin,	[illegible]	[illegible]	[illegible]	[illegible]	[illegible]	[illegible]	[illegible]
Fermanagh,	[illegible]	[illegible]	[illegible]	[illegible]	[illegible]	[illegible]	[illegible]
Galway,	[illegible]	[illegible]	[illegible]	[illegible]	[illegible]	[illegible]	[illegible]
Kerry,	[illegible]	[illegible]	[illegible]	[illegible]	[illegible]	[illegible]	.
Kildare,	[illegible]	[illegible]	[illegible]	[illegible]	[illegible]	.	[illegible]
Kilkenny,	[illegible]	[illegible]	[illegible]	.	[illegible]	-	[illegible]
King's,	[illegible]	[illegible]	[illegible]	[illegible]	[illegible]	.	.
Leitrim,	[illegible]	[illegible]	[illegible]	-	[illegible]	[illegible]	.
Limerick,	[illegible]	[illegible]	[illegible]	[illegible]	[illegible]	.	-
Londonderry,	[illegible]	[illegible]	[illegible]	[illegible]	[illegible]	[illegible]	[illegible]
Longford,	[illegible]	[illegible]	[illegible]	[illegible]	[illegible]	[illegible]	[illegible]
Louth and Drogheda, County of Town,	[illegible]	[illegible]	[illegible]	.	[illegible]	[illegible]	[illegible]
Mayo,	[illegible]	[illegible]	[illegible]	[illegible]	[illegible]	.	[illegible]
Meath,	[illegible]	[illegible]	[illegible]	[illegible]	[illegible]	[illegible]	[illegible]
Monaghan,	[illegible]	[illegible]	[illegible]	[illegible]	[illegible]	[illegible]	[illegible]
Queen's,	[illegible]	[illegible]	[illegible]	[illegible]	[illegible]	.	.
Roscommon,	[illegible]	[illegible]	[illegible]	[illegible]	[illegible]	.	.
Sligo,	[illegible]	[illegible]	[illegible]	[illegible]	[illegible]	-	.
Tipperary,	[illegible]	[illegible]	[illegible]	[illegible]	[illegible]	-	[illegible]
Tyrone,	[illegible]	[illegible]	[illegible]	[illegible]	[illegible]	[illegible]	[illegible]
Waterford,	[illegible]	[illegible]	[illegible]	.	[illegible]	[illegible]	-
Westmeath,	[illegible]	[illegible]	[illegible]	[illegible]	[illegible]	[illegible]	.
Wexford,	[illegible]	[illegible]	[illegible]	[illegible]	[illegible]	[illegible]	[illegible]
Wicklow,	[illegible]	[illegible]	[illegible]	.	[illegible]	.	.
Provinces.							
Leinster,	[illegible]	[illegible]	[illegible]	[illegible]	[illegible]	[illegible]	[illegible]
Munster,	[illegible]	[illegible]	[illegible]	[illegible]	[illegible]	[illegible]	[illegible]
Ulster,	[illegible]	[illegible]	[illegible]	[illegible]	[illegible]	[illegible]	[illegible]
Connaught,	[illegible]	[illegible]	[illegible]	[illegible]	[illegible]	[illegible]	[illegible]
Total,	[illegible]	[illegible]	[illegible]	[illegible]	[illegible]	[illegible]	[illegible]

Produce of the Crops in the Year 18[illegible]7.

THE CROPS.

Potatoes	Turnips	Mangel Wurzel and Beet Root	Cabbage and Parsnips	[illegible]	[illegible]	[illegible]	Flax	Hay: [illegible]	Hay: [illegible]	COUNTIES.
Tons.	Tons.	Tons.	Tons.	Tons.	Tons.	Tons.	Stones of 14 lb.	Tons.	Tons.	
[illegible]	[illegible]	[illegible]	[illegible]	[illegible]	[illegible]	[illegible]	[illegible]	[illegible]	[illegible]	Antrim.
[illegible]	[illegible]	[illegible]	[illegible]	[illegible]	[illegible]	[illegible]	[illegible]	[illegible]	[illegible]	Armagh.
[illegible]	[illegible]	[illegible]	[illegible]	[illegible]	[illegible]	[illegible]	.	[illegible]	[illegible]	Carlow.
[illegible]	[illegible]	[illegible]	[illegible]	[illegible]	[illegible]	[illegible]	[illegible]	[illegible]	[illegible]	Cavan.
[illegible]	[illegible]	[illegible]	[illegible]	[illegible]	[illegible]	[illegible]	[illegible]	[illegible]	[illegible]	Clare.
[illegible]	[illegible]	[illegible]	[illegible]	[illegible]	[illegible]	[illegible]	[illegible]	[illegible]	[illegible]	Cork.
[illegible]	[illegible]	[illegible]	[illegible]	[illegible]	[illegible]	[illegible]	[illegible]	[illegible]	[illegible]	Donegal.
[illegible]	[illegible]	[illegible]	[illegible]	[illegible]	[illegible]	[illegible]	[illegible]	[illegible]	[illegible]	Down.
[illegible]	[illegible]	[illegible]	[illegible]	[illegible]	[illegible]	[illegible]	.	[illegible]	[illegible]	Dublin.
[illegible]	[illegible]	[illegible]	[illegible]	[illegible]	[illegible]	[illegible]	[illegible]	[illegible]	[illegible]	Fermanagh.
[illegible]	[illegible]	[illegible]	[illegible]	[illegible]	[illegible]	[illegible]	.	[illegible]	[illegible]	Galway.
[illegible]	[illegible]	[illegible]	[illegible]	[illegible]	[illegible]	[illegible]	[illegible]	[illegible]	[illegible]	Kerry.
[illegible]	[illegible]	[illegible]	[illegible]	[illegible]	[illegible]	[illegible]	.	[illegible]	[illegible]	Kildare.
[illegible]	[illegible]	[illegible]	[illegible]	[illegible]	[illegible]	[illegible]	.	[illegible]	[illegible]	Kilkenny.
[illegible]	[illegible]	[illegible]	[illegible]	[illegible]	[illegible]	[illegible]	.	[illegible]	[illegible]	King's.
[illegible]	[illegible]	[illegible]	[illegible]	[illegible]	[illegible]	.	[illegible]	[illegible]	[illegible]	Leitrim.
[illegible]	[illegible]	[illegible]	[illegible]	[illegible]	[illegible]	[illegible]	.	[illegible]	[illegible]	Limerick.
[illegible]	[illegible]	[illegible]	[illegible]	[illegible]	[illegible]	[illegible]	[illegible]	[illegible]	[illegible]	Londonderry.
[illegible]	[illegible]	[illegible]	[illegible]	[illegible]	[illegible]	[illegible]	[illegible]	[illegible]	[illegible]	Longford.
[illegible]	[illegible]	[illegible]	[illegible]	[illegible]	[illegible]	[illegible]	[illegible]	[illegible]	[illegible]	Louth and Drogheda, County of Town.
[illegible]	[illegible]	[illegible]	[illegible]	[illegible]	[illegible]	[illegible]	[illegible]	[illegible]	[illegible]	Mayo.
[illegible]	[illegible]	[illegible]	[illegible]	[illegible]	[illegible]	[illegible]	[illegible]	[illegible]	[illegible]	Meath.
[illegible]	[illegible]	[illegible]	[illegible]	[illegible]	[illegible]	[illegible]	[illegible]	[illegible]	[illegible]	Monaghan.
[illegible]	[illegible]	[illegible]	[illegible]	[illegible]	[illegible]	[illegible]	.	[illegible]	[illegible]	Queen's.
[illegible]	[illegible]	[illegible]	[illegible]	[illegible]	[illegible]	[illegible]	.	[illegible]	[illegible]	Roscommon.
[illegible]	[illegible]	[illegible]	[illegible]	[illegible]	[illegible]	[illegible]	[illegible]	[illegible]	[illegible]	Sligo.
[illegible]	[illegible]	[illegible]	[illegible]	[illegible]	[illegible]	[illegible]	.	[illegible]	[illegible]	Tipperary.
[illegible]	[illegible]	[illegible]	[illegible]	[illegible]	[illegible]	[illegible]	[illegible]	[illegible]	[illegible]	Tyrone.
[illegible]	[illegible]	[illegible]	[illegible]	[illegible]	[illegible]	[illegible]	.	[illegible]	[illegible]	Waterford.
[illegible]	[illegible]	[illegible]	[illegible]	[illegible]	[illegible]	[illegible]	.	[illegible]	[illegible]	Westmeath.
[illegible]	[illegible]	[illegible]	[illegible]	[illegible]	[illegible]	[illegible]	.	[illegible]	[illegible]	Wexford.
[illegible]	[illegible]	[illegible]	[illegible]	[illegible]	[illegible]	[illegible]	.	[illegible]	[illegible]	Wicklow.
										PROVINCES.
[illegible]	[illegible]	[illegible]	[illegible]	[illegible]	[illegible]	[illegible]	[illegible]	[illegible]	[illegible]	Leinster.
[illegible]	[illegible]	[illegible]	[illegible]	[illegible]	[illegible]	[illegible]	[illegible]	[illegible]	[illegible]	Munster.
[illegible]	[illegible]	[illegible]	[illegible]	[illegible]	[illegible]	[illegible]	[illegible]	[illegible]	[illegible]	Ulster.
[illegible]	[illegible]	[illegible]	[illegible]	[illegible]	[illegible]	[illegible]	[illegible]	[illegible]	[illegible]	Connaught.
[illegible]	[illegible]	[illegible]	[illegible]	[illegible]	[illegible]	[illegible]	[illegible]	[illegible]	[illegible]	Total.

TABLE 7.—SHOWING, BY POOR LAW UNIONS, THE EXTENT OF LAND UNDER

[illegible]

... in the Year 1897; the Valuation in 1897; and the Population in 1891—continued.

[illegible]

TABLE 8.—SHOWING, BY POOR LAW UNIONS, THE

POOR LAW UNIONS.	PRODUCE.						
	Corn, Beans, and Peas.						
	Wheat.	Oats.	Barley.	Bere.	Rye.	Beans.	Peas.
	[illegible]	[illegible]	[illegible]	[illegible]	[illegible]	[illegible]	[illegible]
Abbeyleix,	617	[illegible]	[illegible]	.	75	.	.
Antrim,	[illegible]	[illegible]	[illegible]	.	[illegible]	[illegible]	[illegible]
Ardee,	[illegible]	[illegible]	[illegible]	.	[illegible]	[illegible]	[illegible]
Armagh,	[illegible]	[illegible]	[illegible]	.	[illegible]	[illegible]	[illegible]
Athlone,	[illegible]	[illegible]	[illegible]	[illegible]	[illegible]	.	.
Athy,	[illegible]	[illegible]	[illegible]	.	[illegible]	.	.
Bailieborough,	[illegible]	[illegible]	[illegible]	.	[illegible]	.	.
Ballina,	[illegible]	[illegible]	[illegible]	[illegible]	[illegible]	.	.
Ballinasloe,	[illegible]	[illegible]	[illegible]	.	[illegible]	[illegible]	.
Ballinrobe,	[illegible]	[illegible]	[illegible]	.	[illegible]	.	[illegible]
[illegible]	[illegible]	[illegible]	[illegible]	.	[illegible]	[illegible]	[illegible]
[illegible]	[illegible]	[illegible]	[illegible]	[illegible]	[illegible]	[illegible]	.
[illegible]	[illegible]	[illegible]	[illegible]	.	[illegible]	[illegible]	.
[illegible]	[illegible]	[illegible]	[illegible]	.	[illegible]	[illegible]	[illegible]
[illegible]	[illegible]	[illegible]	.	[illegible]	[illegible]	[illegible]	.
[illegible]	[illegible]	[illegible]	[illegible]	[illegible]	[illegible]	[illegible]	[illegible]
Galway,	[illegible]	[illegible]	[illegible]	.	[illegible]	.	[illegible]
[illegible]	[illegible]	[illegible]	[illegible]	.	[illegible]	.	[illegible]
[illegible]	[illegible]	[illegible]	[illegible]	.	[illegible]	[illegible]	.
Gort,	[illegible]	[illegible]	[illegible]	[illegible]	[illegible]	[illegible]	.
[illegible]	[illegible]	[illegible]	[illegible]	[illegible]	[illegible]	.	.

[illegible]	
[illegible]	[illegible]
[illegible]	Antrim.
[illegible]	Ardee.
[illegible]	Armagh.
[illegible]	[illegible]
[illegible]	Athy.
[illegible]	Bailieborough.
[illegible]	Ballina.
[illegible]	[illegible]
[illegible]	[illegible]
[illegible]	Ballycastle.
[illegible]	[illegible]
[illegible]	[illegible]
[illegible]	[illegible]
[illegible]	[illegible]
[illegible]	[illegible]
[illegible]	[illegible]
[illegible]	[illegible]
[illegible]	[illegible]
[illegible]	[illegible]
[illegible]	Bantry.
[illegible]	[illegible]
[illegible]	Belfast.
[illegible]	[illegible]
[illegible]	[illegible]
[illegible]	Boyle.
[illegible]	[illegible]
[illegible]	[illegible]
[illegible]	[illegible]
[illegible]	[illegible]
[illegible]	[illegible]
[illegible]	[illegible]
[illegible]	[illegible]
[illegible]	[illegible]
[illegible]	[illegible]
[illegible]	[illegible]
[illegible]	[illegible]
[illegible]	[illegible]
[illegible]	[illegible]
[illegible]	Cavan.
[illegible]	[illegible]
[illegible]	[illegible]
[illegible]	[illegible]
[illegible]	[illegible]
[illegible]	[illegible]
[illegible]	[illegible]
[illegible]	[illegible]
[illegible]	[illegible]
[illegible]	[illegible]
[illegible]	[illegible]
[illegible]	[illegible]
[illegible]	Cork.
[illegible]	[illegible]
[illegible]	[illegible]
[illegible]	[illegible]
[illegible]	Donegal.
[illegible]	[illegible]
[illegible]	[illegible]
[illegible]	[illegible]
[illegible]	[illegible]
[illegible]	Dublin, North.
[illegible]	Dublin, South.
[illegible]	[illegible]
[illegible]	[illegible]
[illegible]	[illegible]
[illegible]	[illegible]
[illegible]	[illegible]
[illegible]	[illegible]
[illegible]	[illegible]

[illegible]	[illegible]
[illegible]	[illegible]
[illegible]	[illegible]
[illegible]	[illegible]
[illegible]	[illegible]
[illegible]	[illegible]
[illegible]	[illegible]

Produce of the Crops in the Year 1897—continued.

[illegible]	[illegible]	[illegible]	[illegible]	[illegible]	[illegible]	[illegible]	Flax.	Hay [illegible]	Hay [illegible]	Poor Law Unions.
Tons.	Tons.	Tons.	Tons.	Tons.	Tons.	Tons.	Stones (14 lbs.)	Tons.	Tons.	
[illegible]	[illegible]	[illegible]	[illegible]	[illegible]	[illegible]	[illegible]	[illegible]	[illegible]	[illegible]	[illegible]
[illegible]	[illegible]	[illegible]	[illegible]	[illegible]	[illegible]	[illegible]	[illegible]	[illegible]	[illegible]	[illegible]
[illegible]	[illegible]	[illegible]	[illegible]	[illegible]	[illegible]	[illegible]	[illegible]	[illegible]	[illegible]	[illegible]
[illegible]	[illegible]	[illegible]	[illegible]	[illegible]	[illegible]	[illegible]	[illegible]	[illegible]	[illegible]	[illegible]
[illegible]	[illegible]	[illegible]	[illegible]	[illegible]	[illegible]	[illegible]	[illegible]	[illegible]	[illegible]	[illegible]
[illegible]	[illegible]	[illegible]	[illegible]	[illegible]	[illegible]	[illegible]	[illegible]	[illegible]	[illegible]	[illegible]
[illegible]	[illegible]	[illegible]	[illegible]	[illegible]	[illegible]	[illegible]	[illegible]	[illegible]	[illegible]	[illegible]
[illegible]	[illegible]	[illegible]	[illegible]	[illegible]	[illegible]	[illegible]	[illegible]	[illegible]	[illegible]	[illegible]
[illegible]	[illegible]	[illegible]	[illegible]	[illegible]	[illegible]	[illegible]	[illegible]	[illegible]	[illegible]	[illegible]
[illegible]	[illegible]	[illegible]	[illegible]	[illegible]	[illegible]	[illegible]	[illegible]	[illegible]	[illegible]	[illegible]

TABLE [illegible].—Showing the Number of Holdings exceeding one Acre, and Extent of Land under Crops in each Year from 18[illegible] to 1887, by Counties and Provinces—continued.

Counties.	Years.	No. of Holdings	Extent under Crops in Statute Acres in each Year from 18[illegible] to 1887. — Corn, Beans, and Peas.							Other Crops.							[illegible]
Dublin [illegible] Acres	[illegible]	[illegible]	[illegible]	[illegible]	[illegible]	[illegible]	[illegible]	[illegible]	[illegible]	[illegible]	[illegible]	[illegible]	[illegible]	[illegible]	[illegible]	[illegible]	[illegible]
Fermanagh [illegible] Acres	[illegible]	[illegible]	[illegible]	[illegible]	[illegible]	[illegible]	[illegible]	[illegible]	[illegible]	[illegible]	[illegible]	[illegible]	[illegible]	[illegible]	[illegible]	[illegible]	[illegible]
Galway [illegible] Acres	[illegible]	[illegible]	[illegible]	[illegible]	[illegible]	[illegible]	[illegible]	[illegible]	[illegible]	[illegible]	[illegible]	[illegible]	[illegible]	[illegible]	[illegible]	[illegible]	[illegible]

TABLE 8.—Showing the Number of Holdings exceeding one Acre, and Extent of Land under Crops in each Year from 1888 to 1897, by Counties and Provinces—continued.

Counties	Data
Limerick:	[illegible]
Londonderry:	[illegible]
Longford:	[illegible]
Louth and Drogheda Co. of Town:	[illegible]
Mayo:	[illegible]
Meath:	[illegible]
Monaghan:	[illegible]
Queen's:	[illegible]

Table 10.—Showing the Average Rates of Produce to the Statute Acre—continued.

Counties.	Years.	Wheat.	Oats.	Barley.	Bere.	Rye.	Beans.	Peas.	Potatoes.	Potatoes.	Mangel Wurzel and Beet Root.	Cabbage.	Flax.
		[illegible]	[illegible]	[illegible]	[illegible]	[illegible]	[illegible]	[illegible]	[illegible]	[illegible]	[illegible]	[illegible]	[illegible]
	[illegible]	[illegible]	[illegible]	[illegible]	[illegible]	[illegible]	[illegible]	[illegible]	[illegible]	[illegible]	[illegible]	[illegible]	[illegible]
	[illegible]	[illegible]	[illegible]	[illegible]	[illegible]	[illegible]	[illegible]	[illegible]	[illegible]	[illegible]	[illegible]	[illegible]	[illegible]
	[illegible]	[illegible]	[illegible]	[illegible]	[illegible]	[illegible]	[illegible]		[illegible]	[illegible]	[illegible]	[illegible]	[illegible]
	[illegible]	[illegible]	[illegible]	[illegible]	[illegible]	[illegible]		[illegible]	[illegible]	[illegible]	[illegible]	[illegible]	[illegible]
	[illegible]	[illegible]	[illegible]	[illegible]		[illegible]	[illegible]	[illegible]	[illegible]	[illegible]	[illegible]	[illegible]	[illegible]

[illegible]	[illegible]	[illegible]	[illegible]	[illegible]
[illegible]	[illegible]	[illegible]	[illegible]	[illegible]
[illegible]	[illegible]	[illegible]	[illegible]	[illegible]

TABLE 10.—SHOWING THE AVERAGE RATE OF PRODUCE TO THE STATUTE ACRE—continued.

AVERAGE OF PROVINCES.

Provinces.	Years.	Wheat.	Oats.	Barley.	Bere.	Rye.	Beans.	Peas.	Potatoes.	Turnips.	Mangel Wurzel and Beet Root.	Cabbage.	Flax.	Hay.
Leinster,	[illegible]	[illegible]	[illegible]	[illegible]	[illegible]	[illegible]	[illegible]	[illegible]	[illegible]	[illegible]	[illegible]	[illegible]	[illegible]	[illegible]
Munster,	[illegible]	[illegible]	[illegible]	[illegible]	[illegible]	[illegible]	[illegible]	[illegible]	[illegible]	[illegible]	[illegible]	[illegible]	[illegible]	[illegible]
Ulster,	[illegible]	[illegible]	[illegible]	[illegible]	[illegible]	[illegible]	[illegible]	[illegible]	[illegible]	[illegible]	[illegible]	[illegible]	[illegible]	[illegible]
Connaught,	[illegible]	[illegible]	[illegible]	[illegible]	[illegible]	[illegible]	[illegible]	[illegible]	[illegible]	[illegible]	[illegible]	[illegible]	[illegible]	[illegible]

AVERAGE OF IRELAND.

—	Years.	Wheat.	Oats.	Barley.	Bere.	Rye.	Beans.	Peas.	Potatoes.	Turnips.	Mangel Wurzel and Beet Root.	Cabbage.	Flax.	Hay.
Ireland,	[illegible]	[illegible]	[illegible]	[illegible]	[illegible]	[illegible]	[illegible]	[illegible]	[illegible]	[illegible]	[illegible]	[illegible]	[illegible]	[illegible]

[illegible]

[illegible]

[illegible]

TABLE 12.—SHOWING THE QUANTITY OF LIVE STOCK IN EACH YEAR FROM 1888 TO 1897, BY COUNTIES AND PROVINCES

COUNTIES.	Years.	No. of Horses.			Mules and Asses.		No. of Cattle.			No. of Sheep.		No. of Pigs.		No. of Goats.	No. of Poultry.
		[illegible]	[illegible]	[illegible]	[illegible]	[illegible]	[illegible]	[illegible]	[illegible]	[illegible]	[illegible]	[illegible]	[illegible]		
ANTRIM:	[illegible]	[illegible]	[illegible]	[illegible]	[illegible]	[illegible]	[illegible]	[illegible]	[illegible]	[illegible]	[illegible]	[illegible]	[illegible]	[illegible]	[illegible]
	[illegible]	[illegible]	[illegible]	[illegible]	[illegible]	[illegible]	[illegible]	[illegible]	[illegible]	[illegible]	[illegible]	[illegible]	[illegible]	[illegible]	[illegible]
	[illegible]	[illegible]	[illegible]	[illegible]	[illegible]	[illegible]	[illegible]	[illegible]	[illegible]	[illegible]	[illegible]	[illegible]	[illegible]	[illegible]	[illegible]
	[illegible]	[illegible]	[illegible]	[illegible]	[illegible]	[illegible]	[illegible]	[illegible]	[illegible]	[illegible]	[illegible]	[illegible]	[illegible]	[illegible]	[illegible]
Area, [illegible] Acres.	[illegible]	[illegible]	[illegible]	[illegible]	[illegible]	[illegible]	[illegible]	[illegible]	[illegible]	[illegible]	[illegible]	[illegible]	[illegible]	[illegible]	[illegible]
	[illegible]	[illegible]	[illegible]	[illegible]	[illegible]	[illegible]	[illegible]	[illegible]	[illegible]	[illegible]	[illegible]	[illegible]	[illegible]	[illegible]	[illegible]
	[illegible]	[illegible]	[illegible]	[illegible]	[illegible]	[illegible]	[illegible]	[illegible]	[illegible]	[illegible]	[illegible]	[illegible]	[illegible]	[illegible]	[illegible]
	[illegible]	[illegible]	[illegible]	[illegible]	[illegible]	[illegible]	[illegible]	[illegible]	[illegible]	[illegible]	[illegible]	[illegible]	[illegible]	[illegible]	[illegible]
	[illegible]	[illegible]	[illegible]	[illegible]	[illegible]	[illegible]	[illegible]	[illegible]	[illegible]	[illegible]	[illegible]	[illegible]	[illegible]	[illegible]	[illegible]
	[illegible]	[illegible]	[illegible]	[illegible]	[illegible]	[illegible]	[illegible]	[illegible]	[illegible]	[illegible]	[illegible]	[illegible]	[illegible]	[illegible]	[illegible]
ARMAGH:	[illegible]	[illegible]	[illegible]	[illegible]	[illegible]	[illegible]	[illegible]	[illegible]	[illegible]	[illegible]	[illegible]	[illegible]	[illegible]	[illegible]	[illegible]
	[illegible]	[illegible]	[illegible]	[illegible]	[illegible]	[illegible]	[illegible]	[illegible]	[illegible]	[illegible]	[illegible]	[illegible]	[illegible]	[illegible]	[illegible]
	[illegible]	[illegible]	[illegible]	[illegible]	[illegible]	[illegible]	[illegible]	[illegible]	[illegible]	[illegible]	[illegible]	[illegible]	[illegible]	[illegible]	[illegible]
	[illegible]	[illegible]	[illegible]	[illegible]	[illegible]	[illegible]	[illegible]	[illegible]	[illegible]	[illegible]	[illegible]	[illegible]	[illegible]	[illegible]	[illegible]
Area, [illegible] Acres.	[illegible]	[illegible]	[illegible]	[illegible]	[illegible]	[illegible]	[illegible]	[illegible]	[illegible]	[illegible]	[illegible]	[illegible]	[illegible]	[illegible]	[illegible]
	[illegible]	[illegible]	[illegible]	[illegible]	[illegible]	[illegible]	[illegible]	[illegible]	[illegible]	[illegible]	[illegible]	[illegible]	[illegible]	[illegible]	[illegible]
	[illegible]	[illegible]	[illegible]	[illegible]	[illegible]	[illegible]	[illegible]	[illegible]	[illegible]	[illegible]	[illegible]	[illegible]	[illegible]	[illegible]	[illegible]
	[illegible]	[illegible]	[illegible]	[illegible]	[illegible]	[illegible]	[illegible]	[illegible]	[illegible]	[illegible]	[illegible]	[illegible]	[illegible]	[illegible]	[illegible]
	[illegible]	[illegible]	[illegible]	[illegible]	[illegible]	[illegible]	[illegible]	[illegible]	[illegible]	[illegible]	[illegible]	[illegible]	[illegible]	[illegible]	[illegible]
	[illegible]	[illegible]	[illegible]	[illegible]	[illegible]	[illegible]	[illegible]	[illegible]	[illegible]	[illegible]	[illegible]	[illegible]	[illegible]	[illegible]	[illegible]
CARLOW:	[illegible]	[illegible]	[illegible]	[illegible]	[illegible]	[illegible]	[illegible]	[illegible]	[illegible]	[illegible]	[illegible]	[illegible]	[illegible]	[illegible]	[illegible]
	[illegible]	[illegible]	[illegible]	[illegible]	[illegible]	[illegible]	[illegible]	[illegible]	[illegible]	[illegible]	[illegible]	[illegible]	[illegible]	[illegible]	[illegible]
	[illegible]	[illegible]	[illegible]	[illegible]	[illegible]	[illegible]	[illegible]	[illegible]	[illegible]	[illegible]	[illegible]	[illegible]	[illegible]	[illegible]	[illegible]
	[illegible]	[illegible]	[illegible]	[illegible]	[illegible]	[illegible]	[illegible]	[illegible]	[illegible]	[illegible]	[illegible]	[illegible]	[illegible]	[illegible]	[illegible]
Area, [illegible] Acres.	[illegible]	[illegible]	[illegible]	[illegible]	[illegible]	[illegible]	[illegible]	[illegible]	[illegible]	[illegible]	[illegible]	[illegible]	[illegible]	[illegible]	[illegible]
	[illegible]	[illegible]	[illegible]	[illegible]	[illegible]	[illegible]	[illegible]	[illegible]	[illegible]	[illegible]	[illegible]	[illegible]	[illegible]	[illegible]	[illegible]
	[illegible]	[illegible]	[illegible]	[illegible]	[illegible]	[illegible]	[illegible]	[illegible]	[illegible]	[illegible]	[illegible]	[illegible]	[illegible]	[illegible]	[illegible]
	[illegible]	[illegible]	[illegible]	[illegible]	[illegible]	[illegible]	[illegible]	[illegible]	[illegible]	[illegible]	[illegible]	[illegible]	[illegible]	[illegible]	[illegible]
	[illegible]	[illegible]	[illegible]	[illegible]	[illegible]	[illegible]	[illegible]	[illegible]	[illegible]	[illegible]	[illegible]	[illegible]	[illegible]	[illegible]	[illegible]
	[illegible]	[illegible]	[illegible]	[illegible]	[illegible]	[illegible]	[illegible]	[illegible]	[illegible]	[illegible]	[illegible]	[illegible]	[illegible]	[illegible]	[illegible]
CAVAN:	[illegible]	[illegible]	[illegible]	[illegible]	[illegible]	[illegible]	[illegible]	[illegible]	[illegible]	[illegible]	[illegible]	[illegible]	[illegible]	[illegible]	[illegible]
	[illegible]	[illegible]	[illegible]	[illegible]	[illegible]	[illegible]	[illegible]	[illegible]	[illegible]	[illegible]	[illegible]	[illegible]	[illegible]	[illegible]	[illegible]
	[illegible]	[illegible]	[illegible]	[illegible]	[illegible]	[illegible]	[illegible]	[illegible]	[illegible]	[illegible]	[illegible]	[illegible]	[illegible]	[illegible]	[illegible]
	[illegible]	[illegible]	[illegible]	[illegible]	[illegible]	[illegible]	[illegible]	[illegible]	[illegible]	[illegible]	[illegible]	[illegible]	[illegible]	[illegible]	[illegible]
Area, [illegible] Acres.	[illegible]	[illegible]	[illegible]	[illegible]	[illegible]	[illegible]	[illegible]	[illegible]	[illegible]	[illegible]	[illegible]	[illegible]	[illegible]	[illegible]	[illegible]
	[illegible]	[illegible]	[illegible]	[illegible]	[illegible]	[illegible]	[illegible]	[illegible]	[illegible]	[illegible]	[illegible]	[illegible]	[illegible]	[illegible]	[illegible]
	[illegible]	[illegible]	[illegible]	[illegible]	[illegible]	[illegible]	[illegible]	[illegible]	[illegible]	[illegible]	[illegible]	[illegible]	[illegible]	[illegible]	[illegible]
	[illegible]	[illegible]	[illegible]	[illegible]	[illegible]	[illegible]	[illegible]	[illegible]	[illegible]	[illegible]	[illegible]	[illegible]	[illegible]	[illegible]	[illegible]
	[illegible]	[illegible]	[illegible]	[illegible]	[illegible]	[illegible]	[illegible]	[illegible]	[illegible]	[illegible]	[illegible]	[illegible]	[illegible]	[illegible]	[illegible]
	[illegible]	[illegible]	[illegible]	[illegible]	[illegible]	[illegible]	[illegible]	[illegible]	[illegible]	[illegible]	[illegible]	[illegible]	[illegible]	[illegible]	[illegible]
CLARE:	[illegible]	[illegible]	[illegible]	[illegible]	[illegible]	[illegible]	[illegible]	[illegible]	[illegible]	[illegible]	[illegible]	[illegible]	[illegible]	[illegible]	[illegible]
	[illegible]	[illegible]	[illegible]	[illegible]	[illegible]	[illegible]	[illegible]	[illegible]	[illegible]	[illegible]	[illegible]	[illegible]	[illegible]	[illegible]	[illegible]
	[illegible]	[illegible]	[illegible]	[illegible]	[illegible]	[illegible]	[illegible]	[illegible]	[illegible]	[illegible]	[illegible]	[illegible]	[illegible]	[illegible]	[illegible]
	[illegible]	[illegible]	[illegible]	[illegible]	[illegible]	[illegible]	[illegible]	[illegible]	[illegible]	[illegible]	[illegible]	[illegible]	[illegible]	[illegible]	[illegible]
Area, [illegible] Acres.	[illegible]	[illegible]	[illegible]	[illegible]	[illegible]	[illegible]	[illegible]	[illegible]	[illegible]	[illegible]	[illegible]	[illegible]	[illegible]	[illegible]	[illegible]
	[illegible]	[illegible]	[illegible]	[illegible]	[illegible]	[illegible]	[illegible]	[illegible]	[illegible]	[illegible]	[illegible]	[illegible]	[illegible]	[illegible]	[illegible]
	[illegible]	[illegible]	[illegible]	[illegible]	[illegible]	[illegible]	[illegible]	[illegible]	[illegible]	[illegible]	[illegible]	[illegible]	[illegible]	[illegible]	[illegible]
	[illegible]	[illegible]	[illegible]	[illegible]	[illegible]	[illegible]	[illegible]	[illegible]	[illegible]	[illegible]	[illegible]	[illegible]	[illegible]	[illegible]	[illegible]
	[illegible]	[illegible]	[illegible]	[illegible]	[illegible]	[illegible]	[illegible]	[illegible]	[illegible]	[illegible]	[illegible]	[illegible]	[illegible]	[illegible]	[illegible]
	[illegible]	[illegible]	[illegible]	[illegible]	[illegible]	[illegible]	[illegible]	[illegible]	[illegible]	[illegible]	[illegible]	[illegible]	[illegible]	[illegible]	[illegible]
CORK:	[illegible]	[illegible]	[illegible]	[illegible]	[illegible]	[illegible]	[illegible]	[illegible]	[illegible]	[illegible]	[illegible]	[illegible]	[illegible]	[illegible]	[illegible]
	[illegible]	[illegible]	[illegible]	[illegible]	[illegible]	[illegible]	[illegible]	[illegible]	[illegible]	[illegible]	[illegible]	[illegible]	[illegible]	[illegible]	[illegible]
	[illegible]	[illegible]	[illegible]	[illegible]	[illegible]	[illegible]	[illegible]	[illegible]	[illegible]	[illegible]	[illegible]	[illegible]	[illegible]	[illegible]	[illegible]
	[illegible]	[illegible]	[illegible]	[illegible]	[illegible]	[illegible]	[illegible]	[illegible]	[illegible]	[illegible]	[illegible]	[illegible]	[illegible]	[illegible]	[illegible]
Area, [illegible] Acres.	[illegible]	[illegible]	[illegible]	[illegible]	[illegible]	[illegible]	[illegible]	[illegible]	[illegible]	[illegible]	[illegible]	[illegible]	[illegible]	[illegible]	[illegible]
	[illegible]	[illegible]	[illegible]	[illegible]	[illegible]	[illegible]	[illegible]	[illegible]	[illegible]	[illegible]	[illegible]	[illegible]	[illegible]	[illegible]	[illegible]
	[illegible]	[illegible]	[illegible]	[illegible]	[illegible]	[illegible]	[illegible]	[illegible]	[illegible]	[illegible]	[illegible]	[illegible]	[illegible]	[illegible]	[illegible]

TABLE 12.—SHOWING THE QUANTITY OF LIVE STOCK IN EACH YEAR FROM 1888 TO 1897, BY COUNTIES AND PROVINCES—continued.

COUNTIES.	Years.	No. of Horses			Mules and Asses		No. of Cattle.			No. of Sheep.		No. of Pigs.		[illegible]	[illegible]
		[illegible]	[illegible]	[illegible]	[illegible]	[illegible]	[illegible]	[illegible]	[illegible]	[illegible]	[illegible]	[illegible]	[illegible]		
[illegible]	[illegible]	[illegible]	[illegible]	[illegible]	[illegible]	[illegible]	[illegible]	[illegible]	[illegible]	[illegible]	[illegible]	[illegible]	[illegible]	[illegible]	[illegible]
[illegible]	[illegible]	[illegible]	[illegible]	[illegible]	[illegible]	[illegible]	[illegible]	[illegible]	[illegible]	[illegible]	[illegible]	[illegible]	[illegible]	[illegible]	[illegible]

17,0[illegible]	1,3[illegible]	1,8[illegible]	24	456	34,0[illegible]	33,81[illegible]
17,01[illegible]	1,3[illegible]	1,7[illegible]	28	384	[illegible]	[illegible]
17,[illegible]	1,17[illegible]	1,8[illegible]	[illegible]	[illegible]	[illegible]	34,[illegible]
17,[illegible]	1,6[illegible]	1,8[illegible]	[illegible]	333	[illegible]	[illegible]
17,617	1,8[illegible]	2,1[illegible]	[illegible]	[illegible]	36,[illegible]	35,[illegible]
17,621	1,887	1,866	[illegible]	[illegible]	38,4[illegible]	38,4[illegible]
18,[illegible]	2,[illegible]	1,8[illegible]	[illegible]	[illegible]	[illegible]	37,[illegible]
19,[illegible]	1,9[illegible]	1,7[illegible]	[illegible]	[illegible]	[illegible]	[illegible]
19,[illegible]	1,9[illegible]	[illegible]	[illegible]	[illegible]	[illegible]	[illegible]
14,[illegible]	1,[illegible]	1,[illegible]	[illegible]	[illegible]	67,[illegible]	67,[illegible]
[illegible]	1,[illegible]	1,[illegible]	[illegible]	[illegible]	20,[illegible]	19,[illegible]
[illegible]	1,[illegible]	1,[illegible]	[illegible]	[illegible]	20,[illegible]	[illegible]
[illegible]	1,[illegible]	1,[illegible]	[illegible]	[illegible]	[illegible]	[illegible]
[illegible]	1,[illegible]	1,[illegible]	[illegible]	[illegible]	[illegible]	[illegible]
[illegible]	1,[illegible]	1,[illegible]	[illegible]	[illegible]	[illegible]	[illegible]

TABLE 12.—SHOWING THE QUANTITY OF LIVE STOCK IN EACH YEAR FROM 1888 TO 1897 BY COUNTIES AND PROVINCES—*continued*.

[illegible]	Years.	No. of Horses.			Mules and Asses.		No. of Cattle.			No. of Sheep.		No. of Pigs.		[illegible]	[illegible]
		[illegible]	[illegible]	[illegible]	[illegible]	[illegible]	[illegible]	[illegible]	[illegible]	[illegible]	[illegible]	[illegible]	[illegible]		
[illegible]	[illegible]	[illegible]	[illegible]	[illegible]	[illegible]	[illegible]	[illegible]	[illegible]	[illegible]	[illegible]	[illegible]	[illegible]	[illegible]	[illegible]	[illegible]
[illegible]	[illegible]	[illegible]	[illegible]	[illegible]	[illegible]	[illegible]	[illegible]	[illegible]	[illegible]	[illegible]	[illegible]	[illegible]	[illegible]	[illegible]	[illegible]
[illegible]	[illegible]	[illegible]	[illegible]	[illegible]	[illegible]	[illegible]	[illegible]	[illegible]	[illegible]	[illegible]	[illegible]	[illegible]	[illegible]	[illegible]	[illegible]
[illegible]	[illegible]	[illegible]	[illegible]	[illegible]	[illegible]	[illegible]	[illegible]	[illegible]	[illegible]	[illegible]	[illegible]	[illegible]	[illegible]	[illegible]	[illegible]
[illegible]	[illegible]	[illegible]	[illegible]	[illegible]	[illegible]	[illegible]	[illegible]	[illegible]	[illegible]	[illegible]	[illegible]	[illegible]	[illegible]	[illegible]	[illegible]
	[illegible]	[illegible]	[illegible]	[illegible]	[illegible]	[illegible]	[illegible]	[illegible]	[illegible]	[illegible]	[illegible]	[illegible]	[illegible]	[illegible]	[illegible]
	[illegible]	[illegible]	[illegible]	[illegible]	[illegible]	[illegible]	[illegible]	[illegible]	[illegible]	[illegible]	[illegible]	[illegible]	[illegible]	[illegible]	[illegible]
	[illegible]	[illegible]	[illegible]	[illegible]	[illegible]	[illegible]	[illegible]	[illegible]	[illegible]	[illegible]	[illegible]	[illegible]	[illegible]	[illegible]	[illegible]
	[illegible]	[illegible]	[illegible]	[illegible]	[illegible]	[illegible]	[illegible]	[illegible]	[illegible]	[illegible]	[illegible]	[illegible]	[illegible]	[illegible]	[illegible]
	[illegible]	[illegible]	[illegible]	[illegible]	[illegible]	[illegible]	[illegible]	[illegible]	[illegible]	[illegible]	[illegible]	[illegible]	[illegible]	[illegible]	[illegible]
[illegible]	[illegible]	[illegible]	[illegible]	[illegible]	[illegible]	[illegible]	[illegible]	[illegible]	[illegible]	[illegible]	[illegible]	[illegible]	[illegible]	[illegible]	[illegible]
[illegible]	[illegible]	[illegible]	[illegible]	[illegible]	[illegible]	[illegible]	[illegible]	[illegible]	[illegible]	[illegible]	[illegible]	[illegible]	[illegible]	[illegible]	[illegible]
[illegible]	[illegible]	[illegible]	[illegible]	[illegible]	[illegible]	[illegible]	[illegible]	[illegible]	[illegible]	[illegible]	[illegible]	[illegible]	[illegible]	[illegible]	[illegible]
[illegible]	[illegible]	[illegible]	[illegible]	[illegible]	[illegible]	[illegible]	[illegible]	[illegible]	[illegible]	[illegible]	[illegible]	[illegible]	[illegible]	[illegible]	[illegible]
	[illegible]	[illegible]	[illegible]	[illegible]	[illegible]	[illegible]	[illegible]	[illegible]	[illegible]	[illegible]	[illegible]	[illegible]	[illegible]	[illegible]	[illegible]
	[illegible]	[illegible]	[illegible]	[illegible]	[illegible]	[illegible]	[illegible]	[illegible]	[illegible]	[illegible]	[illegible]	[illegible]	[illegible]	[illegible]	[illegible]
	[illegible]	[illegible]	[illegible]	[illegible]	[illegible]	[illegible]	[illegible]	[illegible]	[illegible]	[illegible]	[illegible]	[illegible]	[illegible]	[illegible]	[illegible]
	[illegible]	[illegible]	[illegible]	[illegible]	[illegible]	[illegible]	[illegible]	[illegible]	[illegible]	[illegible]	[illegible]	[illegible]	[illegible]	[illegible]	[illegible]
	[illegible]	[illegible]	[illegible]	[illegible]	[illegible]	[illegible]	[illegible]	[illegible]	[illegible]	[illegible]	[illegible]	[illegible]	[illegible]	[illegible]	[illegible]
	[illegible]	[illegible]	[illegible]	[illegible]	[illegible]	[illegible]	[illegible]	[illegible]	[illegible]	[illegible]	[illegible]	[illegible]	[illegible]	[illegible]	[illegible]

TABLE 12.—SHOWING THE QUANTITY OF LIVE STOCK IN EACH YEAR FROM 1888 TO 1897, BY COUNTIES AND PROVINCES—continued.

PROVINCES.

PROVINCES.	Year.	No. of Horses.			Mules and Asses.		No. of Cattle.			No. of Sheep.		No. of Pigs.		No. of Goats.	No. of Poultry.
		Two years and upwards.	One year and under two.	Under one year.	No. of Mules.	No. of Asses.	Two years and upwards.	One year and under two.	Under one year.	One year and upwards.	Under one year.	One year and upwards.	Under one year.		
LEINSTER:	[illegible]	[illegible]	[illegible]	[illegible]	[illegible]	[illegible]	[illegible]	[illegible]	[illegible]	[illegible]	[illegible]	[illegible]	[illegible]	[illegible]	[illegible]
	[illegible]	[illegible]	[illegible]	[illegible]	[illegible]	[illegible]	[illegible]	[illegible]	[illegible]	[illegible]	[illegible]	[illegible]	[illegible]	[illegible]	[illegible]
	[illegible]	[illegible]	[illegible]	[illegible]	[illegible]	[illegible]	[illegible]	[illegible]	[illegible]	[illegible]	[illegible]	[illegible]	[illegible]	[illegible]	[illegible]
	[illegible]	[illegible]	[illegible]	[illegible]	[illegible]	[illegible]	[illegible]	[illegible]	[illegible]	[illegible]	[illegible]	[illegible]	[illegible]	[illegible]	[illegible]
Area, [illegible] Acres.	[illegible]	[illegible]	[illegible]	[illegible]	[illegible]	[illegible]	[illegible]	[illegible]	[illegible]	[illegible]	[illegible]	[illegible]	[illegible]	[illegible]	[illegible]
	[illegible]	[illegible]	[illegible]	[illegible]	[illegible]	[illegible]	[illegible]	[illegible]	[illegible]	[illegible]	[illegible]	[illegible]	[illegible]	[illegible]	[illegible]
	[illegible]	[illegible]	[illegible]	[illegible]	[illegible]	[illegible]	[illegible]	[illegible]	[illegible]	[illegible]	[illegible]	[illegible]	[illegible]	[illegible]	[illegible]
	[illegible]	[illegible]	[illegible]	[illegible]	[illegible]	[illegible]	[illegible]	[illegible]	[illegible]	[illegible]	[illegible]	[illegible]	[illegible]	[illegible]	[illegible]
	[illegible]	[illegible]	[illegible]	[illegible]	[illegible]	[illegible]	[illegible]	[illegible]	[illegible]	[illegible]	[illegible]	[illegible]	[illegible]	[illegible]	[illegible]
	[illegible]	[illegible]	[illegible]	[illegible]	[illegible]	[illegible]	[illegible]	[illegible]	[illegible]	[illegible]	[illegible]	[illegible]	[illegible]	[illegible]	[illegible]
MUNSTER:	[illegible]	[illegible]	[illegible]	[illegible]	[illegible]	[illegible]	[illegible]	[illegible]	[illegible]	[illegible]	[illegible]	[illegible]	[illegible]	[illegible]	[illegible]
	[illegible]	[illegible]	[illegible]	[illegible]	[illegible]	[illegible]	[illegible]	[illegible]	[illegible]	[illegible]	[illegible]	[illegible]	[illegible]	[illegible]	[illegible]
	[illegible]	[illegible]	[illegible]	[illegible]	[illegible]	[illegible]	[illegible]	[illegible]	[illegible]	[illegible]	[illegible]	[illegible]	[illegible]	[illegible]	[illegible]
	[illegible]	[illegible]	[illegible]	[illegible]	[illegible]	[illegible]	[illegible]	[illegible]	[illegible]	[illegible]	[illegible]	[illegible]	[illegible]	[illegible]	[illegible]
Area, [illegible] Acres.	[illegible]	[illegible]	[illegible]	[illegible]	[illegible]	[illegible]	[illegible]	[illegible]	[illegible]	[illegible]	[illegible]	[illegible]	[illegible]	[illegible]	[illegible]
	[illegible]	[illegible]	[illegible]	[illegible]	[illegible]	[illegible]	[illegible]	[illegible]	[illegible]	[illegible]	[illegible]	[illegible]	[illegible]	[illegible]	[illegible]
	[illegible]	[illegible]	[illegible]	[illegible]	[illegible]	[illegible]	[illegible]	[illegible]	[illegible]	[illegible]	[illegible]	[illegible]	[illegible]	[illegible]	[illegible]
	[illegible]	[illegible]	[illegible]	[illegible]	[illegible]	[illegible]	[illegible]	[illegible]	[illegible]	[illegible]	[illegible]	[illegible]	[illegible]	[illegible]	[illegible]
	[illegible]	[illegible]	[illegible]	[illegible]	[illegible]	[illegible]	[illegible]	[illegible]	[illegible]	[illegible]	[illegible]	[illegible]	[illegible]	[illegible]	[illegible]
	[illegible]	[illegible]	[illegible]	[illegible]	[illegible]	[illegible]	[illegible]	[illegible]	[illegible]	[illegible]	[illegible]	[illegible]	[illegible]	[illegible]	[illegible]
ULSTER:	[illegible]	[illegible]	[illegible]	[illegible]	[illegible]	[illegible]	[illegible]	[illegible]	[illegible]	[illegible]	[illegible]	[illegible]	[illegible]	[illegible]	[illegible]
	[illegible]	[illegible]	[illegible]	[illegible]	[illegible]	[illegible]	[illegible]	[illegible]	[illegible]	[illegible]	[illegible]	[illegible]	[illegible]	[illegible]	[illegible]
	[illegible]	[illegible]	[illegible]	[illegible]	[illegible]	[illegible]	[illegible]	[illegible]	[illegible]	[illegible]	[illegible]	[illegible]	[illegible]	[illegible]	[illegible]
	[illegible]	[illegible]	[illegible]	[illegible]	[illegible]	[illegible]	[illegible]	[illegible]	[illegible]	[illegible]	[illegible]	[illegible]	[illegible]	[illegible]	[illegible]
Area, [illegible] Acres.	[illegible]	[illegible]	[illegible]	[illegible]	[illegible]	[illegible]	[illegible]	[illegible]	[illegible]	[illegible]	[illegible]	[illegible]	[illegible]	[illegible]	[illegible]
	[illegible]	[illegible]	[illegible]	[illegible]	[illegible]	[illegible]	[illegible]	[illegible]	[illegible]	[illegible]	[illegible]	[illegible]	[illegible]	[illegible]	[illegible]
	[illegible]	[illegible]	[illegible]	[illegible]	[illegible]	[illegible]	[illegible]	[illegible]	[illegible]	[illegible]	[illegible]	[illegible]	[illegible]	[illegible]	[illegible]
	[illegible]	[illegible]	[illegible]	[illegible]	[illegible]	[illegible]	[illegible]	[illegible]	[illegible]	[illegible]	[illegible]	[illegible]	[illegible]	[illegible]	[illegible]
	[illegible]	[illegible]	[illegible]	[illegible]	[illegible]	[illegible]	[illegible]	[illegible]	[illegible]	[illegible]	[illegible]	[illegible]	[illegible]	[illegible]	[illegible]
	[illegible]	[illegible]	[illegible]	[illegible]	[illegible]	[illegible]	[illegible]	[illegible]	[illegible]	[illegible]	[illegible]	[illegible]	[illegible]	[illegible]	[illegible]
CONNAUGHT:	[illegible]	[illegible]	[illegible]	[illegible]	[illegible]	[illegible]	[illegible]	[illegible]	[illegible]	[illegible]	[illegible]	[illegible]	[illegible]	[illegible]	[illegible]
	[illegible]	[illegible]	[illegible]	[illegible]	[illegible]	[illegible]	[illegible]	[illegible]	[illegible]	[illegible]	[illegible]	[illegible]	[illegible]	[illegible]	[illegible]
	[illegible]	[illegible]	[illegible]	[illegible]	[illegible]	[illegible]	[illegible]	[illegible]	[illegible]	[illegible]	[illegible]	[illegible]	[illegible]	[illegible]	[illegible]
	[illegible]	[illegible]	[illegible]	[illegible]	[illegible]	[illegible]	[illegible]	[illegible]	[illegible]	[illegible]	[illegible]	[illegible]	[illegible]	[illegible]	[illegible]
Area, [illegible] Acres.	[illegible]	[illegible]	[illegible]	[illegible]	[illegible]	[illegible]	[illegible]	[illegible]	[illegible]	[illegible]	[illegible]	[illegible]	[illegible]	[illegible]	[illegible]
	[illegible]	[illegible]	[illegible]	[illegible]	[illegible]	[illegible]	[illegible]	[illegible]	[illegible]	[illegible]	[illegible]	[illegible]	[illegible]	[illegible]	[illegible]
	[illegible]	[illegible]	[illegible]	[illegible]	[illegible]	[illegible]	[illegible]	[illegible]	[illegible]	[illegible]	[illegible]	[illegible]	[illegible]	[illegible]	[illegible]
	[illegible]	[illegible]	[illegible]	[illegible]	[illegible]	[illegible]	[illegible]	[illegible]	[illegible]	[illegible]	[illegible]	[illegible]	[illegible]	[illegible]	[illegible]
	[illegible]	[illegible]	[illegible]	[illegible]	[illegible]	[illegible]	[illegible]	[illegible]	[illegible]	[illegible]	[illegible]	[illegible]	[illegible]	[illegible]	[illegible]
	[illegible]	[illegible]	[illegible]	[illegible]	[illegible]	[illegible]	[illegible]	[illegible]	[illegible]	[illegible]	[illegible]	[illegible]	[illegible]	[illegible]	[illegible]

TOTAL OF IRELAND.

IRELAND.	Year.	No. of Horses.			Mules and Asses.		No. of Cattle.			No. of Sheep.		No. of Pigs.		No. of Goats.	No. of Poultry.
		Two years and upwards.	One year and under two.	Under one year.	No. of Mules.	No. of Asses.	Two years and upwards.	One year and under two.	Under one year.	One year and upwards.	Under one year.	One year and upwards.	Under one year.		
TOTAL OF IRELAND:	[illegible]	[illegible]	[illegible]	[illegible]	[illegible]	[illegible]	[illegible]	[illegible]	[illegible]	[illegible]	[illegible]	[illegible]	[illegible]	[illegible]	[illegible]
	[illegible]	[illegible]	[illegible]	[illegible]	[illegible]	[illegible]	[illegible]	[illegible]	[illegible]	[illegible]	[illegible]	[illegible]	[illegible]	[illegible]	[illegible]
	[illegible]	[illegible]	[illegible]	[illegible]	[illegible]	[illegible]	[illegible]	[illegible]	[illegible]	[illegible]	[illegible]	[illegible]	[illegible]	[illegible]	[illegible]
	[illegible]	[illegible]	[illegible]	[illegible]	[illegible]	[illegible]	[illegible]	[illegible]	[illegible]	[illegible]	[illegible]	[illegible]	[illegible]	[illegible]	[illegible]
Area, [illegible] Acres.	[illegible]	[illegible]	[illegible]	[illegible]	[illegible]	[illegible]	[illegible]	[illegible]	[illegible]	[illegible]	[illegible]	[illegible]	[illegible]	[illegible]	[illegible]
	[illegible]	[illegible]	[illegible]	[illegible]	[illegible]	[illegible]	[illegible]	[illegible]	[illegible]	[illegible]	[illegible]	[illegible]	[illegible]	[illegible]	[illegible]
	[illegible]	[illegible]	[illegible]	[illegible]	[illegible]	[illegible]	[illegible]	[illegible]	[illegible]	[illegible]	[illegible]	[illegible]	[illegible]	[illegible]	[illegible]
	[illegible]	[illegible]	[illegible]	[illegible]	[illegible]	[illegible]	[illegible]	[illegible]	[illegible]	[illegible]	[illegible]	[illegible]	[illegible]	[illegible]	[illegible]
	[illegible]	[illegible]	[illegible]	[illegible]	[illegible]	[illegible]	[illegible]	[illegible]	[illegible]	[illegible]	[illegible]	[illegible]	[illegible]	[illegible]	[illegible]
	[illegible]	[illegible]	[illegible]	[illegible]	[illegible]	[illegible]	[illegible]	[illegible]	[illegible]	[illegible]	[illegible]	[illegible]	[illegible]	[illegible]	[illegible]

TABLE 14.—SHOWING, by COUNTIES and PROVINCES, the Total Area under POTATOES in 1897, and the Extent in Statute Acres under each description of that crop.

COUNTIES.	Total area under Potatoes	Extent in Statute Acres under: [illegible]	[illegible]	[illegible]	[illegible]	[illegible]	[illegible]	[illegible]	[illegible]	[illegible]	[illegible]	[illegible]	[illegible]	[illegible]	[illegible]	[illegible]	[illegible]	All others.
	Acres.	Acres.	Acres.	Acres.	Acres.	Acres.	Acres.	Acres.	Acres.	Acres.	Acres.	Acres.	Acres.	Acres.	Acres.	Acres.	Acres.	Acres.
Antrim,	[illegible]	[illegible]	[illegible]	[illegible]	[illegible]	[illegible]	[illegible]	[illegible]	[illegible]	[illegible]	[illegible]	[illegible]	.	[illegible]	[illegible]	.	[illegible]	[illegible]
Armagh,	[illegible]	[illegible]	[illegible]	[illegible]	[illegible]	[illegible]	[illegible]	[illegible]	[illegible]	[illegible]	[illegible]	[illegible]	.	[illegible]	.	[illegible]	[illegible]	[illegible]
Carlow,	[illegible]	[illegible]	[illegible]	[illegible]	[illegible]	[illegible]	[illegible]	[illegible]	[illegible]	[illegible]	[illegible]	[illegible]	.	[illegible]	[illegible]	[illegible]	[illegible]	[illegible]
Cavan,	[illegible]	[illegible]	[illegible]	[illegible]	[illegible]	[illegible]	[illegible]	[illegible]	[illegible]	[illegible]	[illegible]	.	.	[illegible]	.	[illegible]	[illegible]	[illegible]
Clare,	[illegible]	[illegible]	[illegible]	[illegible]	[illegible]	[illegible]	[illegible]	.	[illegible]	[illegible]	[illegible]	.	.	[illegible]	[illegible]	[illegible]	[illegible]	[illegible]
Cork,	[illegible]	[illegible]	[illegible]	[illegible]	[illegible]	[illegible]	[illegible]	[illegible]	[illegible]	[illegible]	[illegible]	[illegible]	.	[illegible]	.	.	[illegible]	[illegible]
Donegal,	[illegible]	[illegible]	[illegible]	[illegible]	[illegible]	[illegible]	[illegible]	[illegible]	[illegible]	[illegible]	[illegible]	[illegible]	[illegible]	[illegible]	[illegible]	.	[illegible]	[illegible]
Down,	[illegible]	[illegible]	[illegible]	[illegible]	[illegible]	[illegible]	[illegible]	[illegible]	[illegible]	[illegible]	[illegible]	[illegible]	.	[illegible]	[illegible]	.	[illegible]	[illegible]
Dublin,	[illegible]	[illegible]	[illegible]	[illegible]	[illegible]	[illegible]	[illegible]	[illegible]	[illegible]	[illegible]	.	.	.	.	[illegible]	.	[illegible]	[illegible]
Fermanagh,	[illegible]	[illegible]	[illegible]	[illegible]	[illegible]	[illegible]	[illegible]	[illegible]	[illegible]	[illegible]	[illegible]	[illegible]	.	[illegible]	.	.	[illegible]	[illegible]
Galway,	[illegible]	[illegible]	[illegible]	[illegible]	[illegible]	[illegible]	[illegible]	[illegible]	.	[illegible]	[illegible]	[illegible]	.	[illegible]	.	[illegible]	[illegible]	[illegible]
Kerry,	[illegible]	[illegible]	[illegible]	[illegible]	[illegible]	[illegible]	[illegible]	[illegible]	[illegible]	[illegible]	[illegible]	.	.	[illegible]	[illegible]	.	[illegible]	[illegible]
Kildare,	[illegible]	[illegible]	[illegible]	[illegible]	[illegible]	[illegible]	[illegible]	[illegible]	[illegible]	[illegible]	[illegible]	.	.	[illegible]	[illegible]	.	[illegible]	[illegible]
Kilkenny,	[illegible]	[illegible]	[illegible]	[illegible]	[illegible]	[illegible]	[illegible]	[illegible]	[illegible]	[illegible]	[illegible]	[illegible]	.	.	.	[illegible]	[illegible]	[illegible]
King's,	[illegible]	[illegible]	[illegible]	[illegible]	[illegible]	[illegible]	[illegible]	[illegible]	[illegible]	[illegible]	[illegible]	[illegible]	.	[illegible]	.	.	[illegible]	[illegible]
Leitrim,	[illegible]	[illegible]	[illegible]	[illegible]	[illegible]	[illegible]	[illegible]	.	[illegible]	[illegible]	[illegible]	[illegible]	.	[illegible]	.	.	[illegible]	[illegible]
Limerick,	[illegible]	[illegible]	[illegible]	[illegible]	[illegible]	[illegible]	[illegible]	[illegible]	[illegible]	[illegible]	[illegible]	[illegible]	.	[illegible]	.	.	[illegible]	[illegible]
Londonderry,	[illegible]	[illegible]	[illegible]	[illegible]	[illegible]	[illegible]	[illegible]	[illegible]	[illegible]	[illegible]	[illegible]	[illegible]	.	[illegible]	.	.	[illegible]	[illegible]
Longford,	[illegible]	[illegible]	[illegible]	[illegible]	[illegible]	[illegible]	[illegible]	[illegible]	[illegible]	[illegible]	[illegible]	[illegible]	.	.	.	[illegible]	[illegible]	[illegible]
Louth and Drogheda, County of Town,	[illegible]	[illegible]	[illegible]	[illegible]	[illegible]	[illegible]	[illegible]	[illegible]	[illegible]	[illegible]	[illegible]	.	.	[illegible]	[illegible]	.	[illegible]	[illegible]
Mayo,	[illegible]	[illegible]	[illegible]	[illegible]	[illegible]	[illegible]	[illegible]	.	[illegible]	[illegible]	[illegible]	[illegible]	.	.	.	.	[illegible]	[illegible]
Meath,	[illegible]	[illegible]	[illegible]	[illegible]	[illegible]	[illegible]	[illegible]	[illegible]	[illegible]	[illegible]	[illegible]	[illegible]	.	[illegible]	[illegible]	[illegible]	[illegible]	[illegible]
Monaghan,	[illegible]	[illegible]	[illegible]	[illegible]	[illegible]	[illegible]	[illegible]	[illegible]	[illegible]	[illegible]	[illegible]	[illegible]	.	[illegible]	.	.	[illegible]	[illegible]
Queen's,	[illegible]	[illegible]	[illegible]	[illegible]	[illegible]	[illegible]	[illegible]	[illegible]	.	[illegible]	[illegible]	[illegible]	.	[illegible]	.	[illegible]	[illegible]	[illegible]
Roscommon,	[illegible]	[illegible]	[illegible]	[illegible]	[illegible]	[illegible]	[illegible]	[illegible]	[illegible]	[illegible]	[illegible]	[illegible]	.	[illegible]	[illegible]	.	[illegible]	[illegible]
Sligo,	[illegible]	[illegible]	[illegible]	[illegible]	[illegible]	[illegible]	[illegible]	.	[illegible]	[illegible]	[illegible]	[illegible]	.	.	.	.	[illegible]	[illegible]
Tipperary,	[illegible]	[illegible]	[illegible]	[illegible]	[illegible]	[illegible]	[illegible]	[illegible]	.	[illegible]	[illegible]	[illegible]	.	[illegible]	.	[illegible]	[illegible]	[illegible]
Tyrone,	[illegible]	[illegible]	[illegible]	[illegible]	[illegible]	[illegible]	[illegible]	[illegible]	[illegible]	[illegible]	[illegible]	[illegible]	.	[illegible]	.	.	[illegible]	[illegible]
Waterford,	[illegible]	[illegible]	[illegible]	[illegible]	[illegible]	[illegible]	[illegible]	[illegible]	[illegible]	[illegible]	[illegible]	[illegible]	.	[illegible]	.	.	[illegible]	[illegible]
Westmeath,	[illegible]	[illegible]	[illegible]	[illegible]	[illegible]	[illegible]	[illegible]	[illegible]	[illegible]	[illegible]	[illegible]	[illegible]	.	.	[illegible]	[illegible]	[illegible]	[illegible]
Wexford,	[illegible]	[illegible]	[illegible]	[illegible]	[illegible]	[illegible]	[illegible]	[illegible]	[illegible]	[illegible]	[illegible]	[illegible]	.	[illegible]	.	[illegible]	[illegible]	[illegible]
Wicklow,	[illegible]	[illegible]	[illegible]	[illegible]	[illegible]	[illegible]	[illegible]	[illegible]	[illegible]	[illegible]	[illegible]	[illegible]	.	[illegible]	[illegible]	.	[illegible]	[illegible]
PROVINCES.																		
Leinster,	[illegible]	[illegible]	[illegible]	[illegible]	[illegible]	[illegible]	[illegible]	[illegible]	[illegible]	[illegible]	[illegible]	[illegible]	.	[illegible]	[illegible]	[illegible]	[illegible]	[illegible]
Munster,	[illegible]	[illegible]	[illegible]	[illegible]	[illegible]	[illegible]	[illegible]	[illegible]	[illegible]	[illegible]	[illegible]	[illegible]	.	[illegible]	[illegible]	[illegible]	[illegible]	[illegible]
Ulster,	[illegible]	[illegible]	[illegible]	[illegible]	[illegible]	[illegible]	[illegible]	[illegible]	[illegible]	[illegible]	[illegible]	[illegible]	[illegible]	[illegible]	[illegible]	[illegible]	[illegible]	[illegible]
Connaught,	[illegible]	[illegible]	[illegible]	[illegible]	[illegible]	[illegible]	[illegible]	[illegible]	[illegible]	[illegible]	[illegible]	[illegible]	.	[illegible]	[illegible]	[illegible]	[illegible]	[illegible]
Total of Ireland, 1897,	[illegible]	[illegible]	[illegible]	[illegible]	[illegible]	[illegible]	[illegible]	[illegible]	[illegible]	[illegible]	[illegible]	[illegible]	[illegible]	[illegible]	[illegible]	[illegible]	[illegible]	[illegible]
Percentage in 1897,	100·0	[illegible]	[illegible]	[illegible]	[illegible]	[illegible]	[illegible]	[illegible]	[illegible]									
Total of Ireland, 1896,	[illegible]	[illegible]	[illegible]	[illegible]	[illegible]	[illegible]	[illegible]	[illegible]	[illegible]	[illegible]	[illegible]	[illegible]	[illegible]	[illegible]	[illegible]	[illegible]	[illegible]	[illegible]
Percentage in 1896,	100·0	[illegible]	[illegible]	[illegible]	[illegible]	[illegible]	[illegible]	[illegible]	[illegible]									

* [illegible]
† [illegible]

TABLE 15.—SHOWING, by POOR LAW UNIONS, the Total extent in STATUTE ACRES under POTATOES in [illegible] and the extent under each description of that Crop.

Poor Law Unions	[illegible]	[illegible]	[illegible]	[illegible]	[illegible]	[illegible]	[illegible]	[illegible]	[illegible]	[illegible]	[illegible]	[illegible]	[illegible]	[illegible]	[illegible]	[illegible]
[illegible]	[illegible]	[illegible]	[illegible]	[illegible]	[illegible]	[illegible]	[illegible]	[illegible]	[illegible]	[illegible]	[illegible]	[illegible]	[illegible]	[illegible]	[illegible]	[illegible]

[illegible]	[illegible]
[illegible]	[illegible]
[illegible]	[illegible]
[illegible]	[illegible]
[illegible]	[illegible]
[illegible]	[illegible]
[illegible]	[illegible]
[illegible]	[illegible]

TABLE 16.—SHOWING, by COUNTIES, the average rate of Produce per Statute Acre of the principal descriptions of POTATOES planted in Ireland in 1897.

COUNTIES.	AVERAGE RATE OF PRODUCE PER STATUTE ACRE OF														
	[illegible]	[illegible]	[illegible]	[illegible]	[illegible]	[illegible]	[illegible]	[illegible]	[illegible]	[illegible]	[illegible]	[illegible]	[illegible]	[illegible]	[illegible]
Antrim,	[illegible]	[illegible]	[illegible]	[illegible]	[illegible]	[illegible]	[illegible]	77	[illegible]	[illegible]	[illegible]	.	[illegible]	.	.
Armagh,	[illegible]	[illegible]	[illegible]	[illegible]	[illegible]	[illegible]	[illegible]	[illegible]	[illegible]	[illegible]	[illegible]	.	[illegible]	.	-
Carlow,	[illegible]	[illegible]	[illegible]	[illegible]	[illegible]	[illegible]	[illegible]	.	[illegible]	-	.	.	.	[illegible]	[illegible]
Cavan,	[illegible]	[illegible]	[illegible]	41	-	[illegible]	[illegible]	[illegible]	.	[illegible]	.	.	[illegible]	.	-
Clare,	[illegible]	[illegible]	[illegible]	[illegible]	[illegible]	[illegible]	.	19	18	[illegible]	.	.	.	-	[illegible]
Cork,	[illegible]	[illegible]	[illegible]	[illegible]	[illegible]	[illegible]	[illegible]	.	[illegible]	[illegible]	[illegible]	.	[illegible]	.	-
Donegal,	[illegible]	[illegible]	[illegible]	[illegible]	[illegible]	[illegible]	[illegible]	[illegible]	[illegible]	[illegible]	[illegible]	[illegible]	[illegible]	.	-
Down,	[illegible]	[illegible]	[illegible]	[illegible]	[illegible]	[illegible]	[illegible]	[illegible]	.	[illegible]	[illegible]	.	[illegible]	-	-
Dublin,	[illegible]	[illegible]	-	75	[illegible]	.	[illegible]	[illegible]	.	.	.	.	.	[illegible]	
Fermanagh,	[illegible]	[illegible]	[illegible]	[illegible]	[illegible]	[illegible]	[illegible]	[illegible]	.	[illegible]	[illegible]	.	[illegible]	.	-
Galway,	[illegible]	[illegible]	-	[illegible]	.	[illegible]	[illegible]	.	[illegible]	[illegible]	.	.	[illegible]	.	[illegible]
Kerry,	[illegible]	[illegible]	[illegible]	[illegible]	[illegible]	[illegible]	[illegible]	[illegible]	[illegible]	[illegible]	.	.	-	.	-
Kildare,	[illegible]	[illegible]	[illegible]	[illegible]	[illegible]	[illegible]	[illegible]	[illegible]	[illegible]	[illegible]	.	-	[illegible]	[illegible]	.
Kilkenny,	[illegible]	[illegible]	[illegible]	[illegible]	[illegible]	[illegible]	[illegible]	[illegible]	.	[illegible]	[illegible]	.	-	.	[illegible]
King's,	[illegible]	[illegible]	[illegible]	[illegible]	[illegible]	[illegible]	[illegible]	[illegible]	.	[illegible]	[illegible]	.	[illegible]	.	-
Leitrim,	[illegible]	[illegible]	41	[illegible]	.	[illegible]	.	[illegible]	[illegible]	[illegible]	[illegible]	.	[illegible]	.	.
Limerick,	[illegible]	[illegible]	[illegible]	[illegible]	[illegible]	[illegible]	.	[illegible]	-	.	.	.	[illegible]	.	.
Londonderry,	[illegible]	[illegible]	[illegible]	[illegible]	[illegible]	[illegible]	[illegible]	[illegible]	[illegible]	[illegible]	[illegible]	.	[illegible]	.	.
Longford,	[illegible]	[illegible]	[illegible]	[illegible]	.	[illegible]	.	-	[illegible]	.	[illegible]	.	.	-	.
Louth and Drogheda, County of Town.	[illegible]	[illegible]	[illegible]	[illegible]	[illegible]	[illegible]	[illegible]	[illegible]	-	[illegible]	.	.	[illegible]	[illegible]	-
Mayo,	[illegible]	[illegible]	[illegible]	[illegible]	[illegible]	[illegible]	-	[illegible]	.	[illegible]	[illegible]	-	.	-	.
Meath,	[illegible]	[illegible]	[illegible]	[illegible]	[illegible]	[illegible]	[illegible]	[illegible]	[illegible]	-	[illegible]	-	[illegible]	41	.
Monaghan,	[illegible]	[illegible]	[illegible]	[illegible]	[illegible]	61	[illegible]	[illegible]	[illegible]	[illegible]	[illegible]	-	[illegible]	.	.
Queen's,	[illegible]	[illegible]	.	[illegible]	[illegible]	.	[illegible]	.	[illegible]	[illegible]	[illegible]	.	[illegible]	.	[illegible]
Roscommon,	[illegible]	[illegible]	[illegible]	[illegible]	-	.	[illegible]	.	.	[illegible]	[illegible]	.	.	.	.
Sligo,	[illegible]	[illegible]	[illegible]	[illegible]	[illegible]	[illegible]	.	-	[illegible]	.	[illegible]	-	.	-	.
Tipperary,	[illegible]	[illegible]	[illegible]	[illegible]	.	[illegible]	[illegible]	.	-	[illegible]	[illegible]	.	[illegible]	.	.
Tyrone,	[illegible]	[illegible]	[illegible]	[illegible]	[illegible]	[illegible]	[illegible]	[illegible]	.	[illegible]	[illegible]	.	[illegible]	-	.
Waterford,	[illegible]	[illegible]	[illegible]	[illegible]	[illegible]	[illegible]	[illegible]	-	.	-	.	.	.	-	-
Westmeath,	[illegible]	[illegible]	[illegible]	[illegible]	[illegible]	[illegible]	[illegible]	[illegible]	.	[illegible]	.	.	.	.	[illegible]
Wexford,	[illegible]	[illegible]	[illegible]	[illegible]	[illegible]	[illegible]	[illegible]	[illegible]	.	[illegible]	[illegible]	.	.	-	[illegible]
Wicklow,	[illegible]	41	[illegible]	[illegible]	[illegible]	.	[illegible]	[illegible]	-	[illegible]	[illegible]	-	.	[illegible]	-

TABLE 17.—Showing, by Counties and Provinces, the Number of Boars

PROVINCES AND COUNTIES	Number of BOARS …											
	White Pork.							Sweet Pork.				
	Large Yorkshire.		Middle Yorkshire.		Small Yorkshire.		Total.	Berkshire.		[illegible]		Total.
	Bred in Ireland.	Imported.	Bred in Ireland.	Imported.	Bred in Ireland.	Imported.		Bred in Ireland.	Imported.	Bred in Ireland.	Imported.	
LEINSTER.												
Carlow,	[illegible]	.	[illegible]	.	.	.	12	.	[illegible]	.	.	[illegible]
Dublin,	[illegible]	[illegible]	[illegible]	.	[illegible]	.	[illegible]	[illegible]	[illegible]	.	.	[illegible]
Kildare,	[illegible]	[illegible]	[illegible]	.	.	.	[illegible]		[illegible]	.	.	[illegible]
Kilkenny,	[illegible]	[illegible]	[illegible]	.	[illegible]	.	[illegible]	[illegible]	.	.	.	[illegible]
King's,	[illegible]	[illegible]	[illegible]	.	[illegible]	.	[illegible]	[illegible]	.	.	.	[illegible]
Longford,	[illegible]	[illegible]	[illegible]	.	.	.	[illegible]	[illegible]	.	.	.	[illegible]
Louth,	[illegible]	.	[illegible]	[illegible]	[illegible]	.	[illegible]	.	[illegible]	.	.	[illegible]
Meath,	[illegible]	.	[illegible]	.	.	.	[illegible]	[illegible]	.	.	.	[illegible]
Queen's,	[illegible]	[illegible]	[illegible]	.	.	.	[illegible]	[illegible]	.	.	.	[illegible]
Westmeath,	[illegible]	.	[illegible]	.	[illegible]	.	[illegible]	.	.	.	.	.
Wexford,	[illegible]	[illegible]	[illegible]	[illegible]	[illegible]	.	[illegible]	[illegible]	.	[illegible]	.	[illegible]
Wicklow,	[illegible]	.	[illegible]	.	[illegible]	.	[illegible]	[illegible]	.	.	.	[illegible]
Total of Leinster,	[illegible]	[illegible]	[illegible]	[illegible]	[illegible]	.	[illegible]	[illegible]	[illegible]	[illegible]	.	[illegible]
MUNSTER.												
Clare,	[illegible]	.	[illegible]	.	.	.	[illegible]	[illegible]	.	.	.	[illegible]
Cork, E. R.,	[illegible]	[illegible]	[illegible]	.	[illegible]	.	[illegible]	[illegible]	[illegible]	.	.	[illegible]
Cork, W. R.,	[illegible]	.	[illegible]	.	[illegible]	.	[illegible]	[illegible]	.	.	.	[illegible]
Kerry,	[illegible]	.	[illegible]	[illegible]	[illegible]	.	[illegible]	.	.	.	[illegible]	[illegible]
Limerick,	[illegible]	[illegible]	[illegible]	.	[illegible]	.	[illegible]	.	.	.		.
Tipperary, N. R.,	[illegible]	[illegible]	[illegible]	.	[illegible]	.	[illegible]	.	.	.	.	.
Tipperary, S. R.,	[illegible]	.	[illegible]	.	[illegible]	.	[illegible]	[illegible]	.	.		[illegible]
Waterford,	[illegible]	.	[illegible]	[illegible]	.	.	[illegible]	.	.	.	.	.
Total of Munster,	[illegible]	[illegible]	[illegible]	[illegible]	[illegible]	.	[illegible]	[illegible]	[illegible]	.	[illegible]	[illegible]
ULSTER.												
Antrim,	[illegible]	[illegible]	[illegible]	.	[illegible]	.	[illegible]	[illegible]	[illegible]	.	.	[illegible]
Armagh,	[illegible]	.	[illegible]	.	[illegible]	.	[illegible]	[illegible]	.	.	.	[illegible]
Cavan,	[illegible]	.	[illegible]	.	[illegible]	.	[illegible]	[illegible]	.	.	.	[illegible]
Donegal,	[illegible]	.	[illegible]	.	[illegible]	.	[illegible]	[illegible]	.	.	.	[illegible]
Down,	[illegible]	.	[illegible]	.	[illegible]	.	[illegible]	.	.	.	.	.
Fermanagh,	[illegible]	.	[illegible]	[illegible]	[illegible]	.	[illegible]	[illegible]	.	.	.	[illegible]
Londonderry,	[illegible]	.	[illegible]	[illegible]	[illegible]	.	[illegible]	[illegible]	.	.	.	[illegible]
Monaghan,	[illegible]	.	[illegible]	.	[illegible]	.	[illegible]	[illegible]	.	.	.	[illegible]
Tyrone,	[illegible]	[illegible]	[illegible]	.	[illegible]	.	[illegible]	[illegible]	.	.	.	[illegible]
Total of Ulster,	[illegible]	[illegible]	[illegible]	[illegible]	[illegible]	.	[illegible]	[illegible]	[illegible]	.	.	[illegible]
CONNAUGHT.												
Galway,	[illegible]	[illegible]	[illegible]	[illegible]	[illegible]	.	[illegible]	[illegible]	.	[illegible]	.	[illegible]
Leitrim,	[illegible]	.	[illegible]	.	[illegible]	.	[illegible]	[illegible]	.	.	.	[illegible]
Mayo,	[illegible]	[illegible]	[illegible]	[illegible]	[illegible]	[illegible]	[illegible]	[illegible]	.	.	.	[illegible]
Roscommon,	[illegible]	.	[illegible]	.	[illegible]	.	[illegible]	[illegible]	.	.		[illegible]
Sligo,	[illegible]	.	[illegible]	[illegible]	[illegible]	.	[illegible]	[illegible]	.	.	.	[illegible]
Total of Connaught,	[illegible]	[illegible]	[illegible]	[illegible]	[illegible]	[illegible]	[illegible]	[illegible]	.	[illegible]	.	[illegible]
Total of Ireland,	[illegible]	[illegible]	[illegible]	[illegible]	[illegible]	[illegible]	[illegible]	[illegible]	[illegible]	[illegible]	[illegible]	[illegible]

kept for Breeding Purposes in Ireland in the Year 1897.

[illegible]									[illegible]			Provinces and Counties.
[illegible]			[illegible]			[illegible]						
Bred in Ireland.	Imported.	Total.	Bred in Ireland.	Imported.	Total.	Bred in Ireland.	Imported.	Total.	Bred in Ireland.	Imported.	Total.	
												Leinster.
.	.	.	[illegible]	.	[illegible]	[illegible]	.	[illegible]	[illegible]	[illegible]	[illegible]	Carlow.
.	.	.	[illegible]	.	[illegible]	[illegible]	.	[illegible]	[illegible]	[illegible]	[illegible]	Dublin.
.	.	.	[illegible]	.	[illegible]	[illegible]	.	[illegible]	[illegible]	[illegible]	[illegible]	Kildare.
.	.	.	[illegible]	.	[illegible]	[illegible]	.	[illegible]	[illegible]	[illegible]	[illegible]	Kilkenny.
.	.	.	[illegible]	.	[illegible]	[illegible]	.	[illegible]	[illegible]	[illegible]	[illegible]	King's.
.	.	.	[illegible]	.	[illegible]	[illegible]	.	[illegible]	[illegible]	[illegible]	[illegible]	Longford.
.	.	.	[illegible]	.	[illegible]	[illegible]	.	[illegible]	[illegible]	[illegible]	[illegible]	Louth.
.	.	.	[illegible]	.	[illegible]	.	.	.	[illegible]	.	[illegible]	Meath.
.	.	.	[illegible]	.	[illegible]	[illegible]	.	[illegible]	[illegible]	[illegible]	[illegible]	Queen's.
.	.	.	[illegible]	.	[illegible]	[illegible]	.	[illegible]	[illegible]	.	[illegible]	Westmeath.
.	.	.	[illegible]	.	[illegible]	[illegible]	.	[illegible]	[illegible]	[illegible]	[illegible]	Wexford.
.	.	.	[illegible]	.	[illegible]	[illegible]	.	[illegible]	[illegible]	.	[illegible]	Wicklow.
.		.	[illegible]	.	[illegible]	[illegible]	.	[illegible]	[illegible]	[illegible]	[illegible]	Total of Leinster.
												Munster.
.	.	.	[illegible]	.	[illegible]	[illegible]	.	[illegible]	[illegible]	.	[illegible]	Clare.
[illegible]	.	[illegible]	[illegible]	.	[illegible]	[illegible]	.	[illegible]	[illegible]	[illegible]	[illegible]	Cork, E. R.
.	.	.	[illegible]	.	[illegible]	[illegible]	.	[illegible]	[illegible]	.	[illegible]	Cork, W. R.
.	[illegible]	[illegible]	[illegible]	.	[illegible]	[illegible]	.	[illegible]	[illegible]	[illegible]	[illegible]	Kerry.
[illegible]	.	[illegible]	[illegible]	.	[illegible]	[illegible]	[illegible]	[illegible]	[illegible]	[illegible]	[illegible]	Limerick.
.	[illegible]	[illegible]	[illegible]	.	[illegible]	[illegible]	.	[illegible]	[illegible]	[illegible]	[illegible]	Tipperary, N. R.
.	.	.	[illegible]	.	[illegible]	[illegible]	.	[illegible]	[illegible]	.	[illegible]	Tipperary, S. R.
.	.	.	[illegible]	.	[illegible]	[illegible]	.	[illegible]	[illegible]	.	[illegible]	Waterford.
[illegible]	[illegible]	[illegible]	[illegible]	.	[illegible]	[illegible]	[illegible]	[illegible]	[illegible]	[illegible]	[illegible]	Total of Munster.
												Ulster.
.	.	.	[illegible]	.	[illegible]	[illegible]	.	[illegible]	[illegible]	[illegible]	[illegible]	Antrim.
[illegible]	.	[illegible]	[illegible]	.	[illegible]	[illegible]	.	[illegible]	[illegible]	.	[illegible]	Armagh.
.	.	.	[illegible]	.	[illegible]	[illegible]	.	[illegible]	[illegible]	.	[illegible]	Cavan.
.	.	.	[illegible]	.	[illegible]	[illegible]	.	[illegible]	[illegible]	.	[illegible]	Donegal.
[illegible]	.	[illegible]	[illegible]	.	[illegible]	[illegible]	.	[illegible]	[illegible]	.	[illegible]	Down.
.	.	.	[illegible]	.	[illegible]	[illegible]	.	[illegible]	[illegible]	.	[illegible]	Fermanagh.
.	.	.	[illegible]	.	[illegible]	[illegible]	.	[illegible]	[illegible]	[illegible]	[illegible]	Londonderry.
.	.	.	[illegible]	.	[illegible]	[illegible]	.	[illegible]	[illegible]	.	[illegible]	Monaghan.
.	.	.	[illegible]	.	[illegible]	[illegible]	.	[illegible]	[illegible]	[illegible]	[illegible]	Tyrone.
[illegible]	.	[illegible]	[illegible]	.	[illegible]	[illegible]	.	[illegible]	[illegible]	[illegible]	[illegible]	Total of Ulster.
												Connaught.
.	.	.	[illegible]	.	[illegible]	[illegible]	.	[illegible]	[illegible]	[illegible]	[illegible]	Galway.
.	.	.	[illegible]	.	[illegible]	[illegible]	.	[illegible]	[illegible]	.	[illegible]	Leitrim.
.	.	.	[illegible]	.	[illegible]	[illegible]	.	[illegible]	[illegible]	[illegible]	[illegible]	Mayo.
[illegible]	.	[illegible]	[illegible]	.	[illegible]	[illegible]	.	[illegible]	[illegible]	.	[illegible]	Roscommon.
.	.	.	[illegible]	.	[illegible]	[illegible]	.	[illegible]	[illegible]	[illegible]	[illegible]	Sligo.
[illegible]	.	[illegible]	[illegible]	.	[illegible]	[illegible]	.	[illegible]	[illegible]	[illegible]	[illegible]	Total of Connaught.
[illegible]	[illegible]	[illegible]	[illegible]	.	[illegible]	[illegible]	[illegible]	[illegible]	[illegible]	[illegible]	[illegible]	Total of Ireland.

The following statements have been received from persons who have made Ensilage in Ireland in 1887.

PROVINCE OF

No. of Return.	Dimensions of Silos—Length, Breadth, Depth.	Materials of Silos.			Whether [illegible] or open.	[illegible]	Has Ensilage been made [illegible] this year?
		Walls.	Floor.	Roof.			
[illegible]	—	—	—	—	—	—	[illegible]
[illegible]	—	—	—	—	—	—	[illegible]
[illegible]	[illegible] feet by [illegible] feet; [illegible] feet deep.	Concrete,	Concrete,	Wood,	Sheltered,	Partly [illegible]	No.
[illegible]	—	—	—	—	—	—	Yes, [illegible]
	[illegible] feet by [illegible] feet; [illegible] feet deep.	—	Clay,	—	[illegible]	[illegible]	[illegible]
[illegible]	[illegible]	Concrete,	Concrete,	Galvanised [illegible]	Yes,	[illegible]	No.
[illegible]	—	—	—	—	—	—	[illegible]
[illegible]	—	—	—	—	—	—	[illegible]
[illegible]	—	—	—	—	—	—	[illegible]

E.

inserted in those cases where permission has been given to include them.

PROVINCE OF

[illegible]	[illegible]	[illegible]	[illegible]	[illegible]			[illegible]	[illegible]	[illegible]
				[illegible]	[illegible]	[illegible]			
KING'S COUNTY.									
[illegible]	-	1		-	-	-	-	-	[illegible]
[illegible]	-	1	-	-	-	-	-	-	[illegible]
[illegible]	-	1	-	-	-	-	-	-	[illegible]
[illegible]	-	1	-	-	-	-	-	-	[illegible]
[illegible]	-	1	-	-	-	-	-	-	[illegible]
[illegible]	-	1	-	[illegible]	-	[illegible]	[illegible]	-	[illegible]
[illegible]	-	1	-	-	-	-	-	-	[illegible]
[illegible]	-	1	-	-	-	-	-	-	[illegible]
LONGFORD COUNTY.									
[illegible]	-	1	-	-	-	-	[illegible]	-	[illegible]
[illegible]	-	1	-	-	-	-	-	-	-
MEATH COUNTY									
[illegible]	-	1	-	-	-	-	-	-	[illegible]

LEINSTER—continued.

[illegible]	[illegible]	[illegible]		[illegible]	[illegible]	[illegible]
		[illegible]	[illegible]			
[illegible]	[illegible]	—	—	[illegible]	[illegible]	[illegible]
[illegible]	[illegible]	[illegible]		[illegible]	[illegible]	[illegible]
[illegible]	[illegible]	[illegible]	[illegible]	[illegible]	[illegible]	[illegible]
[illegible]	[illegible]	—	—	[illegible]	[illegible]	[illegible]
[illegible]	[illegible]	—	—	[illegible]	[illegible]	[illegible]
[illegible]	[illegible]	[illegible]	[illegible]	[illegible]	[illegible]	[illegible]
[illegible]	[illegible]	—	—	[illegible]	[illegible]	[illegible]
[illegible]	[illegible]	[illegible]		[illegible]	[illegible]	[illegible]
[illegible]	[illegible]	[illegible]	[illegible]	[illegible]	[illegible]	[illegible]
—	—	—	—	—	[illegible]	[illegible]
[illegible]	[illegible]	[illegible]		[illegible]	—	

–	–	–	–
–	–	–	–
–	–	–	–
–	–	–	–
–	–	–	–
[illegible]	[illegible]	[illegible]	[illegible]
–	–	–	–
–	–	–	–
–	–	–	–
–	–	–	–
–	–	–	–
–	–	–	–

–	–	–	–	–
[illegible]	[illegible]	[illegible]	[illegible]	[illegible]
–	–	–	–	–
–	–	–	–	–
–	–	–	–	–
–	–	–	–	–
[illegible]	[illegible]	[illegible]	[illegible]	[illegible]

[illegible]	[illegible]	Temperature.		[illegible]	[illegible]	Remarks.
		[illegible]	[illegible]			
[illegible]	[illegible]	[illegible]		[illegible]	[illegible]	[illegible]
—	[illegible]	—	—	[illegible]	[illegible]	—
[illegible]	[illegible]	[illegible]		[illegible]	[illegible]	[illegible]
[illegible]	[illegible]	[illegible]		[illegible]	[illegible]	—
[illegible]	[illegible]	—	—	[illegible]	[illegible]	[illegible]
[illegible]	[illegible]	[illegible]		[illegible]	[illegible]	[illegible]
[illegible]	[illegible]	[illegible]		[illegible]	[illegible]	[illegible]
[illegible]	[illegible]	[illegible]		[illegible]	[illegible]	[illegible]
[illegible]	[illegible]	[illegible]		[illegible]	[illegible]	[illegible]
[illegible]	[illegible]	[illegible]		[illegible]	[illegible]	[illegible]
[illegible]	[illegible]	[illegible]		[illegible]	[illegible]	—
[illegible]	[illegible]	[illegible]		[illegible]	[illegible]	[illegible]

—	—	—	—	—	—	[illegible]
—	—	—	—	—	—	[illegible]
—	—	—	—	—	—	[illegible]
[illegible]	[illegible]	[illegible]	[illegible]	[illegible]	[illegible]	[illegible]
[illegible]	Do.	Do.	[illegible]	Do.	Do.	
[illegible]	Do.	Do.	Do.	Do.	Do.	
—	—	—	—	—	—	[illegible]
—	—	—	—	—	—	[illegible]
—	—	—	—	—	—	[illegible]
—	—	—	—	—	—	[illegible]
[illegible]	[illegible]	[illegible]	[illegible]	[illegible]	[illegible]	[illegible]
[illegible]	[illegible]	[illegible]	[illegible]	[illegible]	[illegible]	Do.
—	—	—	—	—	—	Do.
—	[illegible]	[illegible]	[illegible]	Do.	[illegible]	—

LEINSTER—continued.

[illegible]	[illegible]	[illegible]		[illegible]	[illegible]	[illegible]
		[illegible]	[illegible]			
[illegible]	[illegible]	[illegible]	[illegible]	[illegible]	[illegible]	[illegible]
[illegible]	[illegible]	[illegible]	[illegible]	[illegible]	[illegible]	[illegible]
[illegible]	[illegible]	[illegible]	[illegible]	[illegible]	[illegible]	[illegible]
[illegible]	[illegible]	[illegible]	[illegible]	[illegible]	[illegible]	[illegible]
[illegible]	[illegible]	[illegible]	[illegible]	[illegible]	[illegible]	[illegible]
[illegible]	[illegible]	[illegible]	—	[illegible]	[illegible]	[illegible]
[illegible]	[illegible]	—	—	[illegible]	[illegible]	[illegible]
[illegible]	[illegible]	—	—	—	[illegible]	[illegible]
[illegible]	[illegible]	[illegible]	[illegible]	[illegible]	[illegible]	—
[illegible]	[illegible]	[illegible]	—	[illegible]	[illegible]	[illegible]
[illegible]	[illegible]	[illegible]	[illegible]	[illegible]	[illegible]	[illegible]
[illegible]	[illegible]	—	—	—	[illegible]	[illegible]

Dimensions of Excavation, Length, Breadth, Depth.	Materials of Silo.			Whether Drained or not.	Situation, "Above," "Below," "Partly Below," or "Above" Surface.	Has Ensilage kept, [illegible]
	Walls.	Floor.	Roof.			
—	—	—	—	—	—	[illegible]
—	[illegible]	[illegible]	[illegible]	No.	[illegible]	No.
[illegible]	[illegible]	[illegible]	[illegible]	[illegible]	[illegible]	[illegible]
[illegible]	[illegible]	[illegible]	[illegible]	No.	[illegible]	[illegible]
Do.	Do.	Do.	Do.	Do.	Do.	
[illegible]	[illegible]	[illegible]	[illegible]	[illegible]	[illegible]	No.
Do.	Do.	Do.	Do.	Do.	Do.	
[illegible]	[illegible]	Concrete.	[illegible]	No.	[illegible]	No.
—	—	—	—	—	—	[illegible]
—	—	—	—	—	—	[illegible]
[illegible]	[illegible]	[illegible]	[illegible]	[illegible]	[illegible]	—
[illegible]	[illegible]	Clay.	[illegible]	No.	[illegible]	[illegible]
[illegible]	Do.	Do.	Do.	Do.	Do.	
[illegible]	[illegible]	Clay.	[illegible]	[illegible]	[illegible]	—
—	—	—	—	—	—	[illegible]

[illegible]		[illegible]	[illegible]	[illegible]
[illegible]	[illegible]	[illegible]	[illegible]	[illegible]
Not observed.		[illegible]	[illegible]	—
[illegible]		[illegible]	[illegible]	[illegible]
[illegible]		I do not [illegible]	[illegible]	[illegible]
[illegible]		—	[illegible]	[illegible]
—		I [illegible]	[illegible]	[illegible]

[illegible]									
[illegible]	[illegible]	[illegible]	[illegible]	[illegible]	[illegible]	[illegible]	[illegible]	[illegible]	[illegible]
[illegible]	[illegible]	[illegible]	—	—	—	—	—	—	[illegible]
[illegible]	[illegible]	[illegible]	—	—	—	—	—	—	[illegible]
[illegible]	[illegible]	[illegible]	—	—	—	—	—	—	—

PROVINCE OF

[illegible]									
[illegible]	[illegible]	[illegible]	—	—	—	—	—	—	[illegible]
[illegible]	[illegible]		[illegible]	[illegible]	[illegible]	[illegible]	[illegible]	[illegible]	—
[illegible]	[illegible]	[illegible]	—	—	[illegible]	—	—	—	[illegible]
[illegible]	[illegible]	[illegible]	[illegible]	[illegible]	[illegible]	[illegible]	[illegible]	[illegible]	[illegible]
[illegible]	[illegible]	[illegible]	—	—	—	—	—	—	[illegible]
[illegible]	[illegible]	[illegible]	[illegible]	[illegible]	[illegible]	[illegible]	[illegible]	[illegible]	—
[illegible]	[illegible]	[illegible]	—	—	—	—	—	—	[illegible]
[illegible]									
[illegible]		[illegible]	—	—	—	—	—	—	[illegible]

MUNSTER—continued.

[illegible]	[illegible]	Temperature.		[illegible]	[illegible]	Remarks.
		[illegible]	[illegible]			
[illegible]	Meadow [illegible]	No record.		—	[illegible]	[illegible]
[illegible]	[illegible]	[illegible]		—	[illegible]	[illegible]
[illegible]	[illegible]	[illegible]	[illegible]	About [illegible] lbs.	[illegible]	[illegible]
—	—	—	—	—	—	[illegible]

ULSTER.

[illegible]	[illegible]	[illegible]		[illegible]	[illegible]	—
[illegible]	Meadow [illegible]	—	—	[illegible]	[illegible]	[illegible]
[illegible]	Aftergrass.	[illegible]		—	[illegible]	[illegible]
Cannot say.	[illegible]	Cannot say.		[illegible]	[illegible]	[illegible]
[illegible]	Aftergrass.	[illegible]	[illegible]	[illegible]	—	[illegible]
[illegible]	Meadow [illegible]	—	—	[illegible]	[illegible]	[illegible]
[illegible]	[illegible]	[illegible]		[illegible]	[illegible]	[illegible]
[illegible]	[illegible]	[illegible]		[illegible]	[illegible]	[illegible]

—	—	—	—	—	—	[illegible]
—	—	—	—	—	—	[illegible]
[illegible] feet by [illegible] feet, [illegible] feet deep.	[illegible]	[illegible]	[illegible]	Flat.	Partly below.	No.
[illegible] feet by [illegible] feet, [illegible] feet deep.	[illegible]	[illegible]	[illegible]	Natural drainage.	Partly below.	No.
[illegible] feet by [illegible] feet, [illegible] feet deep.	[illegible]	[illegible]	[illegible]	[illegible]	[illegible]	Not for [illegible] purposes.
[illegible] feet by [illegible] feet, [illegible] feet deep.	[illegible]	Clay.	[illegible]	No.	Below.	[illegible]
—	—	—	—	—	—	[illegible]
[illegible] feet by [illegible] feet, [illegible] feet deep.	[illegible]	[illegible]	Wood.	[illegible]	[illegible]	[illegible]
[illegible] feet by [illegible] feet, [illegible] feet deep. Do.	[illegible]	[illegible]	[illegible]	[illegible]	[illegible]	[illegible]
—	—	—	—	—	—	In a [illegible].

ULSTER—continued.

[illegible]	[illegible]	[illegible]		[illegible]	[illegible]	Remarks.
		[illegible]	[illegible]			
—	[illegible]	—	—	—	[illegible]	[illegible]
[illegible]	[illegible]	—	—	[illegible]	[illegible]	[illegible]
[illegible]	[illegible]	[illegible]	[illegible]	[illegible]	[illegible]	[illegible]
[illegible]	[illegible]	—	—	[illegible]	[illegible]	[illegible]
[illegible]	[illegible]	—	[illegible]	[illegible]	[illegible]	[illegible]
[illegible]	[illegible]	[illegible]		[illegible]	[illegible]	—
[illegible]	[illegible]	[illegible]		[illegible]	[illegible]	[illegible]
[illegible]	[illegible]	—	—	[illegible]	[illegible]	[illegible]
[illegible]	[illegible]	[illegible]		[illegible]	[illegible]	[illegible]
[illegible]	Ordinary grass.	[illegible]		[illegible]	[illegible]	[illegible]

PROVINCE OF

[illegible]	[illegible]			[illegible]	[illegible]	[illegible]
	Walls.	Floor.	Roof.			
[illegible]	[illegible]	[illegible]	[illegible]	[illegible]	[illegible]	[illegible]
—	—	—	—	—	—	[illegible]
—	—	—	—	—	—	[illegible]
[illegible]		—	—	—	—	[illegible]
—	[illegible]	—	—	—	—	[illegible]
—	—	—	—	—	—	[illegible]
—	—	—	—	—	—	[illegible]
—	—	—	—	—	—	[illegible]
[illegible]	[illegible]	[illegible]	[illegible]	[illegible]	[illegible]	[illegible]
—	—	—	—	—	—	[illegible]

CONNAUGHT.

[illegible]	[illegible]	[illegible]		[illegible]	[illegible]	[illegible]
		[illegible]	[illegible]			
[illegible]	[illegible]	Not taken.		[illegible]	[illegible]	[illegible]
—	—	—	—	—	—	[illegible]
[illegible]	[illegible]	Not taken.		[illegible]	[illegible]	[illegible]
[illegible]	[illegible]	[illegible]		[illegible]	[illegible]	—
[illegible]	[illegible]	No record kept.		[illegible]	[illegible]	—
[illegible]	[illegible]	—	—	[illegible]	[illegible]	—
[illegible]	[illegible]	[illegible]		[illegible]	[illegible]	[illegible]
[illegible]	[illegible]	—	—	[illegible]	[illegible]	—
[illegible]	[illegible]	[illegible]	[illegible]	[illegible]	[illegible]	[illegible]
—	—	—	—	—	[illegible]	[illegible]

[illegible]		Whether Drained or not.	[illegible]
Floor.	Roof.		
—	—	—	—
—	—	—	—

CONNAUGHT—continued.

[illegible]	[illegible]	[illegible]		[illegible]	[illegible]	Remarks.
		[illegible]	[illegible]			
[illegible]	[illegible]	—	—	About [illegible]	[illegible]	—

THE WEATHER.

Abstract of Meteorological Observations registered at the Ordnance Survey Office (Height above the Sea 155·3 Feet), Phœnix Park, Dublin, during the year 1897:—

The barometer stood highest in 1897, on the 21st November, at 9 P.M., wind calm, when it was 30·675 inches; it was lowest at 9 P.M. on 29th December, when it was 28·[illegible] inches, wind S.S.W. The highest temperature of the air during the year was 79·0 degrees of Fahrenheit on 10th July, and the lowest 13·7 degrees on 17th January. The greatest quantity of rain which fell in a day (24 hours) was 1·020 inches on 1st September, with wind S.W. The point from which the wind chiefly prevailed was the W.; it blew from that direction on 88 days, at 9 A.M. The strongest wind was from the W.S.W. on the 14th March, when the pressure was 4·30 lbs. per square foot.

1897	Barometer. Corrected for Altitude and reduced to 32° Fah.							Thermometer.											
	[illegible]	[illegible]	[illegible]	[illegible]	[illegible]	[illegible]	[illegible]	[illegible]	[illegible]	[illegible]	[illegible]	[illegible]	[illegible]	[illegible]	[illegible]	[illegible]	[illegible]	[illegible]	[illegible]
January,	[illegible]	[illegible]	[illegible]	[illegible]	[illegible]	[illegible]	[illegible]	[illegible]	[illegible]	[illegible]	[illegible]	[illegible]	[illegible]	[illegible]	[illegible]	[illegible]	[illegible]	[illegible]	[illegible]
February,	[illegible]	[illegible]	[illegible]	[illegible]	[illegible]	[illegible]	[illegible]	[illegible]	[illegible]	[illegible]	[illegible]	[illegible]	[illegible]	[illegible]	[illegible]	[illegible]	[illegible]	[illegible]	[illegible]
March,	[illegible]	[illegible]	[illegible]	[illegible]	[illegible]	[illegible]	[illegible]	[illegible]	[illegible]	[illegible]	[illegible]	[illegible]	[illegible]	[illegible]	[illegible]	[illegible]	[illegible]	[illegible]	[illegible]
April,	[illegible]	[illegible]	[illegible]	[illegible]	[illegible]	[illegible]	[illegible]	[illegible]	[illegible]	[illegible]	[illegible]	[illegible]	[illegible]	[illegible]	[illegible]	[illegible]	[illegible]	[illegible]	[illegible]
May,	[illegible]	[illegible]	[illegible]	[illegible]	[illegible]	[illegible]	[illegible]	[illegible]	[illegible]	[illegible]	[illegible]	[illegible]	[illegible]	[illegible]	[illegible]	[illegible]	[illegible]	[illegible]	[illegible]
June,	[illegible]	[illegible]	[illegible]	[illegible]	[illegible]	[illegible]	[illegible]	[illegible]	[illegible]	[illegible]	[illegible]	[illegible]	[illegible]	[illegible]	[illegible]	[illegible]	[illegible]	[illegible]	[illegible]
July,	[illegible]	[illegible]	[illegible]	[illegible]	[illegible]	[illegible]	[illegible]	[illegible]	[illegible]	[illegible]	[illegible]	[illegible]	[illegible]	[illegible]	[illegible]	[illegible]	[illegible]	[illegible]	[illegible]
August,	[illegible]	[illegible]	[illegible]	[illegible]	[illegible]	[illegible]	[illegible]	[illegible]	[illegible]	[illegible]	[illegible]	[illegible]	[illegible]	[illegible]	[illegible]	[illegible]	[illegible]	[illegible]	[illegible]
September,	[illegible]	[illegible]	[illegible]	[illegible]	[illegible]	[illegible]	[illegible]	[illegible]	[illegible]	[illegible]	[illegible]	[illegible]	[illegible]	[illegible]	[illegible]	[illegible]	[illegible]	[illegible]	[illegible]
October,	[illegible]	[illegible]	[illegible]	[illegible]	[illegible]	[illegible]	[illegible]	[illegible]	[illegible]	[illegible]	[illegible]	[illegible]	[illegible]	[illegible]	[illegible]	[illegible]	[illegible]	[illegible]	[illegible]
November,	[illegible]	[illegible]	[illegible]	[illegible]	[illegible]	[illegible]	[illegible]	[illegible]	[illegible]	[illegible]	[illegible]	[illegible]	[illegible]	[illegible]	[illegible]	[illegible]	[illegible]	[illegible]	[illegible]
December,	[illegible]	[illegible]	[illegible]	[illegible]	[illegible]	[illegible]	[illegible]	[illegible]	[illegible]	[illegible]	[illegible]	[illegible]	[illegible]	[illegible]	[illegible]	[illegible]	[illegible]	[illegible]	[illegible]
Total,	[illegible]	[illegible]	[illegible]	-	-	-	-	-	-	-	[illegible]	[illegible]	[illegible]	-	[illegible]	[illegible]	[illegible]	[illegible]	[illegible]
Mean,	[illegible]	[illegible]	[illegible]	-	-	-	-	-	-	-	[illegible]	[illegible]	[illegible]	-	[illegible]	[illegible]	[illegible]	[illegible]	[illegible]

1897	Rain.			Cloud.	[illegible]		Wind.																
	[illegible]	[illegible]	[illegible]	[illegible]	[illegible]	[illegible]	N.	[illegible]	N.E.	[illegible]	E.	[illegible]	S.E.	[illegible]	S.	[illegible]	S.W.	[illegible]	W.	[illegible]	N.W.	[illegible]	Calm.
January,	[illegible]	[illegible]	[illegible]	[illegible]	[illegible]	[illegible]	[illegible]	[illegible]	[illegible]	[illegible]	[illegible]	[illegible]	[illegible]	[illegible]	[illegible]	[illegible]	[illegible]	[illegible]	[illegible]	[illegible]	[illegible]	[illegible]	[illegible]
February,	[illegible]	[illegible]	[illegible]	[illegible]	[illegible]	[illegible]	[illegible]	[illegible]	[illegible]	[illegible]	[illegible]	[illegible]	[illegible]	[illegible]	[illegible]	[illegible]	[illegible]	[illegible]	[illegible]	[illegible]	[illegible]	[illegible]	[illegible]
March,	[illegible]	[illegible]	[illegible]	[illegible]	[illegible]	[illegible]	[illegible]	[illegible]	[illegible]	[illegible]	[illegible]	[illegible]	[illegible]	[illegible]	[illegible]	[illegible]	[illegible]	[illegible]	[illegible]	[illegible]	[illegible]	[illegible]	[illegible]
April,	[illegible]	[illegible]	[illegible]	[illegible]	[illegible]	[illegible]	[illegible]	[illegible]	[illegible]	[illegible]	[illegible]	[illegible]	[illegible]	[illegible]	[illegible]	[illegible]	[illegible]	[illegible]	[illegible]	[illegible]	[illegible]	[illegible]	[illegible]
May,	[illegible]	[illegible]	[illegible]	[illegible]	[illegible]	[illegible]	[illegible]	[illegible]	[illegible]	[illegible]	[illegible]	[illegible]	[illegible]	[illegible]	[illegible]	[illegible]	[illegible]	[illegible]	[illegible]	[illegible]	[illegible]	[illegible]	[illegible]
June,	[illegible]	[illegible]	[illegible]	[illegible]	[illegible]	[illegible]	[illegible]	[illegible]	[illegible]	[illegible]	[illegible]	[illegible]	[illegible]	[illegible]	[illegible]	[illegible]	[illegible]	[illegible]	[illegible]	[illegible]	[illegible]	[illegible]	[illegible]
July,	[illegible]	[illegible]	[illegible]	[illegible]	[illegible]	[illegible]	[illegible]	[illegible]	[illegible]	[illegible]	[illegible]	[illegible]	[illegible]	[illegible]	[illegible]	[illegible]	[illegible]	[illegible]	[illegible]	[illegible]	[illegible]	[illegible]	[illegible]
August,	[illegible]	[illegible]	[illegible]	[illegible]	[illegible]	[illegible]	[illegible]	[illegible]	[illegible]	[illegible]	[illegible]	[illegible]	[illegible]	[illegible]	[illegible]	[illegible]	[illegible]	[illegible]	[illegible]	[illegible]	[illegible]	[illegible]	[illegible]
September,	[illegible]	[illegible]	[illegible]	[illegible]	[illegible]	[illegible]	[illegible]	[illegible]	[illegible]	[illegible]	[illegible]	[illegible]	[illegible]	[illegible]	[illegible]	[illegible]	[illegible]	[illegible]	[illegible]	[illegible]	[illegible]	[illegible]	[illegible]
October,	[illegible]	[illegible]	[illegible]	[illegible]	[illegible]	[illegible]	[illegible]	[illegible]	[illegible]	[illegible]	[illegible]	[illegible]	[illegible]	[illegible]	[illegible]	[illegible]	[illegible]	[illegible]	[illegible]	[illegible]	[illegible]	[illegible]	[illegible]
November,	[illegible]	[illegible]	[illegible]	[illegible]	[illegible]	[illegible]	[illegible]	[illegible]	[illegible]	[illegible]	[illegible]	[illegible]	[illegible]	[illegible]	[illegible]	[illegible]	[illegible]	[illegible]	[illegible]	[illegible]	[illegible]	[illegible]	[illegible]
December,	[illegible]	[illegible]	[illegible]	[illegible]	[illegible]	[illegible]	[illegible]	[illegible]	[illegible]	[illegible]	[illegible]	[illegible]	[illegible]	[illegible]	[illegible]	[illegible]	[illegible]	[illegible]	[illegible]	[illegible]	[illegible]	[illegible]	[illegible]
Total,	[illegible]	[illegible]	-	[illegible]	[illegible]	[illegible]	[illegible]	[illegible]	[illegible]	[illegible]	[illegible]	[illegible]	[illegible]	[illegible]	[illegible]	[illegible]	[illegible]	[illegible]	[illegible]	[illegible]	[illegible]	[illegible]	[illegible]
Mean,	-	-	-	[illegible]	[illegible]	[illegible]	-	[illegible]	-	[illegible]	-	[illegible]	-	[illegible]	-	[illegible]	-	[illegible]	-	[illegible]	-	[illegible]	-

METEOROLOGICAL OBSERVATIONS

FOR EACH MONTH OF THE YEAR 1897.

By J. W. MOORE, Esq., M.D., F.R.C.P.I., F.R. MET. SOC.

(Extracted from the *Dublin Journal of Medical Science.*)

JANUARY.—Opening with a brilliantly fine day, January, 1897, proved a cold, changeable month. Between the 3rd and the 10th, inclusive, there was an abundant rainfall with S.E. winds, owing to the presence of depressions over the Atlantic off the S.W. of Ireland. The weather was open at this time, but after the 14th frequent frosts occurred, and a good deal of snow fell from time to time, particularly in the N. of Scotland, where the weather was at times extremely severe.

In Dublin the arithmetical mean temperature (38·1°) was much below the average (41·4°); the mean dry bulb readings at 9 a.m. and 9 p.m. were 37·9°. In the thirty-two years ending with 1896, January was coldest in 1881 (M. T. = 33·4°), and warmest in 1873 (M. T. = 46·6°). In 1895 the M. T. was 35·4°, and in 1896 it was 44·3°. As a general rule, January in Dublin is not colder, but a shade warmer, than December. This is owing to the full development in January of a winter area of low pressure over the Atlantic, to the northwestward of the British Isles, and to a resulting prevalence of S.W. winds in their vicinity. January, 1897, proved an exception to this rule, the M. T. being 3·3° below that of December, 1896 (41·4°).

The mean height of the barometer was 29·918 inches, or 0·044 inch above the corrected average value for January—namely, 29·874 inches. The mercury rose to 30·434 inches at 9 p.m. of the 1st, and fell to 29·284 inches at 7.30 a.m. of the 20th. The observed range of atmospheric pressure was, therefore, 1·150 inches.

The mean temperature deduced from daily readings of the dry bulb thermometer at 9 a.m. and 9 p.m. was 37·3°, or 3·5° below the value for December, 1896. Using the formula, *Mean Temp.* = *Min.* + (*max.* — *min.* × ·52), the M. T. becomes 38·3°, compared with a twenty-five years' average of 41·3°. The arithmetical mean of the maximal and minimal readings was 38·1°, compared with a twenty-five years' average of 41·6°. On the 3rd the thermometer in the screen rose to 51·3°—wind, S. to S.W.; on the 17th the temperature fell to 25·0°—wind, W. The minimum on the grass was 21·3°, also on the 17th.

The rainfall was 2·654 inches, distributed over 17 days. The average rainfall for January in the twenty-five years, 1865–89, inclusive, was 2·200 inches, and the average number of rainy days was 17·3. The rainfall, therefore, was above, while the rainy days were equal to, the average. In 1877 the rainfall in January was very large—4·391 inches on 23 days; in 1869, also, 4·258 inches fell—on, however, only 18 days. But the record rainfall for January was in 1895—namely, 5·711 inches on 24 days, or nearly eight times as much as the rainfall for January, 1896 (·720 inch).

In 1876 only ·406 inch was measured on but 8 days; and in 1880 the rainfall was only ·869 inch on but 8 days.

The atmosphere was foggy on the 5th, 10th, 11th, 13th, 15th, 16th, 17th, 18th, and 27th. High winds were noted on 11 days, reaching the force of a gale on 4 days—the 5th, 6th, 7th and 22nd. Snow or sleet fell on the 18th, 22nd, 23rd, 24th, and 26th. Hail fell on the 18th, 20th, 22nd, 23rd, and 26th. Temperature exceeded 50° in the screen on only 2 days—the 2nd and 3rd; while it fell to or below 32° in the screen on 12 nights, compared with only 3 nights in 1896, 19 in 1895, 7 in 1894, 4 in 1893, 15 in 1892, 7 in 1891, 1 night in 1890, and 3 nights in 1889. The minima on the grass were 32°, or less, on 21 nights, compared with 8 nights in 1896, 29 in 1895, 17 in 1894, 10 in 1893, 25 in 1892, 21 in 1891, 15 in 1890, and 10 in 1889.

New Year's Day, 1897, was brilliantly fine—not a cloud showed in the sky from morning till night. Saturday, the 2nd, was less fair, but on the whole fine and mild, although at times cloudy.

Interesting from a meteorological point of view, the weather of the week ended Saturday, the 9th, was very unsettled and inclement. At the beginning of the period depressions were still passing northwards outside the Western Coasts of Ireland and Scotland, so that S. and S.W. winds prevailed, with rains and bright intervals alternately. Monday was fair and sunny in Dublin, although a heavy dash of rain occurred in the evening. Tuesday broke cold, damp, and foggy, and as the day advanced the wind became S.E. and freshened until at night it blew a gale with heavy rain. From that time to the close of the week, storm, gloom, and rain were paramount. This state of things was brought about by the gradual advance across Northern Europe south-westwards of an anticyclone, in which the barometer rose above 30·70 inches in Sweden on Friday morning; while, at the same time, deep depressions approached the S.W. of Ireland on Wednesday morning (barometer down to 28·90 inches at Valentia Island) and the mouth of the English Channel on Friday morning. The north-easterly course of the system in each case was arrested by the high pressure area over Scandinavia. Gales from S.E. to E. prevailed, the sky remained densely clouded, and rain fell in large quantities, especially in the S.W. and S. of England and the S. and E. of Ireland. Temperature gave way considerably on Friday and Saturday, which were dull and cold in the extreme. In Dublin the mean height of the barometer was 29·709 inches, pressure ranging between 30·098 inches at 9 a.m. of Sunday (wind, S.) and 29·139 inches at 9 p.m. of Wednesday (wind, E.S.E.) The corrected mean temperature was 43·4°. The mean dry bulb reading at 9 a.m. and 9 p.m. was 42·0°. On Sunday the screened thermometers rose to 51·3°. On Tuesday they fell to 33·1°. Rain fell daily to the total amount of 1·771 inches, ·373 inch being measured on Wednesday. The prevailing winds were S.S.W., S.E., and E.

Much finer and generally colder weather was experienced in the period ended Saturday, the 16th. Until Tuesday the distribution of atmospheric pressure remained much the same as it had been during the previous week. Thus, an anticyclone was found over Scandinavia and the North of Russia, while the barometer was relatively low to the S.W. of our Islands. Gradients, however, were not at all so steep, and the S.E. gales accordingly subsided. Sunday was gloomy, damp, and finally wet and foggy in Dublin. Gloom and fog prevailed also on Monday. On Tuesday a new depression appeared off the coast of Kerry, renewing the strong S.E. winds and bringing a considerable fall of rain to the County Cork. A complete change now took place. The Scandinavian anticyclone moved away eastwards and partially dispersed, while a new area of high barometer advanced upon the N.W. of Ireland from the Atlantic. This system developed rapidly until on Thursday morning the barometer rose above 30·40 inches in the West of Ireland. Light to moderate N.E. winds resulted, and showers of hail and snow began to fall along the east coast of both Great Britain and Ireland. In Dublin the ground was covered with snow on Saturday morning, and calms and dense fogs prevailed. The mean height of the barometer at this station was 29·945 inches, pressure ranging between 29·544 inches at 9 a.m. of Sunday (wind, S.E.) and 30·380 inches at 9 a.m. of Thursday (wind, N.) The corrected mean temperature was 35·3°. The mean dry bulb temperature at 9 a.m. and 9 p.m. was 34·7°. On Monday the screened thermometers rose to 44·6°, on Saturday they fell to 26·1. The rainfall was ·097 inch on two days, ·078 inch being measured on Sunday. The prevalent winds were S.E. and afterwards N.W. A little hail fell on Friday, snow on Saturday.

During the week ended Saturday, the 23rd, cold, and at times very cold, weather prevailed and at its close snow lay thickly on the ground in snow districts. On Sunday a very sharp frost occurred in Dublin, the thermometer falling to 25·0° in the screen and to 21·2° on the ground. A beautiful sunny, yet frosty, day followed. On Monday morning sharp frost was reported from England, while the cold relaxed in both Scotland and Ireland. The northern half of the British Isles now came under the influence of an area of high atmospheric pressure, which stretched across the North Sea from Scandinavia. At the same time the barometer fell in France as depressions moved north-eastwards across the Peninsula and the Mediterranean. As a result, strong easterly winds set in on Tuesday night, accompanied by bitterly cold weather and showers of hail and sleet or snow. At 8 a.m. of Wednesday the barometer stood a little above 30·5 inches in the Hebrides. This system of high pressure afterwards moved southwards and dispersed, while a rapid reduction of pressure over Scandinavia took place and a well-marked cyclonic system travelled southwards across Central Europe during the last two days of the week. This disturbance brought northerly and north-easterly gales to the British and Irish coasts, as well as heavy falls of snow and hail. In Dublin a small blizzard was felt on Friday afternoon, and at 3.40 p.m. a bright flash of lightning was quickly followed by a loud peal of thunder. On Saturday snow lay in this city to the depth of about 2 inches. The mean atmospheric pressure was 30·002 inches, the barometer rising to 30·294 inches at 9 a.m. of Wednesday (wind, E.N.E.), and falling to 29·744 inches at 11 p.m. of Thursday (wind, W.N.W.) The corrected mean temperature was 35·1°. The mean dry bulb temperature at 9 a.m. and 9 p.m. was 34·0°. On Sunday the screened thermometers fell to 25·0°, on Wednesday they rose to 42·0°. The rainfall (which consisted chiefly of snow and hail) was equal to ·250 inch, ·218 inch being measured on Friday. There were three "rainy" days. The prevalent wind was N.E. Thunder and lightning occurred on Friday.

Cold, changeable weather prevailed throughout the week ended Saturday, the 30th. After Thursday, however, the frost broke up, and a considerable fall of rain occurred on Friday night and Saturday morning in connection with a large and deep atmospheric depression which crossed the British Islands towards the east at that time. Sunday opened with sharp frost, but a rapid thaw set in as the day advanced, and there were light showers of rain in the afternoon. These changes were due to the approach of a deep depression which lay over the Shetlands on Monday morning, when the barometer was down to 28·95 inches at Sumburgh Head. The system subsequently crossed the North Sea in a south-easterly direction. It caused a violent snowstorm and severe frost in the North of Scotland—the melted snow yielded 1·5 inches of rain in the gauge at Wick on Tuesday morning. This represents some 18 inches of snow on the level. On Wednesday a high pressure system appeared off the West of Ireland and the weather moderated. A gradual rise of temperature now took place, spreading south-eastwards over the kingdom. On Friday the anticyclone in the West dispersed as a new and deep depression approached Ireland from the Atlantic. In front of the disturbance the wind for a while backed to S., and rain set in with a further increase of temperature—in Dublin, however, only to 48·5°. Early on Saturday the wind again veered to N.W. in the rear of the centre of low pressure, and temperature gave way—sleet and snow falling on the Dublin and Wicklow mountains. The mean barometric pressure was 29·814 inches, the observed range being from 30·469 inches at 9 p.m. of Wednesday (wind, W.N.W.), to 29·284 inches at 7.30 a.m. of Saturday (wind, N.W.). The corrected mean temperature was 35·5°. The mean dry bulb reading at 9 a.m. and 9 p.m. was 34·7°. On Sunday the screened thermometers fell to 23·9°, on Saturday they rose to 48·8°. The rainfall was ·201 inch on four days, ·190 inch being registered on Friday. The prevalent wind was W.N.W.

Sunday, the 31st, was fair to cloudy, overcast, and finally rainy.

In Dublin the rainfall up to January 31st, 1897, amounted to 2·694 inches on 17 days, compared with 5·711 inches on 24 days in 1895, only ·780 inch on 14 days in 1896, and with a twenty-five years' average (1865–1889) of 2·200 inches on 17·3 days.

At Knockdolian, Greystones, Co. Wicklow, the rainfall was 3·600 inches on 20 days, compared with only ·446 inch on 7 days in 1896, and 6·190 inches on 19 days in 1895. The heaviest falls in 24 hours were ·580 inch on the 4th, and ·620 inch on the 5th.

At Clonsevin, Killiney, Co. Dublin, the rainfall was 3·040 inches on 20 days, ·440 inch being measured on the 6th. The average fall for the 13 years, 1885–1896, was 2·225 inches on 16·5 days. Snow fell on the 14th, 15th, and 22nd. In 1894, the rainfall was 3·260 inches on 23 days, in

1893 it was 1·940 inches on 14 days, in 1836 it was ·700 inch on 9 days. In 1891, only ·47 inch fell on, however, 11 days.

At the National Hospital for Consumption, Newcastle, Co. Wicklow, rain fell on 18 days in January, the total measurement being 3·673 inches. On the 6th, ·870 inch was registered; on the 8th, ·530 inch; and on the 3rd, ·510 inch. At this climatological station the thermometer in the screen sank to 32° or lower on 10 nights. The highest temperature in the shade was 47·0° on the 7th; the lowest was 27·8° on the 24th. Snow fell on the 16th, 22nd, 24th, and 25th.

FEBRUARY.—Taken as a whole, this was one of the mildest Februaries on record in Dublin. There was scarcely any frost even on the ground, and the sky was often densely clouded. The first third of the month was gloomy and wet in Ireland, intensely cold in the North and North-east of Scotland, where the thermometer fell on the 4th to zero at Nairn and Lairg, and to −1° at Braemar. The minimum at Aberdeen at this time was 9°, whereas the thermometer rose at that place to 64° on the 22nd and to 61° on the 26th. Equatorial winds were prevalent during the greater part of the month.

In Dublin the mean temperature (45·0°) was 3·2° above the average (41·8°); the mean dry bulb readings at 9 a.m. and 9 p.m. were 45·1°. In the thirty-two years ending with 1890, February was coldest in 1873 (M. T. = 34·3°), and warmest in 1869 (M. T. = 44·7°).

The mean height of the barometer was 30·001 inches, or 0·146 inch above the average value for February—namely, 29·855 inches. The mercury rose to 30·513 inches at 9 p.m. of the 22nd, having fallen to 28·709 inches at 9 p.m. of the 1st. The observed range of atmospheric pressure was, therefore, 1·804 inches.

The mean temperature deduced from daily readings of the dry bulb thermometer at 9 a.m. and 9 p.m. was 45·1°, or 11·8° above the value for February, 1895. Using the formula, *Mean Temp.* = *Min.* + (*max.*—*min.* × ·30), the M. T. is 46·0°, compared with a twenty-five (1865–1889) years' average of 42·6°. On the 19th the thermometer in the screen rose to 55·7°—wind, S.W.; on the 1st the temperature fell to 35·0°—wind, E.S.E. The minimum on the grass was 29·0°, on the 24th.

The rainfall was 1·385 inches, distributed over 10 days. The average rainfall for February in the twenty-five years, 1865–89, inclusive, was 2·180 inches and the average number of rainy days was 17·2. The rainfall, therefore, and also the rainy days, were below the average. In 1883 the rainfall in February was large—3·732 inches on 17 days; in 1879, also, 3·706 inches fell on 23 days. On the other hand, in 1891, only ·042 inch was measured on but 2 days. The rainfall in 1891 was much the smallest recorded in February for very many years. The record is probably unparalleled in Dublin—·042 inch on 2 days. Neither hail, nor sleet, nor snow fell.

The atmosphere was foggy on 7 days—namely, the 3rd, 4th, 5th, 10th, 12th, 16th, and 17th. The amount of cloud—73·6 per cent.—was much above the average—66 per cent. High winds were noted on 7 days, and reached the force of a gale on the 19th, 20th, 24th, 25th, and 26th. A lunar halo was seen on the 10th.

The temperature reached or exceeded 50° in the screen on 14 days, and it never once fell below 32°, compared with as many as 16 nights in 1895, and only 1 night in 1894. The minima on the grass were 32°, or less, on only 4 nights, compared with every night in 1895, and 10 nights in 1894. The thermometer never failed to rise to or above 40° in the screen during the daytime.

The weather was exceedingly unsettled—cold, wet, gloomy, and foggy—during the greater part of the period ended Saturday, the 6th. But the most striking feature in the meteorology of the period was the occurrence of intense frost in the N. and N.E. of Scotland from the morning of the 1st to the evening of the 4th. This local area of cold was brought about by a combination of circumstances—namely, a country deeply covered with snow, a clear sky, and a tolerably calm atmosphere. The town of Nairn suffered most severely from the resulting chill—the minima in the screen there being 13°, 13°, 7°, 0°, 5°, and 20° respectively. This hyperborean cold had an extraordinary effect on the weather in England and Ireland, for it seemed to stop the Atlantic depressions in their passage north-eastwards—the result was gloom, fog, and downpours of rain or heavy falls of wet snow. The steepness of the thermometric gradients over Western Europe was extreme on Tuesday, the 2nd, when a warm S.W. air-current blew across France with gale force. At 8 a.m. of that day the thermometer read 52° at Lorient and Jersey, 31° in Paris, 37° in London, but 10° at Nairn and 17° at Wick. In the course of the day it rose to 56° in Paris, but did not exceed 38° in London. At 8 a.m. of Wednesday the reading at Nairn was 10°, at Nice 55°, or a difference of 45° F. The maximum at Nice on that day was 70°. On Tuesday a trough of low atmospheric pressure stretched from the south of Ireland eastwards to the Netherlands, and on Friday a well-defined cyclonic system was found over the English Channel. These systems caused heavy rains in France, Ireland, and England. In Dublin the barometer ranged between 29·209 inches at 9 p.m. of Monday (wind, E.S.E.), and 29·695 inches at 9 p.m. of Wednesday (wind, S.E.). On Monday the screened thermometers fell to 35·0°, on Thursday they rose to 49·5°. The rainfall was ·671 inch on six days, ·369 inch being measured on Tuesday. The prevailing winds were easterly.

A very decided advance in temperature was observed during the week ended Saturday, the 13th, the weather of which was of the south-westerly type—open, cloudy and damp. Between Monday and Friday a large area of low atmospheric pressure travelled slowly north-eastwards from the N.W. of Scotland to the N. of Scandinavia. From Wednesday a shallower depression was found over the S. and S.W. of Ireland. The latter disturbance equalised pressure, and so caused a temporary fall of temperature on Wednesday. This was followed by easterly and south-easterly breezes; gloom and fog succeeding on Friday, when a sharp frost visited the Scottish stations, the screened thermometer falling to 29° at Ardrossan, 25° at Stornoway, 20° at Leith, 16° at Wick, and

24° at Nairn. At the beginning of the week intense cold still held in the Baltic and Gulf of Bothnia—at Haparanda the minimum on Sunday was −24°, on Monday it was −27°. The corresponding values at Hernösand were −18° and −17°. At 8 a.m. of Tuesday the thermometer at this latter station stood 83° higher than at 8 a.m. of Monday. In Dublin the mean height of the barometer was 30·032 inches, pressure ranging between 29·841 inches at 9 a.m. of Tuesday (wind, W.) and 30·163 inches at 9 a.m. of Wednesday (wind, calm). The range of pressure was therefore small. The mean temperature was 45·2°, the mean dry bulb reading at 9 a.m. and 9 p.m. being 44·8°. On Wednesday the screened thermometers fell to 36·0°; on Saturday they rose to 53·0°. Rain fell on 4 days to the amount of ·377 inch, ·240 inch being registered on Monday. The prevailing winds were westerly, but an easterly breeze blew from Wednesday evening to Friday at noon.

Weather of the south-westerly type—open, cloudy, and often damp—was in evidence throughout the week ended Saturday, the 20th, and temperature again showed a substantial advance, although a temporary chill occurred on the morning of Wednesday the 17th. At the beginning of the period very intense cold held over the North of Europe—at 8 a.m. of Sunday the thermometer read −17° F. at Haparanda on the Gulf of Bothnia, on Monday morning it marked −5° at Hernösand and −6° at Karlstad in Sweden. A change then took place, as a large and deep depression reached the N.W. of Norway from the westward, and a general thaw set in all over Scandinavia—the 8 a.m. temperatures at Karlstad for the rest of the week were 28°, 42°, 39°, 35°, and 31° respectively. The south-westerly current, which flowed over the British Islands at the periphery of the depression in the far north, brought with it unusual warmth, so that on Friday the thermometer rose almost to 60° in the screen in Dublin. It should also be mentioned that an anticyclone existed over France, Germany, and the southern parts of the British Isles from Monday, so that at times the S.W. winds were very dry and somewhat searching in character. This was notably the case early on Thursday morning and again on Saturday. At 9 a.m. of Thursday the relative humidity was only 58 per cent. in Dublin. On Saturday evening a heavy fall of rain occurred and there was a fresh S.W. to W. gale. The mean atmospheric pressure was 30·215 inches, the barometer rising to 30·563 inches at 9 a.m. of Tuesday (wind, S.W.), and falling to 29·863 inches at 8 p.m. of Saturday (wind, W.S.W.) The mean temperature was 47·3°. The mean dry bulb temperature at 9 a.m. and 9 p.m. was 45·9°. On Wednesday the screened thermometers fell to 37·1°, on Friday they rose to 59·7°. The rainfall was ·267 inch on three days, ·211 inch being measured on Saturday. The prevailing winds were S.W. and W. Gales occurred on Thursday and Saturday.

Stormy, open, cloudy weather was prevalent throughout the week ended Saturday, the 27th; but except in the north and west of Ireland the rainfall was not heavy. The distribution of atmospheric pressure over northern and western Europe was eminently calculated to produce westerly gales. Thus, an area of high atmospheric pressure, near the centre of which the barometer stood at 30·7 inches or upwards, stretched from the Bay of Biscay eastwards across France, while a constant succession of depressions swept north-eastwards across the Norwegian Sea and Norway. At the very beginning of the period a well-marked secondary depression moved rapidly over the British Isles towards E.N.E., the centre reaching Holland at 8 a.m. of Sunday. This disturbance caused strong S.W. to N.W. gales, which were, however, of short duration. In its rear the barometer rose quickly, so that by 8 a.m. of Monday it reached 30·70 inches at Brest and Lorient. On this day a warm wave swept over our Islands, the maximal thermometric reading being 64° at Aberdeen. On Wednesday morning the barometric gradient was very steep—pressure ranging from 30·71 inches in Paris to 29·03 inches at Bodö, in Norway. Twenty-four hours later a new and deep depression had advanced to the neighbourhood of the Hebrides, so that south-westerly gales again sprang up in Ireland, Scotland, and parts of England. Heavy rain was reported from Valentia (·60 inch), Belmullet (·65 inch), and Stornoway (·50 inch). On Friday afternoon the wind moderated and temperature gave way. Saturday was a beautiful, sunny, spring-like day. In Dublin the mean height of the barometer was 30·233 inches, pressure ranging between 30·589 inches at 9 p.m. of Monday (wind, W. by N.) and 29·705 inches at 7 15 a.m. of Thursday (wind, S.W.). The mean temperature was 49·7°. The mean dry bulb reading at 9 a.m. and 9 p.m. was 48·5°. On Thursday the screened thermometers rose to 56·0°, on Saturday they fell to 37·8°. The rainfall was ·131 inch on two days, ·109 inch being registered on Wednesday.

Sunday, the 28th, was dull, threatening, and showery in the day-time. In the evening the sky cleared and temperature fell.

In Dublin the rainfall up to February 28th, 1897, amounted to 4·069 inches on 38 days compared with only 1·389 inches on 24 days in 1896, 6·356 inches on 33 days in 1895, 4·741 inches on 39 days in 1894, 4·909 inches on 41 days in 1893, 3·817 inches on 29 days in 1892, ·714 inch on 16 days in 1891, and a twenty-five years' (1865-1889) average of 4·430 inches on 34·5 days.

At Knockdolian, Greystones, Co. Wicklow, 1·330 inches of rain fell in February on 17 days. The heaviest fall in 24 hours was ·180 inch on the 3rd. The total fall to February 28th inclusive was 5·190 inches on 37 days, compared with only 1·940 inches on but 17 days in the corresponding period of 1896.

The rainfall in February at Cloneevin, Killiney, Co. Dublin, amounted to 1·23 inches on 18 days. The average rainfall for February during 11 years (1885-95) at this station is 1·481 inches on 13·5 days. The greatest rainfall in 24 hours was ·18 inch on the 5th. Since January 1, the rainfall was 4·81 inches on 38 days, compared with 1·64 inches on 19 days in the same period in 1896.

At the National Hospital for Consumption, Newcastle, Co. Wicklow, rain fell on 15 days in February, the total measurement being 1·718 inches. On the 4th, ·281 inch was registered. At this climatological station there was no frost in the screen during the month, the minimum being 33·4° on the 1st. The maximal temperature was 58·9° on the 25th. On 10 days the thermometer rose above 60° in the screen. Since January 1 the rainfall has been 5·50 inches on 34 days.

MARCH.—Like March, 1896, this was a changeable, wild and rainy month, with a cyclonic distribution of pressure. During the first half temperature was low. A warm spell followed, but temperature again fell briskly on Sunday, the 28th, and the month closed cold and ungenial. Compared with February, the mean temperature showed a falling off of one degree Fahr. Notwithstanding, the progress of vegetation was very rapid, and on the last day the trees presented quite a vernal appearance.

In Dublin the arithmetical mean temperature (45·3°) was about two degrees above the average (43·1°); the mean dry bulb readings at 9 a.m. and 9 p.m. were 43·8°. In the thirty-one years ending with 1896, March was coldest in 1867 and 1883 (M. T.=39·0°), and warmest in 1893 (M. T.=48·1°); and in 1859 (M. T.=47·3°). In 1896 the M. T. was 45·1°.

The mean height of the barometer was 29·543 inches, or 0·373 inch below the corrected average value for March—namely, 29·916 inches. The mercury rose to 30·081 inches at 9 a.m. of the 7th, and fell to 28·771 inches at 11 p.m. of the 2nd. The observed range of atmospheric pressure was, therefore, 1·310 inches.

The mean temperature deduced from daily readings of the dry bulb thermometer at 9 a.m. and 9 p.m. was 43·8°, or 1·3° below the value for February, 1897. Using the formula, *Mean Temp.* = *Min.* + (*max.*—*min.* × ·465), the M. T. becomes 45·1°. The arithmetical mean of the maximal and minimal readings was 45·3°, compared with a twenty-five years' average of 43·1°. On the 21st the thermometer in the screen rose to 61·6°—wind, S.W.; on the 30th the temperature fell to 29·0°—wind, calm. The minimum on the grass was 25·0° also on the 30th.

The rainfall was 3·980 inches, distributed over 24 days. The average rainfall for March in the twenty-five years, 1865–89, inclusive, was 2·051 inches, and the average number of rainy days was 16·3. The rainfall, therefore, and also the rainy days were considerably above the average. In 1867 the rainfall in March was very large—4·972 inches on 22 days. On the other hand, the smallest March rainfall was ·753 inch on 8 days in 1893. In 1896, 3·310 inches fell on 23 days.

The atmosphere was more or less foggy in the city on 2 days—viz., the 21st and 30th. High winds were noted on 19 days, reaching the force of a gale on nine occasions—the 4th, 11th, 12th, 14th, 17th, 19th, 22nd, 24th, and 26th. Snow or sleet occurred on the 1st, 3rd, 4th, 9th, 12th, and 14th; and hail fell on the 1st, 3rd, 5th, 10th, 16th, 25th, and 29th. The temperature exceeded 50° in the screen on 14 days, compared with 11 days in 1896, 13 in 1895, 22 in 1894, 26 in 1893, only 7 in 1892, 9 in 1891, and 12 in 1890. It only once fell below 32° in the screen. In March, 1892, frost had occurred in the shade on as many as 16 nights. The minima on the grass were 32°, or less, on 9 nights, compared with 3 nights in 1896, 10 in 1895, 12 each in 1894 and 1893, 23 in 1892, 20 in 1891, and 16 in 1890. The thermometer once rose to 60° in the screen, but never failed to reach 40°. In March, 1892, the thermometer did not rise to 40° in the screen on 9 days. Solar halos were seen on the 9th, 11th, 24th, 27th, and 30th. Lunar halos appeared on the 8th, 12th, and 13th. Thunder was heard on the 17th, lightning was seen on the 1st and 3rd.

Cyclonic conditions, and very rough, cold, changeable weather held over North-western Europe throughout the period ended Saturday, the 6th. On Sunday, February 28, an atmospheric depression had advanced quickly from S.W., passing along the western shores of Ireland and Scotland and causing squally, showery weather. At 8 a.m. of Monday, the 1st, this disturbance was central off the N. of Scotland. Fair intervals and passing showers of cold rain or sleet and hail prevailed during the day, and at night snow fell in the W. of Ireland. Early on Tuesday morning a dense sheet of cirro-stratus cloud overspread the sky as a much larger and deeper depression approached the British Isles from S.W. The centre of this cyclonic system travelled across Wales and Central England during the following night, and was found over Yorkshire and Lincolnshire on Wednesday morning, when the barometer was down to 28·54 inches at York and 28·58 inches at Spurn Head. Violent S.W. to W. gales blew in France, Belgium, and the S. of England. Hail and sleet squalls, accompanied by thunder and lightning in some districts, swept across Ireland and Scotland. On Thursday morning the disturbance was found over Denmark, where it was rapidly filling up; but another deep depression had already reached the N.W. of Ireland from the Atlantic. A renewal of the gales and showers resulted from the approach of this new disturbance, and thunderstorms again occurred in several places. On Friday the weather began to moderate and Saturday was a fine, dry, and sunny day. In Dublin barometric pressure increased from 28·771 inches at 11 p.m. of Tuesday (wind, W.S.W.) to 30·045 inches at 9 p.m. of Saturday (wind, N.W.). On Tuesday the screened thermometers fell to 32·9°, on Saturday they rose to 50·8°. The rainfall was ·800 inch on five days, ·251 inch being measured on Tuesday. W. and W.S.W. winds prevailed. Lightning was seen on Monday and Wednesday.

The week ending Saturday, March 13, was very broken—cold, rainy, and stormy. Only Sunday was fine throughout, but on several days there were fine intervals. A violent rainstorm occurred on Thursday evening, and much snow fell on the Dublin and Wicklow mountains during the week. Even on the lowlands sleet and hail were often mingled with the rain. The persistent presence of an anticyclone over Scandinavia and Lapland, with intense cold in those regions, contrasted remarkably with the disturbed state of the atmosphere and the unstable temperature in the British Isles and over France. On Sunday morning, indeed, the barometer stood uniformly rather high, but by Monday morning a V-shaped depression had advanced over Ireland, throwing the weather into a wet and dull condition. At night a lunar halo was seen, and this was followed by a solar halo on Tuesday forenoon. The day was mild, but towards evening a sudden chill spread across Ireland from W. to E., causing heavy rain and sleet, while thunder and lightning occurred at Belmullet. At 8 a.m. of Wednesday the barometer ranged from 30·55 inches at Hernösand (Sweden) to 29·40 inches at Wick. Showers of cold rain and hail were very prevalent on this day, and thunder and lightning were reported from the S.E. of England. On Thursday evening the most serious depression of the week advanced to the Bristol Channel, thence passing northwards to the Irish Sea. It caused a downpour of rain and sleet in many districts. Saturday was chiefly fine, but at night a lunar halo and a falling barometer heralded the approach of a new disturbance from the Atlantic. In Dublin the mean atmospheric pressure for the week was 29·712 inches, the barometer falling from 30·041 inches at 9 a.m. of Sunday (wind, N.W.) to 29·328 inches at 11 p.m. of Thursday (wind, E.). The corrected mean temperature was 42·1°. The mean dry bulb reading at 9 a.m. and 9 p.m. was 41·8°. The shade thermometer fell to 33·0° on Sunday and rose to 53·1° on Tuesday. The prevailing winds were S.S.E. and W. Rain fell daily to the amount of 1·277 inches, ·735 inch being registered on Thursday.

Another spell of cyclonic conditions and unsettled, squally, showery weather signalised the week ended Saturday, the 20th. Deep atmospheric depressions appeared in the S.W. at the beginning and in the N.W. towards the close of the period. In the extreme N.E. (over Northern Russia and Lapland) the barometer stood relatively high and the cold was at times very intense—on Thursday, for example, the thermometer fell to -20° at Haparanda, on the Gulf of Bothnia, and the 8 a.m. temperature at that station was -12°, or 44° below the freezing point. On Sunday morning a large depression was central off the S.W. of Kerry. Thence the system travelled in a circuitous route to Wales, over which country it was found on Monday morning. At that time the weather was dull, cold, and wet in Dublin, with a light N.E. wind. The disturbance subsequently travelled north-north-westwards to the North Channel and the wind backed in Ireland to W. and S.W. On Tuesday a new depression passed in a northerly direction along the west coast of Ireland. The reduction of pressure went on until 2 p.m. of Wednesday, when the barometer read only 28·75 inches at Malin Head. On and after Thursday there was a brisk recovery of pressure in the S.W. and S., so that on Saturday morning the barometer reached 30·07 inches in Dublin. During the disturbed period up to Friday, squalls and showers accompanied by thunder and lightning were prevalent in Ireland and England. Hail and sleet or snow fell in Scotland on Monday. In Dublin the mean height of the barometer was 29·440 inches, the range of pressure being from 29·003 inches at 9 a.m. of Tuesday (wind, S.) to 30·067 inches at 7 a.m. of Saturday (wind, N., light). The corrected mean temperature was 46·1°. The mean dry bulb reading at 9 a.m. and 9 p.m. was 45·1°. On Sunday the screened thermometers fell to 36·8°; on Saturday they rose to 56·9°. Rain fell on 6 days to the amount of ·898 inch, ·339 inch being measured on Monday. Thunder was heard on Wednesday.

A continuance of cyclonic conditions is to be noted in the week ended Saturday, the 27th, but there was a great advance in temperature, and the rainfalls, although frequent, were not heavy. A succession of deep depressions passed northwards or north-eastwards along the western coasts of Ireland and Scotland at short intervals, causing fresh S.W. to W. gales and showers in most exposed districts. In the extreme north of Europe the weather remained very cold throughout, although at Haparanda the thermometer on Wednesday morning stood 20° higher than it had done 24 hours previously, at -23° compared with—4°. Sunday was very mild in Ireland and England—the thermometer rose in the shade to 61° at Parsonstown, Oxford, and in London; to 62° in Dublin and at Loughborough; and to 64° at Cambridge. In Dublin S.W. or W. gales occurred on Monday, Wednesday, and Friday—the force of the wind being especially great on Wednesday. The high temperature and frequent showers gave vegetation so great an impetus that at the close of the week even forest trees were quickly assuming a leafy covering—in fact vegetation appeared to be a month in advance. On Saturday temperature showed a tendency to give way. In Dublin the mean height of the barometer was 29·713 inches, pressure ranging from 29·094 inches at 9 a.m. of Sunday (wind, calm) to 30·210 inches at 7 p.m. of Saturday (wind, W.). The corrected mean temperature was 52·7°. The mean dry bulb temperature at 9 a.m. and 9 p.m. was 50·7°. On Sunday the screened thermometers rose to 61·6°; on Saturday they fell to 35·9°. The rainfall was ·170 inch on six days, ·053 inch being measured on Friday and ·053 inch on Saturday. The prevailing winds were S.W. and W.

On Sunday, the 28th, a brisk and sudden fall of temperature occurred in the forenoon, and showers of cold rain and hail fell in the afternoon. The cold spell thus ushered in lasted to the end of the month, a very sharp frost prevailing on the night of the 29th–30th, when the screened thermometer fell to 23° at Loughborough and Shields, 26° at Parsonstown and various British stations, 27° at Oxford, Leith, and Aberdeen, and 29° in London and Dublin. At this time the centre of a large and deep atmospheric depression (29·70 inches and less) lay over the South of Scandinavia, a cold northerly current of air being in this way drawn over the British Isles.

The rainfall in Dublin during the three months ending March 31st amounted to 7·069 inches on 57 days, compared with 4·638 inches on 47 days in 1896, 8·034 inches on 51 days in 1895, 6·093 inches on 58 days in 1894, 5·195 inches on 49 days in 1893, 4·808 inches on 46 days in 1892, only 1·650 inches on but 32 days in 1891, 7·470 inches on 53 days in 1890, and a twenty-five years' average of 6·411 inches on 51·0 days (1865–1889, inclusive).

At Knockdolian, Greystones, Co. Wicklow, 3·758 inches of rain fell on 24 days during March; and the total rainfall since January 1, 1897, equals 8·945 inches on 61 days. The corresponding figures for 1896 are 2·706 inches on 25 days, the total rainfall since January 1 having been 4·730 inches on 49 days. The maximal fall in 24 hours was ·740 inch on the 2nd.

The rainfall in March at Cloneevin, Killiney, Co. Dublin, was 3·23 inches on 23 days, compared with 2·01 inches on 23 days in 1896, 2·29 inches on 21 days in 1895, 1·11 inches on 16 days in 1894, ·93 inch on 9 days in 1893, ·95 inch on 10 days in 1892, and a twelve years' (1885–96) average of 1·873 inches on 15·2 days. The maximum in the 12 years was 3·35 inches in 1888, the minimum was ·93 inch in 1893. At this station the total rainfall since January 1, was 7·38 inches on 61 days, compared with a fall of 4·23 inches on 42 days in the first quarter of 1896, 8·08 inches on 52 days, in that of 1895, and 5·56 inches on 53 days in that of 1894. On the 11th, ·84 inch fell.

At the National Hospital for Consumption, Newcastle, Co. Wicklow, the rainfall in March was 4·499 inches on 23 days, 1·017 inches being registered on the 2nd, and ·749 inch on the 11th. The highest shade temperature at this climatological station was 59·1° on the 21st, the lowest was 29·9° on the 10th. Since January 1st, 10·066 inches of rain had fallen at the hospital on 57 days.

April.—A cold, changeable, rainy month. In Dublin rain fell on as many as 22 days, including snow or sleet on 2 and hail on 5. The barometer was very unsteady, and the distribution of atmospheric pressure was for the most part cyclonic. A finer and drier period, associated with a tolerably high barometer and easterly winds, set in on the 21st and lasted for a few days, but winter lingered to the close in Ireland, though in England some genial warmth was enjoyed in the daytime after the 25th. The amount of cloud was, in Dublin, 12 per cent. in excess of what it had been in April, 1896.

In Dublin the arithmetical mean temperature (46·0°) was 1·7° below the average (47·7°); the mean dry bulb readings at 9 a.m. and 9 p.m. were 45·0°. In the thirty-two years ending with 1896, April was coldest in 1879 (the cold year) (M. T. = 44·3°), and warmest in 1893 (M. T. = 51·8°). The month of April, 1893, was the warmest for at least 50 years, yet it was only half a degree warmer than April, 1896, which was 3° warmer than the month now under discussion.

The mean height of the barometer was 29·818 inches, or 0·032 inch below the average value for April—namely, 29·850 inches. The mercury rose to 30·289 inches at 9 a.m. of the 10th, and fell to 29·281 inches at 9 a.m. of the 1st. The observed range of atmospheric pressure was, therefore, 1·008 inches.

The mean temperature deduced from daily readings of the dry bulb thermometer at 9 a.m. and 9 p.m. was 45·0°, or only 1·8° above the value for March, 1897. Using the formula, *Mean Temp. = Min. + (max. — min. × ·476)*, the value is 45·6°, or 1·6° below the average mean temperature for April, calculated in the same way, in the twenty-five years, 1865–89, inclusive (47·4°). The arithmetical mean of the maximal and minimal readings was 46·0°, compared with a twenty-five years' (1865–1889 inclusive) average of 47·7°. On the 25th the thermometer in the screen rose to 59·7°—wind, N.W.; on the 2nd the temperature fell to 29·0°—wind, N.W. The minimum on the grass was 28·0° also on the 2nd.

The rainfall was 2·485 inches, distributed over 22 days. The average rainfall for April in the twenty-five years, 1865–89, inclusive, was 2·035 inches, and the average number of rainy days was 15·2. The rainfall and the rainy days, therefore, were considerably above the average. In 1877 the rain fall in April was very large—4·707 inches on 21 days; in 1885 also, 3·526 inches fell on 20 days, and in 1894, 3·123 inches on 20 days. On the other hand, in 1873, only ·498 inch was measured on 8 days; in 1870, only ·835 inch fell, also on 8 days, and in 1896, only ·883 inch on 16 days.

Fog was observed on the 21st. High winds were noted on 10 days, reaching the force of a gale on the 3rd and 18th. Hail fell on the 1st, 14th, 15th, 19th, and 30th. The temperature rose to 50° in the screen on 22 days. It never rose to 60°, and once fell to 32° in the screen, and on 6 nights below 32° on the grass. The mean lowest temperature on the grass was 37·7°, compared with 40·0° in 1896, 37·8° in 1895, 40·0° in 1894, 35·2° in 1893, 33·8° in 1892, 34·1° in 1891 and 1890, 34·6° in 1889, 34·0° in 1888, and 31·6° in 1887. Solar halos were seen on the 8th and 16th, lunar halos on the 10th and 15th. Snow or sleet fell on the 1st and 14th.

The month opened with very unsettled, winterly weather. On the morning of Thursday, the 1st, a deep depression (28·74 inches at Jersey) was found to have travelled quickly eastwards up the English Channel, its centre at 8 a.m. being midway between the Isle of Wight and Cherbourg. Heavy rain and warm S.W. winds prevailed in France, while cold N.E. winds and sleet were experienced in England, the weather being still colder and drier in Scotland and Ireland. In the afternoon snow and hail fell heavily in Dublin. Another sharp frost followed at night. Friday was fair and cold. A new disturbance in the S.W. brought gloom, cold rain, and a piercing S.E. wind to the Irish stations on Saturday. The rainfall of these first three days amounted to ·194 inch, ·136 inch being registered on the 3rd, none on the 2nd, and ·058 inch on the 1st.

Another period of cold, unsettled, rainy weather has to be recorded in the week ended Saturday, the 10th. A number of circular but not very deep atmospheric depressions drifted slowly across Western Europe in an easterly or south-easterly direction. The centres of these systems mostly passed across Wales, the S.W. of England and Brittany, and in these districts the rainfall was exceptionally heavy. Sunday was cold and wet at first, then dull and dreary on the east coast of Ireland, though fair at Holyhead. Rain fell heavily on Monday and Tuesday nights. Wednesday was a raw, cold day in Dublin, and thunder and lightning occurred in London with sleet and rain. Thursday morning was frosty; a solar halo appeared in the forenoon, and the afternoon was wet. On Friday also dull rainy weather prevailed, as a V-shaped depression passed eastward across Ireland. Between 5 and 6 p.m. the sky darkened and a sudden shift of wind from S.W. to N. took place with close rain. The sky cleared at night and temperature again became very low. Saturday proved a beautiful springlike day—a ridge of high barometer having advanced over Ireland in the rear of Friday's V-shaped depression. In Dublin the mean height of the barometer was 29·883 inches, pressure ranging between 29·301 inches at 9 a.m. of Wednesday (wind W.N.W.) and 30·280 inches at 9 a.m. of Saturday (wind N.N.W.). The corrected mean temperature was 43·4°. The mean dry bulb temperature at 9 a.m. and 9 p.m. was 43·5°. On Friday the screened thermometers rose to 51·1°; on Thursday they fell to 31·8°. The wind was variable—chiefly south-easterly. Rain fell on six days to the amount of ·737 inch, ·349 inch being registered on Tuesday.

Comparatively fine and springlike in parts of England—particularly the South and South-east—the weather during the week ended Saturday the 17th remained extremely broken and inclement in Ireland, the South-west of England, Wales and Scotland. A large anticyclone was found lying over Northern Europe up to and including Thursday, but in this period areas of low pressure were passing in rapid succession either northwards or north-eastwards along the western shores of Ireland and Scotland. Hence the prevalent strong southerly to westerly winds and frequent showers. Early on Wednesday morning the wind veered to W.N.W. in Ireland, and a bitterly cold day followed, showers of hail, sleet and snow falling at frequent intervals. At night there was clear moonlight and temperature was very low—37·0° at 9 p.m. Thunder and lightning occurred over Central England on this day. The two succeeding days were changeable, squally and showery. A brief spell of fair, dry weather was enjoyed in the east of Ireland on the afternoon of Good Friday, but thunderstorms occurred in England. A sheet of cirro-stratus, in which a solar halo was seen at first, overspread the sky on Friday evening. Saturday was wet and windy but mild at first, then showery, and finally clear and cold as well as dry. In Dublin the mean height of the barometer was 29·722 inches, pressure ranging between 29·323 inches at 9 p.m. of Tuesday (wind S.S.W.), and 30·012 inches at 9 p.m. of Thursday (wind W.S.W.). The corrected mean temperature was 46·5°. The mean dry bulb temperature was 45·8°. On Saturday the screened thermometers rose to 50·1°; on Thursday they sank to 37·1°. Rain fell daily to the total amount of ·530 inch, ·209 inch being measured on Friday. The wind was first south-easterly, then westerly.

The most noteworthy feature in the weather of the week ended Saturday the 24th was the cessation of the rainfall after Wednesday, and the substitution of strong easterly (or polar) winds, dry and searching in character, for the westerly (or equatorial) winds which had so long prevailed. On Easter Day, April 18, a sharply-defined cyclone lay over Denmark, the station Fanö reporting a barometric reading of 29·20 inches at 8 a.m., whereas atmospheric pressure reached 30·10 inches at Valentia Island, Kerry. Fresh N.W. winds blew all over the British Islands, but the weather, although cool, was chiefly dry. On Monday a new disturbance advanced over Ireland, causing a wet afternoon. At 6 p.m. a heavy hail shower passed across Dublin and a brisk fall of temperature took place. Brilliant rainbows were seen in the evening. On Tuesday yet another depression approached Ireland, where rain fell heavily in the afternoon. This system apparently travelled away southwards as an area of high barometer developed over Scotland and the Norwegian Sea. With this re-adjustment of atmospheric pressure came a spell of strong, dry, cold easterly winds and much bright sunshine. As is usual in such a polar current, the atmosphere was very hazy—indeed, on Wednesday thick vapour fog prevailed for some time. On Friday a large depression was found over the Peninsula, moving north-eastwards to France and Central Europe. The effect was to increase the force of the easterly wind and to break up the fine weather in the extreme S. and S.E. In Dublin the mean height of the barometer was 29·917 inches, pressure ranging from 29·571 inches at 9 p.m. of Tuesday (wind, S.E.) to 30·210 inches at 9 p.m. of Thursday (wind, E.). The corrected mean temperature was 44·3°. The mean dry bulb reading at 9 a.m. and 9 p.m. was 46·2°. On Sunday the screened thermometers rose to 55·0°; on Tuesday they sank to 38·7°. The rainfall was ·533 inch, ·431 inch being registered on Tuesday. The prevailing winds were at first N.W., then E.

Comparatively favourable and spring-like weather occurred in the closing period (25th–30th). In Ireland there was very little warmth, but over the south and south-east of England the daily maxima were considerably above 60° on and after Monday. At the beginning an area of high barometer held over Northern Europe, while depressions were found over the Bay of Biscay and the Peninsula, as well as in the Mediterranean Basin. Hence easterly winds, low temperatures, and hazy but dry weather held in the British Islands and Central Europe. Tuesday morning broke dull and rainy in Dublin but the afternoon proved fair. In the evening a severe thunderstorm with heavy rain and hail passed across parts of London—large quantities of hail falling in and about Streatham and Tooting. On Wednesday also electrical disturbances took place in various parts of both France and England in connection with a number of shallow atmospheric depressions which slowly approached from S.W. On Thursday a more decided depression appeared in the N.W., causing rain at first and afterwards cold showers and hail on Friday. During the ensuing night the thermometers sank to 33·0° in the screen, and to 27·9° on the grass in Dublin. In Dublin the barometer rose to 30·085 inches at 9 p.m. of Wednesday (wind, W.), and sank to 29·701 inches at 9 a.m. of Friday (wind, W.N.W.). On Wednesday the screened thermometers both rose to 59·7° and fell to 43·7°. The rainfall was ·150 inch on four days, ·080 inch falling on Thursday. The prevalent winds were E. and W.N.W.

The rainfall in Dublin during the four months ending April 30th amounted to 9·454 inches on 70 days, compared with 9·741 inches on 63 days in 1896, 10·233 inches on 65 days in 1895, 9·161 inches on 73 days in 1894, 6·912 inches on 56 days in 1893, 5·622 inches on 61 days in 1892, only 3·203 inches on 42 days in 1891, 9·015 inches on 59 days in 1890, and a twenty-five years' average of 8·460 inches on 66·8 days.

At Knockdolian, Greystones, Co. Wicklow, the rainfall amounted to 4·136 inches on 19 days. The heaviest falls in 24 hours were 1·130 inches on the 19th, and ·830 inch on the 6th. The total rainfall in 1897, up to April 30, was 13·030 inches on 60 days, compared with 5·636 inches on 50 days in 1896, 12·370 inches on 54 days in 1895, 12·455 inches on 70 days in 1894, and 5·530 inches on 44 days in 1893.

At Clonsevin, Killiney, Co. Dublin, 3·77 inches of rain fell on 22 days. The maximal fall in 24 hours was ·92 inch on the 5th. The average rainfall in April of the twelve years, 1885–1896, was 1·681 inches on 13·2 days. Since January 1, 1897, 10·30 inches of rain fell at this station on 63 days, compared with 6·77 inches on 50 days in 1896, 11·26 inches on 60 days in 1895, 9·09 inches on 71 days in 1894, and 5·94 inches on 37 days in 1893.

At the National Hospital for Consumption, Newcastle, Co. Wicklow, the rainfall was 3·403 inches on 19 days. On the 5th, ·690 inch was measured; on the 15th, ·630 inch; and on the 20th, ·[illegible] inch. The maximal temperature in the shade was 58·6° on the 17th. The minimal temperature in the screen was 30·1° on the 2nd. The thermometer in the screen fell to or below 32° on two days—the 2nd and 3rd. At this climatological station, 13·481 inches of rain had fallen on 76 days since January 1, 1897.

MAY.—A cold, rather dry month—very showery at the beginning and close, fine and bright in the intervening period, with absolute drought from the 12th to the 24th inclusive, partial drought commencing on the 9th. The prevailing winds were from polar quarters—N.W., N.E., and E. The rainfall was only 58 per cent. of the average for May.

In Dublin the arithmetical mean temperature (50·0°) was decidedly below the average (52·0°); the mean dry bulb readings at 9 a.m. and 9 p.m. were 50·5°. In the thirty-two years ending with 1896, May was coldest in 1869 (M. T. = 49·2°), and warmest in 1833 (M. T. = 56·7°). In 1896 the M. T. was 49·5°; in 1895 it was 54·3°, and in 1894, 49·5°.

The mean height of the barometer was 29·976 inches, or 0·013 inch below the corrected average value for May—namely, 29·989 inches. The mercury rose to 30·436 inches at 9 a.m. of the 18th, and fell to 29·217 inches at 7 p.m. of the 25th. The observed range of atmospheric pressure was, therefore, 1·219 inch.

The mean temperature deduced from daily readings of the dry bulb thermometer at 9 a.m. and 9 p.m. was 50·5°, or 3·8° above the value for April, 1897 (45·0°). Using the formula, *Mean Temp. = Min. + (max.—min. × ·47)*, the value was 50·5°, or 1·1° below the average mean temperature for May, calculated in the same way, in the twenty-five years, 1865–89, inclusive (51·6°). The arithmetical mean of the maximal and minimal readings was 50·0°, compared with a twenty-five years' average of 52·0°. On the 16th the thermometer in the screen rose to 63·6°—wind, E.N.E.; on the 6th the temperature fell to 36·2°—wind, N.W. The minimum on the grass was 33·5° on the 6th.

The rainfall amounted to 1·189 inches, distributed over 14 days. The average rainfall for May in the twenty-five years, 1865–89, inclusive, was 2·020 inches, and the average number of rainy days was 15·4. The rainfall, and—to a less extent—the rainy days, were below the average. In 1886 the rainfall in May was very large—5·472 inches on 21 days; in 1869, also, 4·414 inches fell on 19 days. On the other hand, in 1895, only ·177 inch was measured on but 3 days. In 1896 the fall was only ·190 inch on 7 days.

A solar halo was seen on the 24th. High winds were noted on 12 days, attaining the force of a gale (from W.S.W.) on the 4th only. The atmosphere was slightly foggy on the 20th. Hail fell on the 3rd, 5th, 11th, 12th, and 26th.

During the month the thermometer did not fall below 32° in the screen or on the grass. The mean minimal temperature on the grass was 40·9°, compared with 43·1° in 1896; 41·5° in 1895, 37·0° in 1894, 45·6° in 1893, 41·3° in 1892, 37·7° in 1891, 42·2° in 1890, 42·1° in 1889, 37·3° in 1888, and 37·9° in 1887.

May Day was fine and dry.

The week ended Saturday, the 8th, proved a very changeable showery period; also extremely cold for the time of year until Friday, when the atmosphere became mild and damp, but genial. There was again a cyclonic distribution of barometric pressure in the N.W. and N., while relatively high pressures were found over the Bay of Biscay, France, and Germany. Hence strong winds from westerly (S.W., W., and N.W.) points blew over the British Islands, accompanied by frequent showers of cold rain and hail in the day time, and by clear, very sharp nights. Particularly heavy hail-showers passed over Dublin on Monday and Wednesday. Thunderstorms occurred at Stornoway on Tuesday, Oxford on Wednesday, and Aberdeen on Thursday. On Friday a very considerable increase of temperature took place, and the air became damp and the sky overcast, as some new depressions approached the West of Scotland from the Atlantic. The change was attended by a rather heavy rainfall in Ireland. At the beginning of the week the planet Mercury was well seen after sunset in the north-western sky—on Monday evening the crescent moon and this planet were seen in conjunction. In Dublin the mean height of the barometer was 29·976 inches, pressure ranging between 29·678 inches, at 9 a.m. of Sunday (wind, W. by S.), and 30·134 inches, at 9 p.m. of Thursday and Saturday (wind, W.N.W. and N.W.). The corrected mean temperature was 48·2°. The mean dry bulb temperature at 9 a.m. and 9 p.m. was 48·0°. On Saturday the thermometer rose to 60·0° in the shade, on Thursday it sank to 36·3°. Rainfall amounted to ·657 inch on seven days, ·296 inch being registered on Thursday. The prevailing winds were W.S.W. and W.N.W.

The "cold wave of May" was very typically represented by the weather of the week ended Saturday, the 15th, which up to Friday more resembled a period in February or March than the second week in May. Parching northerly winds of great strength, clouded skies, and particularly low night temperatures prevailed. Along the east coast of Great Britain sleet or snow and hail fell frequently. In France and Germany night frosts of much intensity proved very injurious to vegetation. During the first four days a cyclonic system hovered over the south of Norway and Denmark, while an area of high atmospheric pressure lay off the west of Ireland. Northerly winds and low temperatures were in consequence prevalent throughout the British Isles—a cold wave passing quickly southwards from the Shetlands to the Mediterranean. At 8 a.m. of Monday the thermometer read 31° at Sumburgh Head in the Shetlands, where snow was falling. Tuesday and Wednesday were extremely cold days, and there were slight hail showers in and near Dublin. At inland stations in England, France and Germany, at this time, the thermometer fell at night to or below 32° even in the screen. The anticyclone moved south eastwards on Thursday and was afterwards found over the S. of England and France. The sky remained densely clouded until noon on Saturday, when the clouds dispersed and a sunny afternoon followed. In Dublin the mean height of the barometer was 30·254 inches, the pressure ranging between 30·040 inches at 9 p.m. of Monday (wind, N.N.W.), and 30·441 inches at 9 p.m. of Saturday (wind, E.S.E.). The corrected mean temperature was 46·3°. The mean dry bulb temperature at 9 a.m. and 9 p.m. was 46·2°. On Tuesday the screened thermometer fell to 37·0°, on Saturday they rose to 58·9°. The prevailing wind was N.N.W. The rainfall was only ·001 inch on Tuesday (melted hail). On Saturday morning the thermometer read 68° at Haparanda, within the Arctic Circle, and only 38° at Munich.

An uninterrupted spell of anticyclonic weather has to be recorded in the week ended Saturday, the 22nd. Atmospheric pressure was highest on Sunday, when the barometer read 30·63 inches at Christiansund, on the west coast of Norway. It afterwards gave way intermittently, falling below 30 inches very generally on Saturday. Over Spain, the Mediterranean, and Central Europe at large several shallow depressions were found, and the weather was less settled than in the North of Europe and the British Isles. Owing to the distribution of atmospheric pressure which has just been described, north-easterly winds prevailed and temperature ruled low at night. At stations also on the east coasts of both Great Britain and Ireland the weather was cool even by day. This was especially so at Shields, where in consequence of the prevalence of cloud the thermometer did not rise above 50° from Monday evening to Friday. Inland, however, the heating power of an almost unclouded sun was well marked, London in particular feeling its effect, so that the maxima there were 67°, 75°, 76°, 80°, 73°, and 68° up to Saturday. The cloud canopy which kept the N.E. of England so chilly on Tuesday, Wednesday, and Thursday, extended to the neighbourhood of Dublin on the mornings of Tuesday and Thursday, but by noon in each case the sky had cleared. At times the atmosphere was very hazy, as is usual in anticyclonic easterly winds. In Dublin the mean height of the barometer was 30·188 inches, pressure ranging from 30·446 inches at 9 a.m. of Sunday (wind, E.N.E.), to 29·841 inches at 9 p.m. of Saturday (wind, S.E.). The corrected mean temperature was 53·1°. The mean dry bulb reading at 9 a.m. and 9 p.m. was 53·1°. On Sunday the screened thermometers rose to 63·6°, on Friday they sank to 43·0°. No rain fell. The prevailing wind was N.E. At the Ordnance Survey Office, Phœnix Park, 63·1 hours of bright sunshine were recorded this week.

The week ended Saturday, the 29th, saw the disappearance of the anticyclone which had so long ruled the weather in the N.W. of Europe, and the substitution for it of low pressure areas and their accompanying unsettled, showery conditions. During Sunday and Monday bright, cool, dry weather and north-easterly winds prevailed. On Monday afternoon cirrus cloud overspread the sky from N.W., and a partial solar halo was seen in it at 6·30 p.m. This was the beginning of the change. The barometer began to fall decidedly in all districts, the change being briskest in the north, so that by Tuesday morning a well defined V-shaped depression had formed over Scotland and the N.W. of England. In the afternoon a secondary disturbance advanced eastwards across Ireland, causing a very general though not heavy fall of rain. This disturbance was found over the S.W. of England on Wednesday morning, when the primary depression was still over Scotland with barometer readings below 29·40 inches. A more rapid fall of the barometer in the S.W. led to the formation of a cyclonic system over the south of Ireland and St. George's Channel by Thursday morning. The weather in consequence became more and more unsettled, with a tendency to thundershowers in many places. On Friday morning areas of high atmospheric pressure existed both in Lapland and over the Peninsula, while depressions covered Ireland, England, and Central Europe. In the afternoon heavy thundershowers occurred in Ireland. Saturday was a breezy, showery day; at 8 a.m. the barometer was down to 29·05 inches at Stornoway. In Dublin the mean height of the barometer was 29·679 inches, the range being from 30·097 inches at 9 a.m. of Monday (wind, N.N.E.), to 29·217 inches at 7 p.m. of Friday (wind, S.W.). The corrected mean temperature was 51·8°, the mean dry bulb reading at 9 a.m. and 9 p.m. being 51·7°. The screened thermometers fell to 40·6° on Friday, and rose to 61·6° on Saturday. Rain fell on the last five days of the week to the amount of ·390 inch, ·117 inch being measured on Friday. The wind was variable.

The last two days of the month were changeable, showery and squally, but not unfavourable.

The rainfall in Dublin during the five months ending May 31st amounted to 10·693 inches on 83 days, compared with 8·971 inches on 70 days in 1896, 10·410 inches on 65 days in 1895, 12·709 inches on 96 days in 1894, 7·926 inches on 66 days in 1893, 10·699 inches on 80 days in 1892, only 5·893 inches on 63 days in 1891, 11·485 inches on 76 days in 1890, 10·476 inches on 91 days in 1889, 9·058 inches on 69 days in 1888, 6·469 inches on 43 days in 1887, and a twenty-five years' average of 10·496 inches on 81·6 days.

At Knockdolian, Greystones, Co. Wicklow, the rainfall was 1·040 inches, distributed over 10 days, ·300 inch falling on the 31st and ·210 inch on the 6th. The total fall since January 1st, 1897, equals 14·130 inches on 80 days, compared with 5·716 inches on 58 days in 1896, 17·543 inches on 63 days in 1895, 15·836 inches on 58 days in 1894, and 9·385 inches on 65 days in 1893.

The rainfall at Cloneevin, Killiney, Co. Dublin, was 0·850 inch on 10 days—0·26 inch falling on the 28th. At this station the average rainfall in May in the twelve years, 1885–1896, was 2·081 inches on 13 days. May, 1896, was a very dry month, only 0·08 inch falling on 2 days. Absolute drought prevailed from the 8th to the 24th, both inclusive. Since January 1, 1897, 11·31 inches of rain have fallen on 83 days at Cloneevin.

At the National Hospital for Consumption, Newcastle, Co. Wicklow, the rainfall in May was 0·802 inch on 11 days, ·188 inch being measured on the 28th. Since January 1, 16·294 inches of rain have fallen at this station on 87 days. The maximum shade temperature was 63·8° on the 16th, the minimum was 35·9° on the 4th.

June.—Although the rainfall and rainy days were in excess of the average, and the amount of cloud was large, June, 1897, must be regarded as a favourable month, conducive to health and propitious to vegetation. It is a remarkable fact that with a preponderance of easterly and north-westerly winds, the relative humidity was very high, and radiation temperatures by night were not low. Fog was observed on as many as seven occasions—an unusual feature in June. It is also noteworthy that the percentage of cloud was higher at 9 p.m. (68·3°) than at 9 a.m. (65·7°). There was a very cold spell from the 15th to the 19th.

In Dublin the arithmetical mean temperature (58·7°) was above the average (57·8°) by 0·9°; the mean dry bulb readings at 9 a.m. and 9 p.m. were 57·5°. In the thirty-two years ending with 1890. June was coldest in 1882 (M. T. = 53·8°); and in 1879 (the "cold year") (M. T. = 53·9°). It was warmest in 1887 (M. T. = 62·3°); in 1865 (M. T. = 61·0°); and in 1896 (M. T. = 61·6°).

The mean height of the barometer was 29·999 inches, or 0·082 inch above the corrected average value for June—namely, 29·917 inches. The mercury rose to 30·223 inches at 9 a.m. of the 3rd, and fell to 29·548 inches at 7 a.m. of the 16th. The observed range of atmospheric pressure was, therefore, 0·675 inch.

The mean temperature deduced from daily readings of the dry bulb thermometer at 9 a.m. and 9 p.m. was 57·3°, or 7·0° above the value for May, 1897. Using the formula, *Mean Temp. = Min.* + (max. – min. × ·465), the value was 57·2°, or 1·7° above the average mean temperature for June, calculated in the same way, in the twenty-five years, 1865–89, inclusive (55·5°). The arithmetical mean of the maximal and minimal readings was 58·7°, compared with a twenty-five years' average of 57·8°. On the 22nd the thermometer in the screen rose to 77·7°—wind, S.W.; on the 10th the temperature fell to 41·0°—wind, W.N.W. The minimum on the grass was 40·6°, also on the 10th.

The rainfall amounted to 3·237 inches, distributed over 20 days. The average rainfall for June in the twenty-five years, 1865–89, inclusive, was 1·817 inches, and the average number of rainy days was 13·8. The rainfall and the rainy days, therefore, were much above the average. In 1878 the rainfall in June was very large—5·058 inches on 19 days; in 1879 also 4·046 inches fell on 24 days. On the other hand, in 1880, only ·100 inch was measured on 3 days; in 1887, the rainfall was only ·252 inch, distributed over only 5 days. In 1896, 1·683 inches fell on 14 days.

High winds were noted on 7 days, but the force of a gale was attained only on the 16th and 19th. The atmosphere was more or less foggy on the 2nd, 3rd, 5th, 9th, 23rd, 25th and 26th. Temperature reached or exceeded 70° in the screen on 6 days, compared with 17 days in 1887, only 1 day in 1888, and 3 days in 1896. A thunderstorm occurred on the 12th, and lightning was seen on the 22nd. Solar halos were observed on the 5th and 28th.

Changeable but favourable weather was experienced during the period ended Saturday, the 5th. On Tuesday, June 1st, an anticyclone spread south-westwards from Scandinavia to Scotland, while a shallow trough of low pressure stretched across the southern part of Ireland and England to the East of France. Within this area dull rainy weather was prevalent, and severe thunderstorms occurred in many parts of England, especially over the south-eastern counties. These electrical disturbances afterwards spread northwards with lessening intensity, but Ireland escaped. Towards the close of the period a general and considerable rise of temperature took place and there was a good deal of bright sunshine. Friday, however, was at first dull and rainy in and about Dublin, a very shallow barometric depression having apparently drifted westward from Lancashire and north Wales during Thursday night. The sky cleared about mid-day and very fine summerlike weather set in, lasting to the close of the period. The atmosphere was very thick on Saturday. In Dublin the range of pressure was from 29·911 inches at 9 p.m. of Tuesday, the 1st (wind, E.), to 30·223 inches at 9 a.m. of Thursday (wind, E.). On Thursday the screened thermometers fell to 45·0°, on Saturday they rose to 69·3°. The rainfall was ·310 inch on three days, ·250 inch being registered on Tuesday, the 1st. The prevailing wind was S.E.

Changeable weather was experienced during the week ending Saturday, the 12th, which opened and closed with warmth, the intervening period being very cold for the time of year. A rain storm of much intensity prevailed in Ireland, the southern half of England, and Belgium on Tuesday night, extending into Germany on Wednesday. The measurement of rain during the storm was ·67 inch in Dublin, ·64 inch in London, ·82 inch at Loughborough, 1·13 inches at Oxford, 1·22 inches at Cambridge, and 1·42 inches at Hurst Castle. The rainfall took place near the centre of a long trough of low atmospheric pressure, which stretched on Wednesday morning east-south-eastwards from the S.W. of Ireland to Belgium and the E. of France. To the southward of this line the wind was S.W. to W., to the northward it was easterly in direction, and temperature was very low. From Scotland, at this time, fine, cool, dry weather was reported, with very low night temperatures—at Nairn the screened thermometer fell to 31° on Monday night and to 34° on Tuesday night. The low-pressure system quickly filled up and dispersed, and a brisk rise of the barometer took place. On Thursday moderate gradients for S.W. winds formed over Ireland, where temperature rose fast. On Friday, for the first time this season, the shade thermometer rose above 70° (to 73·8°) in Dublin. Saturday also was fair and warm, but the sky became overcast and the air was heavy and sultry, a few drops of rain falling at intervals. After 9 45 p.m. rain fell heavily, followed by a sharp thunderstorm. In Dublin the mean height of the barometer was 30·050 inches, the range being from 29·720 inches at 7 a.m. of Wednesday (wind, E.N.E.) to 30·180 inches at 8.30 a.m. of Saturday (wind, E.S.E.). The corrected mean temperature was 55·6°, the mean dry bulb reading at 9 a.m. and 9 p.m. being 55·0°. The screened thermometers fell to 41·0° on Wednesday and rose to 73·8° on Friday. The rainfall was 1·030 inches on five days, ·660 inch being recorded on Tuesday. Easterly winds prevailed.

The weather was in a troubled state throughout the week ended Saturday, the 19th—at least in Ireland and Scotland. In England it remained fine and warm until Wednesday, but from that day onward unsettled conditions held there as elsewhere. On Sunday, at 9 a.m., the thermometer stood at 75° in London, and later in the day it reached 84°. At this time a shallow depression lay over the S. of Ireland, causing dull and drizzling weather. By Monday this system had drifted north-eastwards to the North Sea, and had grown deeper, causing heavy rains in parts of Scotland. In Ireland a brisk N.W. wind brought finer and colder weather for the time being. On Tuesday a new and much deeper depression advanced across Ireland. It reached the S. of Scotland by Wednesday morning, having caused a disastrous gale and downpours of rain in many places. At

Ardrossan the rainfall amounted to 2·77 inches up to 8 a.m. of Wednesday. Harsh, cold N.W. winds blew with much violence in the rere of the centre. Scarcely had this disturbance passed away when another followed it, bringing severe S.W. gales to the English Channel. On Saturday again a depression passed over Ireland, where heavy rain fell for several hours. In the evening of this day temperature rose considerably, having been as low as 41° on Friday night. In Dublin the mean atmospheric pressure was 29·853 inches, the barometer rising to 30·211 inches at 9 p.m. of Monday (wind, W.N.W.), and falling to 29·348 inches at 7 a.m. of Friday (wind, N.W.). The corrected mean temperature was 54·7°. The mean dry bulb reading at 9 a.m. and 9 p.m. was 54·6°. On Sunday the shade thermometers rose to 67·0°, on Saturday they fell to 45·0°. The rainfall was 1·113 inches on six days, ·400 inch being measured on Saturday. The prevalent wind was N.W. At Glasgow the rainfall was as much as 4·25 inches, and even at Edinburgh it was 3·27 inches.

A very marked advance in temperature is the most striking feature in the weather-record of the week ending Saturday, the 26th. On Sunday morning the centre of a depression, which had caused a general and in places heavy rainfall the previous day or night, was found over Norfolk. In Ireland the weather was fine and dry, but cloudy, with a brisk N.W. wind. In the afternoon slight rain fell. An anticyclone now began to spread northwards from France, throwing a warm S.W. wind upon the British Isles, where the weather became fine and summerlike. Tuesday—the day set apart for the Queen's Diamond Jubilee celebration—was cloudy to fair in London, brilliant in Dublin, where the thermometer rose to 73·7°. In the evening and at night sheet lightning was observed, thunderstorms being reported from Valentia and Parsonstown. On Wednesday afternoon or in the evening again a brisk fall of temperature occurred in the N. of England and in Ireland, accompanied by a sea fog on the east coast of Ireland. In the centre and S. of England, on the contrary, the heat increased, so that in London the maximum was 88° on Wednesday and 90° on Thursday. At 8 a.m. of this latter day the thermometer read 77° in London, but only 51° at Shields. In the afternoon of Thursday severe thunderstorms broke out over the east and south-east of England, where temperature fell rapidly. The rainfall accompanying the storm amounted to ·30 inch at Brixton in the S. of London. Fine weather held afterwards to the end of the week. In Dublin the mean height of the barometer was 30·044 inches, pressure ranging between 29·842 inches at 9 a.m. of Sunday (wind, N.W.) and 30·228 inches at 9 a.m. of Tuesday (wind, S.W.). The corrected mean temperature was 60·7°. The mean dry bulb reading at 9 a.m. and 9 p.m. was 60·7°. On Sunday the screened thermometers fell to 50·0°, on Tuesday they rose to 73·7°. Rain fell on four days to the amount of ·162 inch, ·133 inch being measured on Wednesday. The wind was generally light in force and variable in direction.

While warm and for the most part summerlike, the weather of the closing period of the month (27th–30th, inclusive) was changeable. On the night of Sunday, the 27th, a heavy fall of rain (·440 inch) took place. The 28th broke foggy and damp, but in the end proved fine. At 5 p.m. a solar halo was seen. Another considerable fall of rain occurred at night. The last two days were fine and warm, after cloudy, dull mornings.

The rainfall in Dublin during the six months ending June 30th amounted to 13·530 inches on 113 days, compared with 7·454 inches on 84 days in 1896, 12·242 inches on 80 days in 1895, 14·341 inches on 109 days in 1894, 9·024 inches on 78 days in 1893, 11·770 inches on 97 days in 1892, 8·748 inches on 77 days in 1891, 12·112 inches on 94 days in 1890, 10·570 inches on 87 days in 1889, 10·113 inches on 87 days in 1888, 6·741 inches on 67 days in 1887, and a twenty-five years' average of 12·812 inches on 93·4 days.

At Knockdolian, Greystones, Co. Wicklow, the rainfall was 4·005 inches, distributed over 14 days. Of this quantity 1·020 inches fell on the 8th, and ·790 inch on the 27th. The total fall since January 1 has been 15·123 inches on 100 days, compared with 7·850 inches on 61 days in the first six months of 1896, 14·270 inches on 67 days in 1895, 17·283 inches on 98 days in 1894, 11·775 inches on 75 days in 1893.

The rainfall at Cloneevin, Killiney, Co. Dublin, amounted to 3·30 inches on 10 days. The greatest fall in 24 hours was 1·21 inches on the 8th. The average rainfall for June in the 12 years 1885–1896, was 1·815 inches on 11·7 days. In 1893, 1·04 inches fell on 12 days, in 1896 1·65 inches fell on 13 days. Since January 1, 1897, 16·60 inches of rain have fallen at this station on 113 days, compared with 6·84 inches on 70 days in the corresponding six months of 1896.

At the National Hospital for Consumption, Newcastle, Co. Wicklow, the rainfall was 4·075 inches on 15 days. On the 8th, 1·020 inches were measured, and on the 27th, ·630 inch. The maximum temperature in the shade was 73·6° on the 29th, the minimum temperature in the shade was 42·0° on the 3rd. At this climatological station the rainfall for the six months ending June 30, amounted to 16·372 inches on 103 days.

July.—A very favourable month, with sufficient rainfall and of average mean temperature. The showers were equably distributed throughout the month. There was a fair amount of bright sunshine. Electrical disturbances were rife and severe in England, but only trifling in Ireland. Very heavy showers of rain and hail fell in the vicinity of Dublin on the 25th and 26th.

In Dublin the arithmetical mean temperature (61·1°) was slightly above the average (60·6°); the mean dry bulb readings at 9 a.m. and 9 p.m. were 60·3°. In the thirty-two years ending with 1896, July was coldest in 1879 (the "cold year") (M.T. = 57·2°). It was warmest in 1887 (M.T. = 63·7°); and in 1868 (the "warm year") (M.T. = 63·6°). In 1896 the M.T. was 60·9°.

The mean height of the barometer was 30·003 inches, or 0·088 inch above the corrected average value for July—namely, 29·915 inches. The mercury marked 30·361 inches at 9 a.m. of the 11th, and fell to 29·601 inches at 7 a.m. of the 20th. The observed range of atmospheric pressure was, therefore, 0·760 inch.

The mean temperature deduced from daily readings of the dry bulb thermometer at 9 a.m. and 9 p.m. was 60·8°, or 3·6° above the value for June, 1887. Using the formula, *Mean Temp.* = *Min.* + (*max.* — *min.* × ·465), the value was 60·6°, or 0·4° above the average mean temperature for July, calculated in the same way, in the twenty-five years, 1865–89, inclusive (60·2°). The arithmetical mean of the maximal and minimal readings was 61·1°, compared with a twenty-five years' average of 60·6°. On the 23rd the thermometer in the screen rose to 75·1°—wind, S.W.; on the 11th the temperature fell to 46·1°—wind, E. The minimum on the grass was 41·3°, also on the 11th.

The rainfall was 1·650 inches, distributed over 12 days. The average rainfall for July in the twenty-five years, 1865–89, inclusive, was 2·429 inches, and the average number of rainy days was 17·2. The rainfall, therefore, was considerably below the average, while the rainy days were still more below it. In 1880 the rainfall in July was very large—6·087 inches on 24 days; in 1884, also, 5·474 inches fell on 18 days; and in 1885, 1·303 inches on 16 days. On the other hand, in 1870, only ·539 inch was measured on 8 days; in 1869 the fall was only ·739 inch on 9 days; and in 1868 only ·741 inch fell on but 5 days.

High winds were noted on 9 days, but attained the force of a gale on only one occasion—the 5th. Temperature reached or exceeded 70° in the screen on 7 days. In July, 1887, temperature reached or exceeded 70° in the screen on no fewer than 17 days. In 1888, the maximum for July was only 68·7°.

A thunderstorm occurred on the evening of the 21st. A solar halo was seen on the 4th. Hail fell on the 5th and 20th. The atmosphere was rather foggy on the 16th, 21st, and 31st.

The weather of the period ended Saturday, the 3rd, was changeable but favourable, with north-westerly to westerly winds and unsteady temperature. On Thursday, the 1st, an anticyclone lay off the W. of Ireland moving south-eastwards. On Friday a series of barometric depressions began to arrive off our N.W. and N. coasts, the wind backed to W. or S.W. and freshened with increasing cloudiness and some showers. The thermometer rose to 71·7° in the shade, having fallen to 53·3° during the previous night. Saturday was a dry but windy day.

The distribution of atmospheric pressure throughout the week ended Saturday, the 10th, was cyclonic in the N.W., N., and N.E., anticyclonic in France and Central Europe. Hence, unsettled weather prevailed in Ireland, Scotland, and Scandinavia, whereas it was comparatively fine in England and on the Continent. The force of the wind was considerable in Ireland and Scotland, amounting to a gale at times at exposed stations. On Sunday a large and rather deep depression passed eastwards across Scandinavia. In its rear, strong, squally and cool northwesterly winds blew over the British Islands—the amount of cloud was large, but very little rain fell except at the exposed Irish stations of Belmullet and Malin Head. At night the wind backed to W.S.W. and freshened to gale force as a new depression approached Scotland from the Atlantic. Near the centre of this system the barometer ultimately fell almost to 29 inches (to 29·01 inches at Sumburgh Head on Tuesday evening). Very cold N.W. winds, with showers of rain and hail, set in as this disturbance moved away to the north-eastward. On Tuesday night the thermometer fell to 46° in Dublin and to 44° at Parsonstown. Thursday was a squally, wet, cold day in Ireland, but fair and bright over the greater part of England. On Friday a rapid increase of atmospheric pressure began, and on Saturday an anticyclone of considerable size covered the greater portion of the British Isles, the result being fine, quiet weather. In Dublin the mean height of the barometer was 29·821 inches, pressure ranging between 29·614 inches at 3 p.m. of Monday (wind, W.S.W.) and 30·233 inches at 9 p.m. of Saturday (wind, S.E.). The corrected mean temperature was 57·7°. The mean dry bulb reading at 9 a.m. and 9 p.m. was 57·0°. The prevalent winds were N.W. and W. Rain fell to the amount of ·327 inch on three days, ·215 inch being measured on Thursday. A perfect solar halo appeared on Sunday afternoon.

Throughout the week ended Saturday, the 17th, the distribution of atmospheric pressure was anticyclonic in the British Islands and their immediate neighbourhood. Fair, summerlike weather was generally prevalent, and there was a large amount of bright sunshine, while scarcely any rain fell. Easterly winds prevailed until Friday, when either calms or variable westerly breezes took their place. On Sunday morning the barometer stood at 30·41 inches at Cambridge. By Monday morning the isobar of 30·4 inches had reformed over Scandinavia, in which neighbourhood it was still found on Tuesday. At this time a shallow depression was forming over the Mediterranean, so that gradients for easterly winds became decided, especially in S.E. of England. The low pressure area subsequently advanced northwards across France, while a more marked depression formed over Germany. These irregularities caused thunder-rains in many parts of the Continent, but the weather remained dry in the United Kingdom until Friday, when some sultry showers fell in the south and west of Ireland. On Saturday the barometer began to fall somewhat decidedly, but the weather was very fine and warm generally. In Dublin the mean height of the barometer was 30·154 inches, pressure varying between 30·361 inches at 9 a.m. of Sunday (wind, E.), and 29·947 inches at 9 p.m. of Wednesday (wind also E.). The corrected mean temperature was 61·3°. The mean dry bulb reading at 9 a.m. and 9 p.m. was 62·5°. On Saturday the shade thermometer rose to 76·9°; on Sunday it fell to 46·1°. Easterly winds prevailed, chiefly light in force. The only rainfall was ·002 inch on Friday, which, however, did not count as a "rainy day."

At the beginning of the week ended Saturday, the 24th, the weather fell into an unsettled, thundery condition owing to the formation of a large and finally complex depression over Ireland, England, the North Sea, France and Belgium. On Sunday afternoon the weather broke in the east of Ireland with a chill and the formation of dense vapour fog on the headlands along the coast. Heavy showers fell early on Monday morning in Dublin, and thunder and lightning occurred in the English Channel. On Tuesday an irregular area of low atmospheric pressure lay over Ireland, England, and Denmark. Thunderstorms had already occurred in the S. and S.E. of England, and rain fell abundantly except in the N. of England and Scotland. During Tuesday and Wednesday electrical disturbances were again prevalent in England, and a sharp thunderstorm passed over Dublin also on Wednesday evening. Earlier in the day a violent thunder and hail storm had visited the northern suburbs of London. The depression subsequently passed on to Denmark, while northerly winds brought a spell of fine weather to the British Islands. On Friday, however, the barometer again gave way in the W., the wind backed to W. and finally to S., and the week closed with a renewal of unsettled weather. In Dublin the mean height of the barometer was 29·824 inches, pressure ranging between 29·601 inches at 7 a.m. of Tuesday (wind, E.N.E.), and 30·048 inches at 9 p.m. of Thursday (wind, W.S.W.). The mean dry bulb thermometer reading at 9 a.m. and 9 p.m. was 61·0°. The corrected mean temperature was 61·3°. On Thursday the screened thermometers fell to 54·2°; on Friday they rose to 73·1°—the highest reading so far recorded this season in Dublin. The rainfall was ·620 inch on four days, ·328 inch being measured as the result of Wednesday's thunderstorm. The prevalent wind was N.N.E.

During the week ended Saturday, the 31st, broken and showery at first, the weather subsequently became fine and warm. On Sunday morning the centre of a large, though not deep, atmospheric depression lay off the Hebrides, where the barometer read 29·10 inches compared with 30·30 inches at Corunna. Fresh S.W. winds were blowing, accompanied by heavy showers in many districts. Thunder and lightning occurred in the course of the day in the N.E. of Ireland, the N. of Scotland, and the N.E. and centre of England. At 8 a.m. of Monday the depression was central between Caithness and the Shetlands, the barometer being down to 29·43 inches. In Ireland the wind had drawn into W. or W.N.W. Heavy showers of rain and hail fell in Dublin at intervals, while thunder and lightning were prevalent all over the centre and east of England and at Aberdeen. A steady and general rise of the barometer now set in, as an anticyclone spread north-eastwards from the Atlantic and Bay of Biscay across the British Islands. While it was forming a considerable fall of warm rain took place in Ireland on Wednesday. By Thursday evening the anticyclone had fully developed, and pressure reached 30·47 inches in the S.W. of Ireland. The last three days of the week were fine and summerlike, but much cloud was reported, and a good deal of fog hung about the coasts and over the Channels. In Dublin the mean height of the barometer was 30·046 inches, pressure ranging between 29·670 inches on Sunday afternoon (wind, W.), and 30·357 inches at 9 a.m. of Friday (wind, W.S.W.). The corrected mean temperature was 62·2°. The mean dry bulb reading at 9 a.m. and 9 p.m. was 61·4°. On Thursday the shade thermometers rose to 71·8°, on Tuesday they fell to 51·3°. The wind was westerly (between S.W. & N.W.) for the most part. The rainfall was ·611 inch on four days, ·283 inch being measured on Monday, when also hail fell.

The rainfall in Dublin during the seven months ending July 31st amounted to 15·600 inches on 123 days, compared with 13·328 inches on 102 days in 1896, 16·785 inches on 90 days in 1895, 16·131 inches on 130 days in 1894, 11·066 inches on 94 days in 1893, 7·933 inches on 80 days in 1887, and a twenty-five years' average of 14·781 inches on 112·6 days.

At Ravenswell, Greystones, Co. Wicklow, the rainfall in July was 1·625 inches on 10 days, compared with 5·720 inches on 10 days in 1896, 3·600 inches on 16 days in 1895, 3·805 inches on 10 days in 1894, and 1·290 inches on 13 days in 1893. Of the total rainfall ·470 inch fell on the 24th, and ·413 inch on the 25th. The total fall since January 1 has been 19·730 inches on 116 days, compared with 13·092 inches on 77 days in 1896, 17·860 inches on 83 days in 1895, 21·104 inches on 113 days in 1894, and 13·466 inches on 80 days in 1893.

At Cloncevin, Killiney, Co. Dublin, the rainfall in July was 1·28 inches on 10 days, compared with a twelve years' average of 2·351 inches on 11·3 days. On the 27th the rainfall was ·24 inch. In July, 1896, 6·78 inches fell on 20 days, in 1895 2·58 inches fell on 17 days, in 1894 4·08 inches fell on 22 days. Since January 1, 1897, 18·04 inches of rain have fallen on 123 days at this station (Cloncevin).

At the National Hospital for Consumption, Newcastle, Co. Wicklow, the rainfall was 1·428 inches on 11 days, ·297 inch being measured on the 18th. At this climatological station 19·737 inches of rain have fallen on 113 days since January 1, 1897. The maximal temperature in the shade in July was 77° on the 18th, the minimum was 42·3° on the 11th. The thermometer rose to or above 70° in the screen on eleven occasions during the month.

AUGUST.—A changeable, showery, windy month, but tolerably warm. In fact great heat prevailed during the first week, which was in all respects summerlike. During the rainy period which followed, temperature did not fall low owing to the prevalence of southerly and south-westerly winds. Thunder and lightning occurred frequently in Great Britain, to a far less extent in Ireland. The wind was often high and squally.

In Dublin the arithmetical mean temperature (60·5°) was decidedly above the average (59·7°); the mean dry bulb readings at 9 a.m. and 9 p.m. were 60·2°. In the thirty-two years ending with 1896, August was coldest in 1881 (M. T. = 57·0°), and warmest in 1893 (M. T. = 63·0°). In 1895 the M.T. was 60·0°; in 1879 (the "cold year"), it was 57·7°; in 1896 it was 58·1°.

The mean height of the barometer was 29·709 inches, or 0·148 inch below the corrected average value for August—namely, 29·857 inches. The mercury marked 30·213 inches at 9 p.m. of the 3rd, and fell to 29·214 inches at 3 p.m. of the 21st. The observed range of atmospheric pressure was, therefore, ·999 inch.

The mean temperature deduced from daily readings of the dry bulb thermometer at 9 a.m. and 9 p.m. was 60·2°, or 1·7° above the value in August, 1896. It was 1·1° below the value for July, 1897. Using the formula, *Mean Temp. = Min. + (max.—min. × ·47)*, the mean temperature was 60·4°, or 1·1° above the average mean temperature for August, calculated in the same way, in the twenty-five years, 1865–89, inclusive (59·3°). The arithmetical mean of the maximal and minimal readings was 60·5°, compared with a twenty-five years' average of 59·7°. On the 4th the thermometer in the screen rose to 70·8°—wind, S.S.E.; on the 19th the temperature fell to 49·2°—wind, W. The minimum on the grass was 43·4°, on the 19th and 27th.

The rainfall was 3·785 inches, distributed over 24 days. The average rainfall for August in the twenty-five years, 1865–89, inclusive, was 2·835 inches, and the average number of rainy days was 15·5. The rainfall, therefore, and the rainy days were considerably in excess of the average. In 1874 the rainfall in August was very large—4·940 inches on 16 days; and in 1868 also, 4·743 inches fell on, however, only 13 days; but the heaviest downpour in August occurred in 1880, when 5·747 inches were registered on 22 days. On the other hand, in 1884, only ·777 inch was measured on 8 days. In 1886, 1·136 inches fell on 18 days.

High winds were noted on as many as 16 days, and attained the force of a gale on three occasions in Dublin—the 17th, 26th, and 27th. Thunder occurred on the 14th, thunder and lightning on the 16th. Temperature reached 70° in the screen on 5 days—all in the first week. The morning of the 1st was foggy.

The most noteworthy feature in the weather of the week ended Saturday, the 7th, was the intensity of the heat which prevailed in most parts of western Europe—particularly in England and France. As is usual, this culminated in violent thunderstorms on Wednesday and Thursday. On both of these days the thermometer touched 90° in the shade at Cambridge—the *London* readings were 85° and 87° respectively. Until Wednesday all parts of the British Islands were under the full influence of an anticyclone, or system of high atmospheric pressure. While of no great intensity, this anticyclone had much staying power, and as the winds were light and the sky comparatively free of cloud the sun's heat had full sway and the thermometer rose higher and higher each day. On Wednesday a decided fall of the barometer occurred in the west, as a large area of low pressure moved in over Ireland from the Atlantic. The fall of the barometer went on gradually until Friday morning, when readings as low as 29·45 inches were reported from the N. and N.W. of Ireland. The wind now veered into W. from S. and a gradual but decided reduction of temperature took place, Saturday proving a cool, cloudy, rather showery day. In Dublin the mean height of the barometer was 29·909 inches, the range being from 30·203 inches at 9 p.m. of Monday (wind, E.N.E.), to 29·561 inches at 9 a.m. of Friday (wind, S.W.). The corrected mean temperature was 64·3°. The mean dry bulb reading at 9 a.m. and 9 p.m. was 63·7°. On Sunday the screened thermometers fell to 55·3°; on Wednesday they rose to 76·8° (the highest reading recorded this season in Dublin). The rainfall was ·911 inch, on two days, ·901 inch being measured on Saturday. Of this large amount, ·890 inch fell in a rainstorm on the morning of Sunday, August 1. The prevalent wind was S.E.

Very changeable, rainy or showery weather held during the week ended Saturday, the 14th, the rainfall being particularly heavy and frequent at the Irish and Scotch stations. In the east and south-east of England spells of fine, dry weather were enjoyed. On Sunday morning an oval-shaped depression had its centre over St. George's Channel, whence it stretched northwestwards to Connaught, and southeastwards to the S.W. of England and the English Channel. From this position the system travelled eastward across England, causing very heavy rains in many places. Monday was very fine, but on Tuesday morning a new disturbance lay off the S.W. of Ireland, whence it travelled northeastwards and caused another downpour of rain in Ireland, Wales, the N. of England and Scotland. Thunderstorms broke out on Wednesday in Great Britain generally. On Friday and Saturday an area of low pressure was found off the N.W. of Ireland and W. of Scotland. This system kept the weather in a showery, squally condition to the close of the week. In Dublin the mean atmospheric pressure was 29·811 inches, the barometer falling to 29·548 inches at 9 a.m. of Sunday (wind, N.E.), and rising to 30·013 inches at 9 a.m. of Thursday (wind, W.). The corrected mean temperature was 60·4°, or 4·0 below that of the previous week. The mean dry bulb reading at 9 a.m. and 9 p.m. was 59·1°. On Monday the screened thermometers rose to 68·6°, on Thursday they sank to 51·9°. The rainfall amounted to ·837 inch on six days, ·430 inch being measured on Tuesday. The prevalent winds were S.S.W. and N.W. Thunder was heard on Saturday afternoon, when thunder, lightning, and hail were observed in the County Kildare.

Very changeable, rainy weather prevailed throughout the week ended Saturday, the 21st. A succession of primary barometric depressions of considerable size and depth passed across the N.W. of Ireland and of Scotland, while their subsidiary or secondary disturbances travelled across the more southern and central portions of the United Kingdom. Strong S.W. to N.W. winds and frequent showers, accompanied by thunder and lightning from time to time, were the result. Temperature was also most unsteady, Wednesday night being particularly cold, while Tuesday and Friday were tolerably warm days. In the S.E. of England intervals of fine, dry, and fairly warm weather were enjoyed, but in Ireland, Wales, the greater part of England and Scotland, rain fell heavily almost daily. In Dublin two showers on Wednesday yielded nearly half an inch of rain in the gauge (·450 inch); of these showers the second was attended with thunder and lightning. On Tuesday the wind rose to the force of a fresh gale from W.S.W. in the forenoon, but it moderated after 2 p.m., and a fine evening followed. In Dublin the mean height of the barometer was 29·588 inches, the range being from 29·832 inches at 9 a.m. of Monday (wind, W.) to 29·240 inches at 3 p.m. of Saturday (wind, W.S.W.). The corrected mean temperature was 57·1°. The mean dry bulb reading at 9 a.m. and 9 p.m. was 55·9°. On Thursday the screened thermometers fell to 45·2°; on Friday they rose to 68·1°. Rain fell daily to the total amount of 1·317 inches, ·450 inch being measured on Wednesday, when thunder and lightning occurred. Westerly winds (between S.S.W. and N.W.) prevailed.

During the week ended Saturday, the 28th, the weather remained changeable as in past weeks, squally and showery with a preponderance of south-westerly winds. In a word, it was of a cyclonic type. The scene of the heaviest rainfall was, however, shifted from Ireland and Scotland to England, and after Tuesday to the S. and S.E. of the last-named country. During Sunday a fresh breeze blew from W.N.W., and the weather, although cloudy, was chiefly fine and dry. On

Monday a new depression advanced over Ireland from the westward, throwing the weather again into an unsettled, showery condition. By Tuesday morning the centre of this disturbance had reached St. George's Channel. It subsequently passed across England in an east-north-easterly direction, causing thunderstorms and heavy rains in that country. In Ireland, after a dull, rainy morning, the weather became bright, with a light breeze from N.E. and later from N. Wednesday was cloudy to fair in Dublin, but the weather remained thundery and showery in the S. and S.E. of England. At night a brisk fall of the barometer heralded the approach of a new depression to the Irish coasts. This system caused a short summer-gale and driving rain on Thursday morning, but the afternoon was fair and sunny. A subsidiary depression formed at this time over England and spread eastwards, so that heavy rains accompanied by thunder were again experienced very generally in Great Britain. Stormy, showery weather lasted to the close of the week. In Dublin the mean atmospheric pressure was 29.621 inches, the barometer falling to 29.414 inches at 1 p.m. of Thursday (wind, S.E. to S.), and rising to 29.780 inches at 9 p.m. of Saturday (wind, S.W.). The corrected mean temperature was 58.0°. The mean dry bulb reading at 9 a.m. and 9 p.m. was 57.2°. On Sunday the minimum was 50.0°, on Thursday the maximum was 66.7° in the shade. Rain fell on six days to the amount of .501 inch, .141 inch being measured on Monday. At Greystones 1.123 inches of rain fell during this week. Southerly and south-westerly winds prevailed.

The last three days were changeable like the greater part of the month. On Sunday, the 29th, a deep depression, in which the barometer fell almost to 29 inches, passed northwards across Ireland. It caused fresh southerly gales and heavy rains, and was followed by showers and squalls alternating with fine, bright intervals to the close of the month.

The rainfall in Dublin during the eight months ending August 31st amounted to 19.398 inches on 140 days, compared with 14.464 inches on 120 days in 1896, 9.444 inches on 96 days during the same period in 1887, and a twenty-five years' average of 17.338 inches on 129.1 days.

At Knockdolian, Greystones, Co. Wicklow, the rainfall in August was 6.193 inches on 27 days, compared with 1.243 inches on 14 days in 1896, and 4.793 inches distributed over 26 days in 1891. Of this quantity .830 inch fell on the 7th. The total fall since January 1 amounts to 25.961 inches on 143 days, compared with 14.387 inches on 91 days in 1896, 19.083 inches on 107 days in 1895, 23.216 inches on 131 days in 1894, 16.841 inches on 106 days in 1893, and 21.296 inches on 108 days in 1892.

At the National Hospital, Newcastle, Co. Wicklow, the rainfall in August was 4.520 inches on 20 days, .807 inch being measured on the 30th and .780 inch on the 7th.

SEPTEMBER.—This month began badly, but proved favourable after the first few days, which were cold and wet. A rainstorm of great violence occurred in the east and south-east of Ireland on the 1st, when 2.700 inches of rain were measured at Greystones, and 1.100 inches in Dublin. An anticyclone formed on the 5th, bringing a week of beautiful weather. On the 29th a severe thunderstorm, accompanied by torrents of rain, passed over the south and south-east of England. The night temperatures were particularly low from time to time.

In Dublin the arithmetical mean temperature (54.5°) was below the average (55.8°); the mean dry bulb readings at 9 a.m. and 9 p.m. were 53.0°. In the thirty-two years ending with 1896, September was coldest in 1886 and in 1892 (M. T. = 53.0°), and warmest in 1865 (M. T. = 61.4°). The three warmest Septembers experienced in Dublin of late years have been—1865 (M. T. = 61.4°), 1880 (M. T. = 59.6°), and 1895 (M. T. = 59.1).

The mean height of the barometer was 29.950 inches, or 0.040 inch above the corrected average value for September—namely, 29.910 inches. The mercury rose to 30.378 inches at 9 a.m. of the 13th, and fell to 28.177 inches at 6.45 p.m. of the 1st. The observed range of atmospheric pressure was, therefore, 1.401 inches.

The mean temperature deduced from daily readings of the dry bulb thermometer at 9 a.m. and 9 p.m. was 53.0°, or 6.2° below the value for August, 1897. Using the formula, *Mean Temp. = Min. + (max. − min. × .476)*, the mean temperature was 54.2°, or 1.3° below the average mean temperature for September, calculated in the same way, in the twenty-five years, 1865–89, inclusive (55.5°). The arithmetical mean of the maximal and minimal readings was 54.5°, compared with a twenty-five years' average of 55.8°. On the 23rd the thermometer in the screen rose to 67.7°—wind, W.S.W.; on the 18th the temperature fell to 40.9°—wind, N.W. The minimum on the grass was 34.8°, on the 11th.

The rainfall was 3.383 inches, distributed over 16 days. The average rainfall for September in the twenty-five years, 1865–89, inclusive, was 2.176 inches, and the average number of rainy days was 14.7. In 1871, the rainfall was very large—4.048 inches on, however, only 15 days. In 1896, no less than 5.073 inches fell on 23 days, establishing a record rainfall for September. On the other hand, in 1865, only .056 inch was measured on but 3 days. In 1884, only .148 inch fell on 8 days; and in 1895, only .543 inch on 7 days.

High winds were noted on eleven days, but attained the force of a gale on only one occasion in Dublin—the 23rd. The atmosphere was foggy on the 9th, 10th, 11th, 16th, 27th, and 30th. Hail fell on the 3rd, 17th, and 18th. A solar halo was seen on the 7th.

The bad weather, which had prevailed since the second week in August, continued throughout the period ending Saturday, the 4th, which may be described as stormy, wet, and finally extremely cold for the time of year. Wednesday, the 1st, broke cloudy and threatening, and the barometer fell fast as a new cyclonic system advanced quickly to St. George's Channel from the south-westward. In Dublin a violent rainstorm began at noon, lasting until 6 p.m. In these six hours nearly an inch of rain (.940 inch) fell, and the wind backed to S.E., E., N.E., and finally N., blowing freshly throughout. By 6.15 p.m. the barometer had fallen to 29·177 inches. Rain again set in at night, so that by 9 a.m. of Thursday, the 2nd, the measurement for the previous twenty-four hours was as much as 1·108 inches, or more than half the average rainfall for September—namely, 2·170 inches. The cyclone subsequently crossed Wales and England, travelling N.E., so that its centre reached Norway on Friday morning. In its rear a remarkable fall of temperature occurred, the thermometer falling to 38° at Stornoway, 39° at Wick, 40° at Parsonstown, and 41° in Dublin early on Friday morning, and on Friday night to between 34° and 36° over Scotland. Heavy hail showers fell on this day, but conditions moderated on Saturday. In Dublin the height of the barometer ranged from 29·177 inches at 6.45 p.m. of Wednesday (wind, N.) to 30·034 inches at 9 p.m. of Saturday (wind, W.N.W.). On Wednesday the screened thermometers rose to 61·5°, on Friday they fell to 41·0°. The rainfall was 1·458 inches on four days, 1·164 inches being recorded on Wednesday. The prevalent wind was N.N.W.

The week ended Saturday, the 11th, happily witnessed a marked change for the better in the weather, which after Wednesday continued fine, sunny and dry to the close of the period. This most fortunate and pleasant change was brought about by the development of an area of high atmospheric pressure (anticyclone) in the extreme N.W.—the very region where the barometer had previously ruled lowest for weeks together. The increase of pressure began on Wednesday and continued until Saturday, when the barometer stood well above 30·4 inches over the greater part of the British Isles. On Sunday the centre of a large depression lay near Hernösand in Sweden, while another area of low pressure was found off the N. of Ireland and W. of Scotland. The latter system caused wet weather in nearly all districts. The primary disturbance and its secondaries then began to pass south-eastwards, while the anticyclone above-mentioned spread in from the N.W. over the United Kingdom. On Wednesday morning a shallow depression over the S.W. of Ireland brought rainy weather to Ireland south of Dundalk, Wales, and the centre of the S. of England. In Scotland and the N. and N.E. of Ireland the weather was brilliantly fine. As this depression passed south-eastwards to France, easterly winds, cloudless skies, and delightful weather became general in the United Kingdom, while heavy rains fell on the Continent. The nights were now very sharp—the thermometer falling in the screen to 34° at Parsonstown on Thursday night. In Dublin the mean pressure was 30·075 inches, the range being from 29·738 inches at 9 a.m. of Sunday (wind, W.) to 30·443 inches at 9 p.m. of Saturday (wind, calm). The corrected mean temperature was 53·3°. The mean dry bulb reading at 9 a.m. and 9 p.m. was 53·0°. On Monday the screened thermometers rose to 63·8°, on Friday they fell to 41·1°. Rain fell on the first four days to the amount of ·370 inch, ·184 inch being measured on Sunday. Westerly winds at first, followed by easterly on Wednesday.

Taken as a whole, the weather of the week ended Saturday, the 18th, was distinctly favourable. At first anticyclonic and genial in point of temperature, it finally became changeable, showery, and cold. But the rains were not torrential, like those of August and the first week of September, and so no further damage was done to the harvest. The barometer stood very high over the British Islands until Wednesday, when the anticyclone, which had brought such fine weather in the middle of the previous week, moved away to the south-westward. On Sunday atmospheric pressure was relatively low both off the N.W. of Norway (29·60 inches at Bodö) and in the Mediterranean Basin. A broad band of high pressure stretched from the South of Ireland (30·51 inches at Roche's Point) to the Baltic. Light variable winds and sunny weather prevailed. The anticyclone reached its fullest development on Monday, when the reading 30·58 inches was reported from several stations, including Dublin. Pressure now gave way—at first slowly and then quickly, so that on Thursday evening signs of a large depression were found between Scotland and Norway. This disturbance afterwards travelled south-eastwards and spread southwards over the whole Kingdom, so that cold N.W. winds and showers of chilly rain and hail became general, thunder and lightning occurring in some places. On Saturday the wind drew into N. in Ireland and the weather became almost wintry. In Dublin the mean height of the barometer was 30·217 inches, pressure ranging between 30·573 inches at 9 a.m. of Monday (wind, S.S.E.), and 29·633 inches at 6 p.m. of Friday (wind, N.W.). The corrected mean temperature was 53·8°. The mean dry bulb reading at 9 a.m. and 9 p.m. was 53·8°. On Tuesday the screened thermometers rose to 66·6°, on Saturday they fell to 40·3°. Rain fell on the last three days to the amount of ·240 inch, ·110 inch being measured on Friday. Hail showers occurred on Friday and Saturday. N.W. winds prevailed.

Although changeable, the weather during the week ended Saturday, the 25th, was on the whole not unfavourable. At first atmospheric depressions were found to the eastward of the North Sea, while the barometer was relatively high off the W. and S.W. of Ireland. Hence cold northerly and north-westerly winds prevailed, and were accompanied by showers at times, especially in Great Britain. Such showers fell in Dublin on Monday night. By Tuesday morning the barometer fell nearly to 29 inches near Christiania (to 29·02 inches at Færder, on the Christiania Fjord). On Wednesday a new and brisk decrease of pressure took place in Ireland and Scotland, as another series of depressions approached our N.W. coasts. Under their influence the wind backed to W. and finally to S.W., while temperature rose fast. On Thursday forenoon the wind rose to gale force, but brilliant and hot sunshine was enjoyed in Dublin. Towards evening clouds overspread the sky, and there were showers of drizzling rain. During the ensuing night rain fell more heavily, and Friday was at first dull, rainy, and squally. In the afternoon of this day, however, it became fine, dry, and cold, and Saturday proved brilliantly fine with a fresh S.W. wind. In Dublin the mean height of the barometer was 29·839 inches, pressure ranging between 29·509 inches at 3.45 p.m. of Thursday (wind, W.S.W.), and 30·037 inches at 9 a.m. of Saturday (wind, S.W.). The corrected mean temperature was 54·0°. The mean dry bulb temperature at 9 a.m. and 9 p.m. was 53·3°. On Sunday the screened thermometers fell to 41·8°, on Thursday they rose to 67·7°. The rainfall was ·237 inch on 3 days, ·142 inch being measured on Thursday. The prevalent winds were—at first N.W., afterwards S.W. The force of the wind was considerable.

The most striking feature of the weather during the closing period of the month—26th to 30th, inclusive—was a violent thunderstorm which passed over the south and south-east of England on Wednesday evening. It was accompanied by very heavy rain and caused loss of life. The rainfall during the storm was 1·03 inches at Brixton, London, 1·18 inches at Oxford, and 1·45 inches at Cambridge. The disturbance was unfelt in Ireland, but extended to France on Thursday. Sunday was very fine after a slight shower in the forenoon. As the day advanced an anticyclone spread westward from the Continent causing a brisk rise of the barometer and still finer weather. On Monday morning a wet vapour fog lay over Ireland, but this soon dispersed. During the next two days the barometer fell steadily and a complex depression formed over the British Islands, leading to the electrical storm of Wednesday night. On Wednesday forenoon a lofty sheet of cirriform cloud was seen from Dublin clearing off from S.S.W. At night the wind shifted in Ireland to N., and an exceptionally heavy electrical shower fell at 8.15 a.m. of Thursday. The weather then remained fine. In Dublin the height of the barometer ranged from 30·290 inches at 9 a.m. of Monday (wind, S.W.) to 29·834 inches at 9 p.m. of Wednesday (wind also S.W.). The extreme range of temperature in the shade, from 45·3° to 64·0°, was recorded on one and the same day—Monday. The rainfall was ·164 inch on two days, ·110 inch being measured on Wednesday. The prevalent winds were S.W.

The rainfall in Dublin during the nine months ending September 30th amounted to 11·871 inches on 165 days, compared with 10·068 inches on 112 days during the same period in 1895, 10·387 inches on 143 days in 1896, and a twenty-five years' average of 10·734 inches on 142·6 days.

At Knockdolian, Greystones, Co. Wicklow, the rainfall was 3·021 inches distributed over 13 days. Of this quantity 2·701 inches fell on the 1st. At this station the rainfall since January 1, 1897, has been 19·570 inches on 168 days, compared with 17·001 inches on 118 days in the same nine months of 1893, 23·804 inches on 137 days in 1894, 23·065 inches on 117 days in 1895, and 21·913 inches on 115 days in 1896.

At Cloneevin, Killiney, Co. Dublin, the rainfall in August was 4·30 inches on 21 days (the maximal fall in 24 hours being ·76 inch on the 29th), compared with a twelve years' average of 2·857 inches on 16·3 days. In September 3·85 inches fell at Cloneevin on 11 days. The maximal fall in 24 hours was 1·49 inches on the 1st. On an average of twelve years the September rainfall at this station has been 1·772 inches on 13·1 days. Since January 1, 1897, 22·01 inches of rain have fallen at Cloneevin on 138 days. The rainfall in the first nine months of the year at Cloneevin was 22·99 inches on 150 days in 1894, 21·36 inches on 120 days in 1895, and 20·30 inches on 120 days in 1896.

At the National Hospital for Consumption, Newcastle, Co. Wicklow, rain fell in measurable quantity on 11 days, during September to the total amount of 3·100 inches. On the 1st the record was as large as 2·300 inches—more than two-thirds of the entire rainfall for the month. The highest temperature in the screen was 69° on the 14th, the lowest was 41° on the 10th.

OCTOBER.—Quite unlike the cold Octobers of 1894, 1895, and 1896, this month was strangely genial and fine—nay more, the temperature of the air actually rose towards the close, thus reversing the seasonal range for the time of year. The weather of the second week was, indeed, rough and wet; but this only accentuated the quietness and mildness of the beginning and end of the month. These features were due to the prevalence of anticyclonic conditions over Western and Central Europe, Ireland getting the benefit of the warmth attending the southerly winds of the area of high atmospheric pressure.

In Dublin the arithmetical mean temperature (52·2°) was much above the average (49·7°); the mean dry bulb readings at 9 a.m. and 9 p.m. were 51·1°. In the thirty-two years ending with 1896, October was coldest in 1869 (M. T. = 44·6°), and in 1896 (M. T. = 45·0°). It was warmest in 1876 (M. T. = 53·1°). In 1863 the M. T. was only 49·9°.

The mean height of the barometer was 30·090 inches, or 0·250 inch above the corrected average value for October, namely, 29·840 inches. The mercury rose to 30·561 inches at 9 a.m. of the 21st, and fell to 29·074 inches at 3 a.m. of the 16th. The observed range of atmospheric pressure was, therefore, as much as 1·487 inches.

The mean temperature deduced from daily readings of the dry bulb thermometer at 9 a.m. and 9 p.m. was 51·1°, or only 1·9° below the value for September. The arithmetical mean of the maximal and minimal readings was 52·2°, compared with a twenty-five years' average of 49·7°. Using the formula, *Mean Temp. = Min. + (max. — min. × ·465)*, the value was 52·1°, or 3·6° above the average mean temperature for October, calculated in the same way, in the twenty-five years, 1865–89, inclusive (48·5°). On the 17th the thermometer in the screen rose to 62·0°—wind, S.; on the 18th, the temperature fell to 35·1°—wind, W.N.W. The minimum on the grass was 33·0°, also on the 18th. The thermometer did not sink to or below 32° in the screen, or even on the grass.

The rainfall was 2·110 inches, distributed over 14 days—the rainfall and the rainy days were decidedly below the average. The average rainfall for October in the twenty-five years, 1865–89, inclusive, was 3·106 inches, and the average number of rainy days was 17·4. In 1880 the rainfall in October was very large—7·358 inches on 18 days. In 1875, also, 7·049 inches fell on 20 days. On the other hand, in 1890, only ·853 inch fell on but 11 days; in 1884, only ·394 inch on but 14 days; and in 1868 only ·836 inch on 15 days.

Lightning was seen on the night of the 18th–19th. High winds were noted on nine days, and attained the force of a gale on three occasions—the 10th, 16th, and 17th. The atmosphere was more or less foggy in Dublin on the 1st, 2nd, 13th, 14th, 20th, 21st, 28th, 30th, and 31st. Hail fell on the 10th. A lunar halo appeared on the 7th. A solar halo was seen on the 29th.

Friday, the 1st, was at first foggy and cloudy, afterwards fine and mild. On Saturday, the 2nd, rain fell at intervals—heavily for an hour in the forenoon and still more heavily in the afternoon—the total measurement was ·322 inch.

Generally favourable weather prevailed during the week ended Saturday, the 9th, which was signalised by a cold snap of some intensity on the Continent and also in England, Ireland and Scotland entirely escaping it owing to the prevalence of S.W. and W. winds and cloudy skies. On Sunday an anticyclone lay off the W. of Ireland, where the barometer stood above 30·4 inches, and a V-shaped depression was found over the North Sea. The latter system had caused a considerable fall of rain during the previous 24 hours, first in Ireland and later on in England. The weather after this remained very fine until Tuesday evening, when rain fell in Ireland, as a large tongue of high atmospheric pressure formed over the Baltic, North Sea, and England, steepening gradients for S. and S.W. winds in Ireland and Scotland, and causing a cold N.E. wind to spring up all over Central Europe. Calms, fogs, and low temperatures set in over England, and a continuous fall of snow occurred at Munich, freezing weather being felt all over Germany, Switzerland, and France. On Thursday night the thermometer fell to 28° in the shade in Paris and at Belfort. Towards the close of the week a new area of high atmospheric pressure was in course of formation off the N.W. of Ireland, in which country temperature was giving way while the weather became fine and dry although cloudy. The mean height of the barometer in Dublin was 30·311 inches, pressure ranging between 30·474 inches at 9 a.m. of Monday (wind, W.N.W.) and 30·070 inches at 3 p.m. of Friday (wind, W.N.W.). The corrected mean temperature was 51·7°. The mean dry bulb reading at 9 a.m. and 9 p.m. was 50·7°. On Monday the screened thermometers fell to 41·1°; on Thursday they rose to 59·2°. The rainfall was ·187 inch on three days, ·140 inch being measured on Tuesday. The prevalent winds were W.N.W. and S.W.

Very unsettled weather prevailed throughout the week ended Saturday, the 16th. Until Wednesday the British Islands were affected by a large depression, which was found near the Shetlands on Sunday morning and moved slowly thence to Scandinavia, becoming deeper and spreading out southwards as it travelled. By 8 a.m. of Tuesday the barometer had fallen to 29·07 inches at Christiansund, on the W. coast of Norway, near the centre of the depression. At first this system caused strong westerly winds, clouds and some rain in most districts, temperature being rather high on Sunday (Dublin, Loughborough and Leith recording 60°, Aberdeen 63°). As the disturbance moved eastward, however, the wind drew into N.W. and N. and the air became much colder, raw and searching. On Monday night the thermometer in the screen fell to 31° at Parsonstown, and 35° in Dublin. Hail, sleet, and snow fell in Scotland on Tuesday. On Wednesday morning, while the cold N.W. winds of the northern depression were still blowing in that country, a new depression appeared off the S.W. of Ireland. Under its influence the wind shifted to E., S.E. or S. over the southern half of the United Kingdom, and temperature rose considerably, while rain fell heavily in Ireland, and in the N.W. and N.E. of England, from time to time. Scotland came within the sphere of the southwestern depression on Friday, so that an easterly gale and heavy rainfall occurred. Lightning was seen on Friday night. During the last three days abrupt changes from foul to fair weather took place, particularly in and near Dublin. In this city the mean height of the barometer was 29·709 inches, the range being from 30·069 inches at 9 a.m. of Sunday (wind, W.) to 29·074 inches at 9 a.m. of Saturday (wind, S.). The corrected mean temperature was 49·0°. The mean dry bulb temperature at 9 a.m. and 9 p.m. was 49·3°. On Sunday the screened thermometers rose to 59·9°, on Tuesday they fell to 36·1°. The rainfall was 1·316 inches on six days, ·437 inch being measured on Thursday. The prevalent winds were W.N.W. and S.S.E.

Opening with unsettled, very rough weather, the week ended Saturday, the 23rd, proved extremely fine and quiet. The change was brought about by the spreading northwestwards and northwards of an anticyclone, which was already forming over Central Europe early on Sunday. At that time a large and deep depression was travelling in a northerly direction across Ireland, where a heavy southerly gale was blowing while rain fell in large quantities—the measurements at 8 a.m. were ·77 inch at Parsonstown, 1·40 inches at Roche's Point, and 1·43 inches at Valentia Island. In Dublin the gale continued to blow for several hours, but the weather became bright and warm at 11.30 a.m., the shade thermometer rising to 62·9°. Gradients for S.W. winds were still rather steep but decreasing, so that the weather became fine and warm as the day advanced. On Tuesday anticyclonic conditions were fully established, the wind died down and calms and fogs became prevalent, especially at night. In the daytime there was less sunshine, so that the diurnal range of temperature was unusually large. On Thursday the screened thermometer at Nairn, in the N.E. of Scotland, rose to 66°, while it fell to 32° during the ensuing night—a range of 34° within a few hours. From Thursday evening to the close of the week easterly and south-easterly breezes prevailed, and clouds increased on Saturday from S.E. At this time the barometer was falling decidedly in the south. In Dublin the mean atmospheric pressure equalled 30·215 inches, the range being from 29·409 inches at 9 a.m. of Sunday (wind, S. by W., blowing a gale), to 30·561 inches at 9 a.m. of Thursday (wind, W., light). The corrected mean temperature was 52·1°. The mean dry bulb reading at 9 a.m. and 9 p.m. was 50·0°. On Sunday the screened thermometers rose to 65·9°; on Thursday they fell to 38·1°. Rain fell on Sunday to the amount of ·163 inch. The prevalent winds were at first S.W., then E.S.E.

Generally favourable weather was experienced in the week ended Saturday, the 30th. In the London district, however, rain fell on Monday and Tuesday, and fog and gloom were very prevalent until Friday, which was bright and very warm. In Dublin conditions were at first much finer, and summerlike warmth was enjoyed on Wednesday, Thursday, and Friday. Saturday, on the contrary, proved dull, damp, and rainy as well as foggy at times. An anticyclone, of which mention was made in last week's report, held its position over the south of Scandinavia, Denmark, and Germany, but depressions appeared to be passing northwards across the Atlantic outside the West of Ireland after Monday. This distribution of atmospheric pressure caused strong southerly winds and warmth in Ireland. On Thursday night a strong southerly gale blew at Belmullet. On Saturday the barometer rose in Ireland, equalising pressure, so that calm, foggy, and finally cooler weather set in. The change was accompanied by a fall of rain. In Dublin the corrected mean height of the barometer was 30·116 inches, pressure ranging between 30·243 inches at 9 a.m. of Sunday (wind, E.), and 29·903 inches at 9 p.m. of Friday (wind, S.S.E.). The corrected mean temperature was 54·9°. The mean dry bulb reading at 9 a.m. and 9 p.m. was 53·6°. On Tuesday the screened thermometers fell to 43·2°, on Thursday they rose to 66·5°. The rainfall was ·178 inch on three days, ·091 inch being measured on Saturday. The prevailing winds were E. and S.S.E. A solar halo was seen on Thursday. The mean temperature was about the same as that of the week ended Saturday, September 4, 1897.

Sunday, the 31st, was very fine and genial.

The rainfall in Dublin during the ten months ending October 31st amounted to 24·081 inches on 170 days, compared with 13·366 inches on 123 days during the same period in 1887 (the dry year), 23·716 inches on 146 days in 1893, 22·032 inches on 158 days in 1896, and a twenty-five years' average of 22·648 inches on 160·4 days.

At Knockdolian, Greystones, Co. Wicklow, the rainfall in October amounted to 3·180 inches on 13 days. Of this quantity ·800 inch fell on the 14th, and ·480 on the 16th. The rainfall at Greystones in October, 1889, was no less than 6·323 inches on 22 days, or more than 11 times as great as the fall in October, 1890, when only ·600 inch fell on 13 days. From January 1st, 1897, up to October 31st, rain fell at Knockdolian on 171 days to the total amount of 32·720 inches. In 1892, the rainfall of the corresponding ten months was 27·133 inches on 140 days; in 1893, 17·601 inches on 133 days; in 1894, 31·221 inches on 154 days; in 1895, 24·270 inches on 131 days; and in 1896, 27·637 inches on 137 days.

At Clonsevin, Killiney, Co. Dublin, the rainfall in October was 2·280 inches on 11 days, compared with ·710 inch on 14 days in 1893, 6·460 inches on 17 days in 1894, 2·650 inches on 14 days in 1895, 4·290 inches on 21 days in 1896, and a twelve years' average (1885-1896) of 3·388 inches on 16·2 days. On the 14th, ·87 inch fell. Since January 1, 1897, 28·10 inches of rain have fallen at this station on 169 days.

At the National Hospital for Consumption, Newcastle, Co. Wicklow, the rainfall in October was 3·176 inches on 13 days. Of this quantity ·970 inch was recorded on the 14th, and ·650 inch on the 16th. The highest temperature in the screen was 62·0° on the 2nd; the lowest was 37·8 on the 18th. At this climatological station the rainfall from January 1 to October 31, inclusive, amounted to 30·684 inches on 157 days.

NOVEMBER.—A dull, mild, foggy month on the whole, but winter burst upon the N.W. of Europe in a violent storm on the 28th and 29th, the barometer falling to 28·45 inches at Fanö, in Denmark, on the morning of the latter day. In Dublin the mean temperature of the entire month was nearly 4° above the average, and that of the week ended Saturday, the 13th, was 54·1°.

In Dublin the arithmetical mean temperature (48·6°) was decidedly above the average (44·7°); the mean dry bulb readings at 9 a.m. and 9 p.m. were 47·6°. In the thirty-two years ending with 1896, November was coldest in 1878 (M. T. = 38·2°), and in 1870 (M. T. = 42·8°), warmest in 1881 (M. T. = 50·3°).

The mean height of the barometer was 30·137 inches, or 0·267 inch above the corrected average value for November—namely, 29·860 inches. The mercury rose to 30·634 inches at 9 p.m. of the 10th, and fell to 29·311 inches at 3 p.m. of the 28th. The observed range of atmospheric pressure was, therefore, 1·323 inches.

The mean temperature deduced from daily readings of the dry bulb thermometer at 9 a.m. and 9 p.m. was 47·8°, or 3·7° below the value for October, and 5·5° below that for September, 1897. The arithmetical mean of the maximal and minimal readings was 48·6°, compared with a twenty-five years' average of 44·7°. On the 12th the thermometer in the screen rose to 60·9°—wind, S.W.; on the 18th the temperature fell to 34·0°—wind, N.N.W. The minimum on the grass was 31·0°, also on the 18th.

The rainfall was 3·422 inches, distributed over 14 days—the rainfall was much above, while the rainy days were considerably below the average. The average rainfall for November in the twenty-five years, 1865-89, inclusive, was 2·632 inches, and the average number of rainy days was 17·0. In 1888, 6·632 inches fell on 26 days. On the other hand, the rainfall in 1896 was only ·664 inch on 9 days. In 1893, 3·648 inches fell on 21 days.

High winds were noted on 11 days, but attained the force of a gale on only one occasion—the 28th. The atmosphere was more or less foggy in Dublin on the 1st, 2nd, 5th, 10th, 11th, 18th, 21st, 22nd, 23rd, 24th, and 25th. Lunar halos were seen on the 8th and 30th. Hail, sleet, and snow fell in the gale of the 28th, when also lightning was seen.

Throughout the period ended Saturday, the 6th, anticyclonic conditions held in the British Isles and Central Europe. Only in the far North on the one hand and over the Peninsula on the other was there a cyclonic distribution of atmospheric pressure with its attendant high winds and rains. The centre of highest barometer lay over the North Sea, the South of Scandinavia and Denmark until Friday morning, when a very shallow depression formed over the North Sea. During the earlier days of the week the air was soft and genial, there was a good deal of bright sunshine, and high temperatures for the time of year were recorded in the daytime. After Wednesday the sky remained densely clouded, and the diurnal range of temperature was small, the thermometer scarcely rising by day, and not falling much by night, owing to the interference with terrestrial radiation by the clouds. During the whole period the area of greatest cold was located over Germany, France and Belgium, and in that region the isotherm of 30° F. was found at 8 a.m. on and after Wednesday. At the hour named on Thursday the thermometer read 47° at Bodö in Norway (lat. 67° N.) and only 25° in Paris and 27° at Munich. In Dublin the barometer rose to 30·396 inches at 9 a.m. of

Saturday (wind, E.S.E.), having fallen to 30·214 inches at 9 p.m. of Wednesday (wind, S.E.). The extreme range of pressure, therefore, amounted to only 0·181 inch. On Tuesday the screened thermometers rose to 59·3°; on Wednesday they fell to 42·0°. Easterly winds prevailed throughout, except for a few hours on Friday, when there was a light north-westerly breeze. The period was rainless.

The week ended Saturday, the 13th, proved the warmest week which had been observed in November for very many years. It was, however, by no means so dry as its predecessor, for rain fell freely on Monday and Friday in Dublin; while much heavier downpours were reported from the S., centre, and W. of Ireland on several days. Until Friday the centre of a large anticyclone was found overlying the south of Scandinavia, Denmark and the Baltic. At 8 a.m. of Wednesday, the barometer read 30·81 inches at Wisby in the Baltic. A tendency to cyclonic conditions was observed on Sunday in Ireland, and local irregularities in atmospheric pressure over Western Europe generally on Monday and Tuesday caused considerable rainfalls in many places. The isobars afterwards became regular and anticyclonic with improving weather, but on and after Thursday the barometer gave way quickly in the west, so that squally southerly winds, high temperatures, and rainfalls took the place of the quiet, dull and foggy weather which had been prevalent, particularly in England. In that country a sudden chill occurred on Wednesday night, the screened thermometers falling to 29° at Cambridge, 32° at Loughborough, and 33° in London and at Oxford. An equally sudden rise of temperature took place early on Friday morning. This last-named day turned out phenomenally warm in Ireland and in Scotland, the thermometer rising to 61° in Dublin and to 60° at Leith and Nairn. In Dublin the mean atmospheric pressure was 29·928 inches, the barometer rising to 30·312 inches at 9 p.m. of Tuesday (wind, S.S.E.) and falling to 29·380 inches at 9 p.m. of Friday (wind, S.W.). The mean temperature was 53·1°. The mean dry bulb reading at 9 a.m. and 9 p.m. was 53·5°. The screened thermometers fell to 46·9° on Monday and rose to 60·9° on Friday. The rainfall was 1·335 inches on five days, ·937 inch being registered on Saturday. The prevailing winds were S.S.E. and S.W.

Mildness was again the predominant characteristic of the weather of the week ended Saturday the 20th, but a "cold snap" of some intensity occurred on Sunday and Monday. A rainstorm prevailed on the east coast of Ireland during the opening hours of the week. It was brought about in connection with a sudden reversal of wind direction and temperature conditions in Scotland and Ireland. At 8 a.m. of Sunday a long curved tongue of low atmospheric pressure stretched from the Bay of Biscay up the Irish Sea and across the South of Scotland to the S.W. of Norway. To the eastward of this curious trough of low barometer, southerly winds and high temperatures prevailed; to the westward, northerly winds, cold rains and sleet, and low temperatures. By 8 a.m. of Monday the thermometer was down to 34° in Dublin, where a reading of 61° had been recorded three days before. A ridge of high pressure now passed quickly eastward across the British Isles, leaving gradients for S.W. winds re-established on Tuesday and Wednesday. Both these days proved dull and rainy in Dublin. On Thursday morning a lofty stratum of cirriform cloud cleared off from S.W. and a fine, bright day ensued. Fine, mild weather afterwards lasted to the end, anticyclonic conditions being fully established on Saturday. At 6 p.m. of Friday the barometer was down to 28·73 inches at Bodö in Norway. In Dublin the mean height of the barometer was 30·127 inches, atmospheric pressure ranging from 29·522 inches at 9 a.m. of Sunday (wind, N.N.W.) to 30·634 inches at 9 p.m. of Saturday (wind, E.). The mean temperature was 47·7°. The mean of the dry bulb readings at 9 a.m. and 9 p.m. was 47·0°. The screened thermometers fell to 34·0° on Monday and rose to 57·7° on Wednesday. The rainfall amounted to ·696 inch on three days, ·583 inch being recorded on Wednesday. The prevailing winds were N.W. and W.S.W.

Dull, foggy, changeable weather ruled during the greater part of the week ended Saturday, the 27th. The general distribution of atmospheric pressure was cyclonic in the North of Europe, anticyclonic in the British Isles and Central Europe. During the first two days a large depression swept eastward across Scandinavia, while the isobar of 30·7 inches lay over the S.E. of England and Germany. On Tuesday the barometer rose in the former, but fell in the latter regions, thus tending to equalise pressure. Much fog prevailed from time to time, and the changes in temperature were sudden and extreme, the thermometer falling fast when the sky cleared, only to rise again as clouds formed. On Thursday morning a shallow depression was found over the mouth of the English Channel. This disturbance caused gloomy wet weather in Ireland, South Wales, and the extreme S.W. of England. A very heavy fall of rain occurred also in Brittany and at Biarritz. The depression quickly filled up, and the anticyclone formed again over England and Germany, so that a rapid decrease of temperature occurred on Thursday night, frost of some intensity being reported on Friday morning, even in London (28°). Meanwhile sudden alternations in pressure off the N.W. of Ireland caused squally S.W. winds, high temperatures and rains in this country. In Dublin the mean height of the barometer was 30·365 inches, pressure ranging from 30·640 inches at 9 p.m. of Sunday (wind, calm) to 29·919 inches at 9 a.m. of Saturday (wind, W.N.W.). The mean temperature was 46·1°. The mean dry bulb reading at 9 a.m. and 9 p.m. was 45·4°. The screened thermometers fell to 37·9° on Tuesday and rose to 54·8° in the early morning hours of Saturday. The rainfall was ·320 inch on three days, ·236 inch being registered on Friday.

The last three days of the month were rough, cold, and unsettled. On Sunday, the 28th, a deep depression travelled southeastwards across the North Sea, becoming deeper as it approached the Continent. It caused violent gales in Ireland at first, and on the 29th in England and on the Continent. Temperature fell fast as the wind veered towards N. in the rear of the storm centre. Lightning and squalls of hail, sleet, and snow were reported from many places on the night of Sunday, the 28th. The 29th was fine and bright in Dublin, but a heavy rainfall (·610 inch) occurred on the 30th.

The rainfall in Dublin during the eleven months ending November 30th amounted to 27·[illegible] inches on 193 days, compared with 15·378 inches on 141 days during the same period in 1887, 27·[illegible] inches on 187 days in 1895, 25·710 inches on 174 days in 1896, and a twenty-five years' average of 25·[illegible] inches on 177·[illegible] days.

At Rockdollan, Greystones, Co. Wicklow, the rainfall in November was 5·[illegible] inches, distributed over 17 days. Of this quantity 2·[illegible] inches fell on the 12th. From January 1st, 1897, up to November 30th, rain fell at that station on 188 days, and to the total amount of 3[illegible]·183 inches. The corresponding figures for 1893 were 19·[illegible] inches on 150 days; for 1894, 33·710 inches on 168 days; for 1895, 31·713 inches on 181 days; and for 1896, 25·[illegible] inches on 147 days.

At Cloneevin, Killiney, Co. Dublin, 2·[illegible] inches of rain fell on 15 days, compared with a twelve years' average of 2·[illegible] inches on 17·0 days. The maximal fall in 24 hours was 1·[illegible] inches on the 12th. Since January 1st, 1897, 2[illegible]·[illegible] inches of rain have fallen at this station on 18[illegible] days. The corresponding figures for 1896 were [illegible]·81 inches on 150 days.

At the National Hospital for Consumption, Newcastle, Co. Wicklow, the rainfall in November was 4·[illegible] inches, distributed over 15 days. The maximal fall in 24 hours was 1·[illegible] inches on the 12th. Since January 1, 1897, the rainfall at Newcastle has amounted to 33·[illegible] inches on 172 days. On November 5th the screened thermometers at the National Hospital rose to 5[illegible]°, on the 16th they fell to 24°.

DECEMBER.—A changeable, open month, with frequent but not heavy rain in the Dublin district, where also frost was almost entirely absent. In the Co. Wicklow, the rainfall was more than double that registered in Dublin, in consequence of the prevailing southerly and south-westerly winds, the rains borne by which were intercepted by the Dublin mountains.

As in December, 1896, large and deep depressions passed north-eastwards across the British Islands during the closing period of the month. Just before this a local frost of great intensity prevailed in the N.E. of Scotland, becoming general in great Britain in the days before Christmas.

In Dublin the arithmetical mean temperature (4[illegible]·[illegible]°) was much above the average (41·[illegible]°); the mean dry bulb readings at 9 a.m. and 9 p.m. were 44·1°. In the thirty-two years ending with 1896, December was coldest in 1878 (M. T. = 3[illegible]·[illegible]°), and in 1874 (M. T. = 3[illegible]·[illegible]°), and warmest, in 1865 (M. T. = 4[illegible]·[illegible]°). In 1896, the M. T. was 41·[illegible]°.

The mean height of the barometer was 29·731 inches, or 0·12[illegible] inch below the corrected average value for December—namely, 29·[illegible] inches. The mercury rose to 30·[illegible] inches at 9 p.m. of the 31st, and fell to 28·710 inches at 11 p.m. of the 22nd. The observed range of atmospheric pressure was therefore, 1·8[illegible] inches.

The mean temperature deduced from daily readings of the dry bulb thermometer at 9 a.m. and 9 p.m. was 44·1°, or 3·7° below the value for November. Using the formula, *Mean Temp. = Min. +* (max.—min × ·[illegible]), the value was 4[illegible]·[illegible]°, or [illegible]·[illegible]° above the average mean temperature for December, calculated in the same way, in the twenty-five years, 1865–89, inclusive (41·5°). The arithmetical mean of the maximal and minimal readings was 44·[illegible]°, compared with a twenty-five years' average of 41·[illegible]°. On the 27th the thermometer in the screen rose to 57·[illegible]°—wind, S.W.; on the 3rd the temperature fell to 3[illegible]·[illegible]°—wind, W. The minimum on the grass was [illegible]·[illegible]°, on the 22nd. There was no frost in the screen, but 1[illegible] days of frost on the grass were recorded.

The rainfall was 1·[illegible] inches, distributed over as many as 1[illegible] days. The average rainfall for December in the twenty-five years, 1865–89, was 2·[illegible] inches, and the average number of rainy days was 16·[illegible]. The rainfall, therefore, was below, while the rainy days were above the average. In 1876 the rainfall in December was very large—7·[illegible] inches on [illegible] days. In 1872, [illegible]·[illegible] inches fell on as many as 24 days; and in 18[illegible] (which was otherwise a fine and dry year), 4·7[illegible] inches fell on as many as [illegible] days. On the other hand, in 1867, only ·771 inch was measured on 13 days; in 18[illegible], only ·74[illegible] inch on 10 days; in 18[illegible], only ·7[illegible] inch on 10 days; and in 1871, only ·7[illegible] inch on 15 days; in 18[illegible], 1·[illegible] inches of rain fell on [illegible] days.

A lunar halo was seen on the [illegible]th. High winds were noted on 15 days, and attained the force of a gale on 7 occasions—the 7th, 8th, 1[illegible]th, 1[illegible]th, [illegible]th, 2[illegible]th, and [illegible]th. The atmosphere was more or less foggy in Dublin on the 2nd, 4th, 5th, 1[illegible]th, 17th, 1[illegible]th, and 22nd. Snow and sleet fell on the [illegible]th. Hail fell on the 14th. Aurora borealis was seen on the 11th. Lightning occurred on the evening of the 14th.

Wednesday, the 1st, was very fine, bright, and bracing in Dublin; but heavy showers of cold rain and hail fell along the coast south of the city, borne in by a strong northerly wind. Thunderstorms occurred at Scilly and Jersey. Thursday was also fine in Ireland generally, sharp frost occurring inland in the morning, a minimum of 2[illegible]° in the shade being reported from Parsonstown. In the S.E. of England a fresh to strong northerly gale prevailed, accompanied by hail showers. On Friday the barometer gave way in the N.W., so that clouds increased, the wind shifted to S.W., temperature rose, and rain set in. Saturday was dull, damp and at times foggy. The rainfall of this period (1st–4th) was ·[illegible] inch on [illegible] days.

A cyclonic distribution of atmospheric pressure, and very changeable, unsettled weather held throughout the week ended Saturday, the 11th. Sunday broke damp and foggy in Dublin, but shortly before noon a warm S.W. wind swept away the fog and caused a brisk rise of temperature to 5[illegible]°. Rain set in at 3 p.m. and lasted throughout the evening. Monday was changeable, rain falling in the forenoon, but it became finer, brighter, and colder later on. On Tuesday a large and ultimately deep depression approached the West of Scotland from the Atlantic. It caused squally S.W. to W. winds and gales with rain. At first temperature rose considerably—to 5[illegible]° at several British stations and to 5[illegible]·[illegible]° in Dublin. At 8 a.m. on Wednesday the barometer ranged from 2[illegible]·[illegible] inches at Sumburgh Head (Shetlands) to 30·47 inches at Lisbon and 30·[illegible] inches in the Azores. In the evening a new depression reached the N. of Scotland from the westward, the barometer sinking to 28·95 inches at Stornoway and 28·89 inches at Wick. This northern depression began to fill up on Thursday, but another disturbance came in over Ireland from W.S.W., so that on Friday the barometer fell to 28·80 inches at Malin Head and to 28·87 inches even in Dublin. Sudden and extreme changes in weather and temperature accompanied these oscillations of atmospheric pressure. On Saturday the barometer rose fast and the weather proved fine, quiet and bright. In Dublin the mean pressure of the air was 29·532 inches, the range being from 30·027 inches at 9 p.m. of Monday (wind, W.) to 28·870 inches at 8.30 p.m. of Friday (wind, W.S.W.). The corrected mean temperature was 43·7°. The mean dry bulb reading at 9 a.m. and 9 p.m. was 41·9°. On Tuesday the screened thermometers rose to 56·6°; on Wednesday they fell to 30·8°. The rainfall was ·487 inch on six days, ·251 inch being measured on Sunday. Westerly (S.W. to W.N.W.) winds were predominant. A perfect lunar halo was seen on Thursday night; a band of auroral light at 6 p.m. of Saturday.

Quiet and calm at its beginning and close, the week ended Saturday, the 18th, was generally unsettled, with frequent rain and squally southerly and south-westerly winds. It blew a fresh gale for several hours on Thursday. Sunday was a beautiful day—fair and calm. There was some fog in the forenoon, but the afternoon was brilliant. This "pet" day was due to the presence of a secondary depression at the mouth of the English Channel. The effect of this was to equalise barometric pressure in Ireland—at 8 a.m. the extreme limit of variation was only ·11 inch, the barometer marking 29·47 inches at Roche's Point, Cork, and 29·36 inches at Malin Head, Donegal. Hence clear skies and light winds or calms prevailed. Near Dublin the grass was white with hoar frost throughout the day. Between Sunday and Friday the weather was determined by a series of large and deep atmospheric depressions which travelled northwards or north-eastwards across the Atlantic, Ireland and Scotland. These caused rains, high temperatures and squalls. On Thursday the shade thermometers rose to 58° at Loughborough and Oxford, 57° in Dublin and at York, Liverpool and Cambridge, and 56° in London. An anticyclone now surged westward from the Continent, causing calm, foggy and colder weather on Friday evening. Saturday was a day of gloom and fog which became wet in the afternoon. In Dublin the mean height of the barometer was 29·554 inches, pressure ranging from 28·963 inches at 9 p.m. of Monday (wind, S.S.E.) to 30·254 inches at 9 p.m. of Saturday (wind, E.). The corrected mean temperature was 46·3°. The mean dry bulb reading at 9 a.m. and 9 p.m. was 46·1°. On Sunday the screened thermometers fell to 33·1°, on Thursday they rose to 56·5°. Rain fell on 4 days to the amount of ·403 inch, ·173 inch being registered on Wednesday. The wind was chiefly southerly and south-westerly.

Throughout the week ended Saturday, the 25th, the British Islands were within the sphere of an anticyclone, the centre of which lay off the east of Scotland at first and was afterwards found over Belgium, Holland, and North Germany. At 8 a.m. of Wednesday the barometer stood at 30·74 inches at Berlin. Owing to this distribution of pressure the wind in Ireland was at first easterly, then south-easterly, and finally southerly or south-westerly. Early on Christmas morning there was a strong and squally southerly wind, and on this day the thermometer rose to 53·6° in the screen in Dublin. As a rule temperature was much higher in Ireland than in Great Britain, where sharp frosts were felt after Monday. In the N.E. of Scotland an area of intense cold became developed on Sunday—at Nairn the thermometer fell in the screen to 21° on Sunday, 18° on Monday, 17° on Tuesday, 14° on Wednesday, and 15° on Thursday. At the same station the highest shade temperature on Monday was 29°; on Tuesday and Wednesday it was 31°. At 8 a.m. of Thursday the thermometer read 21° at Nairn, 22° at Loughborough and Cambridge, 23° at Aberdeen, 24° at Oxford, 25° at Wick, 26° at York, and 27° in London. The isotherm of 30° embraced nearly the whole of Great Britain, while Ireland was from 10° to 15° warmer. Christmas Day proved exceptionally mild and fine. In Dublin the mean height of the barometer was 30·343 inches, pressure ranging between 30·555 inches at 9 p.m. of Tuesday (wind, E.S.E.) and 30·122 inches at 9 p.m. of Friday (wind, S.S.E.). The corrected mean temperature was 43·6°. The mean dry bulb reading at 9 a.m. and 9 p.m. was 43·2°. The screened thermometers fell to 33·5 on Wednesday, and rose to 53·6° on Saturday. The only precipitation was a slight shower on the afternoon of Christmas Day. It yielded no measurable rainfall in the gauge.

Very unsettled and often tempestuous was the weather of the closing period of 1897. Temperature, although very unsteady, ranged high—the mean being some 7° above the average. The weather characteristics just mentioned were brought about by the passage north-eastwards across the Atlantic and British Isles of a succession of large and unusually deep atmospheric depressions. In one of these the barometer sank to 28·19 inches at Stornoway, in the Hebrides, at 8 p.m. of Thursday. On Sunday morning, December 26, frost still held in the midland counties, and the E. and S.E. of England. But in Ireland and Scotland the thermometer stood between 45° and 53°. Next morning it had risen from 16° to 19° in England also, and frost had disappeared from all parts of the British Isles. Southerly and south-westerly gales prevailed on all coasts between Monday and Friday, and rain fell abundantly. Thunder, lightning, and hail were reported from Roche's Point, Co. Cork, on Thursday evening. On Friday afternoon the barometer rose briskly in Ireland, and the wind veered to N.W. with a falling temperature. In Dublin the barometer ranged between 30·061 inches at 9 a.m. of Sunday (wind, S.S.W.) and 28·740 inches at 11 p.m. of Wednesday (wind S.S.E.). On Monday the screened thermometers rose to 57·6°, on Tuesday they fell to 42·4°. S.S.W. winds predominated. Rain fell daily to the total amount of ·446 inch, ·159 being measured on Tuesday.

The rainfall in Dublin during 1897 amounted to 29·346 inches on 211 days, compared with 25·901 inches on 194 days in 1896, 31·249 inches on 194 days in 1895, 29·281 inches on 209 days in 1894, only 20·493 inches on 174 days in 1893, 25·644 inches on 190 days in 1892, 27·820 inches on 184 days in 1891, 27·362 inches on 200 days in 1890, 27·279 inches on 193 days in 1889, 23·679 inches on 190 days in 1888, 16·601 inches on 160 days in 1887, and a twenty-five years' average of 27·696 inches on 194·6 days.

B.

At Knockdolian, Greystones, Co. Wicklow, the rainfall in December, 1897, was 4·700 inches, distributed over 21 days. Of this quantity ·990 inch fell on the 27th. From January 1st to December 31st, 1897, rain fell at Knockdolian on 210 days, to the total amount of 41·935 inches. The corresponding figures for 1893 were 22·525 inches on 170 days; for 1894, 29·776 inches on 186 days; for 1895, 25·185 inches on 174 days; and for 1896, 28·102 inches on 189 days.

Mr. Robert O'Brien Furlong, B.A., writes:—

The rainfall at Cloonevin, Killiney, in December, 1897, was 2·47 inches on 20 days. The maximal fall in 24 hours was ·48 inch on the 13th. The average December rainfall of the eleven years 1885-95, was 2·490 inches on 17 days. The maximal daily fall was 1·43 inches on September 1st. The rainfall for 1897, though less than that of 1895 (—33·66 inches) or 1894 (—32·64 inches) was largely in excess of the average of the eleven years, 1885-95, viz., 25·66 inches. Rain measuring ·01 inch and upwards fell on 204 days, the average of eleven years being 179. There was a period of absolute drought from May 8th to May 24th. On June 11th there was a thunderstorm. Snow fell on January 14th (lightly) 18th (lying to the 19th) and 22nd (lying to the 29th); also on April 1st.

At the National Hospital for Consumption, Newcastle, Co. Wicklow, rain fell during December on 20 days to the amount of 3·685 inches, ·491 inch being measured on the 15th. At this climatological station the highest temperature in the shade was 55·4° on the 7th, the lowest was 33·0° on the 3rd. The rainfall for the year 1897 was 40·193 inches on 194 days, the maximal daily fall having been 2·208 inches on September 1st.

RAINFALL IN 1897,

At 40, Fitzwilliam-square, West, Dublin.

Rain Gauge:—Diameter of funnel, 8 in. Height of top—Above ground, 1 ft. 6 in.; above sea level, 50 ft.

Month.	Total Depth.	Greatest Fall in 24 hours.		Number of Days on which ·01 or more fell.	Month.	Total Depth.	Greatest Fall in 24 hours.		Number of Days on which ·01 or more fell.
	Inches.	Depth.	Date.			Inches.	Depth.	Date.	
January, . .	[illegible]	[illegible]	[illegible]	17	August, . .	[illegible]	[illegible]	[illegible]	[illegible]
February, . .	[illegible]	[illegible]	[illegible]	[illegible]	September, . .	[illegible]	[illegible]	[illegible]	[illegible]
March, . .	[illegible]	[illegible]	[illegible]	[illegible]	October, . .	[illegible]	[illegible]	[illegible]	[illegible]
April, . .	[illegible]	[illegible]	[illegible]	[illegible]	November, . .	[illegible]	[illegible]	[illegible]	[illegible]
May, . .	[illegible]	[illegible]	[illegible]	[illegible]	December, . .	[illegible]	[illegible]	[illegible]	[illegible]
June, . .	[illegible]	[illegible]	[illegible]	[illegible]					
July, . .	[illegible]	[illegible]	[illegible]	[illegible]	Total, . .	[illegible]	—	—	[illegible]

The rainfall was 1·648 inches in excess of the average annual measurement of the twenty-five years, 1865-89, inclusive—viz., 27·696 inches.

It is to be remembered that the rainfall in 1887 was very exceptionally small—18·601 inches, the only approach to this measurement in Dublin being in 1870, when only 20·859 inches fell, in 1884, when the measurement was 20·467 inches, and in 1893 with its rainfall of 20·493 inches. In seven of the twenty-five years in question the rainfall was less than 25 inches.

The scanty rainfall in 1887 was in marked contrast to the abundant downpour in 1886 when 33·264 inches—or as nearly as possible double the fall of 1887—fell on 230 days. Only twice since these records commenced has the rainfall in Dublin exceeded that of 1886—namely, in 1872, when 35·566 inches fell on 234 days, and in 1880, when 34·512 inches were measured on, however, only 185 days.

In 1897 there were 211 rainy days, or days upon which not less than ·005 inch of rain (five-thousandths of an inch) was measured. This was much above the average number of rainy days, which was 194·2 in the twenty-five years, 1865–89, inclusive. In 1868 and 1887—the warm, dry years of recent times—the rainy days were only 160, and in 1870 they were only 165.

The rainfall in 24 hours, from 9 a.m. to 9 a.m., exceeded one inch on two occasions in 1892—viz., May 25th (1·056 inches) and August 16th (1·210 inches). On no occasion in 1893 did one inch of rain fall on a given day in Dublin. In 1894 falls of upwards of an inch of rain in 24 hours were recorded on four occasions, viz., May 15th (1·320 inches); July 24th (1·660 inches); August 25th (1·260 inches); and October 22nd (1·042 inches). In 1895, 1·070 inches fell on January 12th; 1·014 inches on July 24th; and 1·258 inches on July 25th. In 1896, 1·365 inches fell on July 8th; 2·020 inches on July 24th; and 1·355 inches on December 6th; in 1897, 1·166 inches fell on September, 1st.

Included in the 211 rainy days in 1897 are 15 on which snow or sleet fell, and 20 on which there was hail. In January hail was observed on 5 days, in March on 7 days, in April on 5 days, in May on 6 days, in July on 2 days, in September on 3 days, in October, November, and December on 1 day. Snow or sleet fell on 5 days in January, on 6 days in March, on 2 days in April, and also on 1 day in both November and December. Thunder occurred on 6 occasions during the year—once in January, March, June, and July, and twice in August. Lightning was also seen on two occasions in March, and once in June, October, November, and December.

The rainfall in the first six months was 12·930 inches, on 115 days. The rainfall exceeded 3 inches in June (3·257), August (3·786), and November (3·423). In May it was only 1·139 inches on 14 days.

The rainfall was distributed as follows:—7·089 inches fell on 57 days in the first quarter, 6·881 inches on 56 days in the second, 9·021 inches on 59 days in the third, 7·378 inches on 46 days in the fourth and last quarter.

Aurora borealis was observed on December 11th. More or less fog prevailed on 64 occasions—9 in January, 7 in February, 3 in March, 1 in April and May, 7 in June, 3 in July, 1 in August, 6 in September, 9 in October, 11 in November, and 7 in December. High winds were noted on 163 days—19 in January, 7 in February, 19 in March, 16 in April, 13 in May, 7 in June, 9 in July, 16 in August, 11 in September, 9 in October, 11 in November, and 15 in December. The high winds amounted to gales (force 7 or upwards according to the Beaufort scale) on 39 occasions—4 in January, 5 in February, 9 in March, 2 in April, 1 in May, 2 in June, 1 in July, 3 in August, 1 in September, 3 in October, 1 in November, and 7 in December.

Abstract of Meteorological Observations taken at Dublin (40 Fitzwilliam-square, West), during the Year [illegible].

Month.	Abs. Max.	Date.	Abs. Min.	Date.	Mean Daily Max.	Mean Daily Min.	Rainfall.	Rainy Days.	Mean Height of Barometer.	Highest Pressure.	Date.	Lowest Pressure.	Date.	Prevailing Winds.
	°		°		°	°	Ins.		Ins.	Ins.		Ins.		
January,	[illegible]	[illegible]	[illegible]	[illegible]	[illegible]	[illegible]	[illegible]	[illegible]	[illegible]	[illegible]	[illegible]	[illegible]	[illegible]	[illegible]
February,	[illegible]	[illegible]	[illegible]	[illegible]	[illegible]	[illegible]	[illegible]	[illegible]	[illegible]	[illegible]	[illegible]	[illegible]	[illegible]	[illegible]
March,	[illegible]	[illegible]	[illegible]	[illegible]	[illegible]	[illegible]	[illegible]	[illegible]	[illegible]	[illegible]	[illegible]	[illegible]	[illegible]	[illegible]
April,	[illegible]	[illegible]	[illegible]	[illegible]	[illegible]	[illegible]	[illegible]	[illegible]	[illegible]	[illegible]	[illegible]	[illegible]	[illegible]	[illegible]
May,	[illegible]	[illegible]	[illegible]	[illegible]	[illegible]	[illegible]	[illegible]	[illegible]	[illegible]	[illegible]	[illegible]	[illegible]	[illegible]	[illegible]
June,	[illegible]	[illegible]	[illegible]	[illegible]	[illegible]	[illegible]	[illegible]	[illegible]	[illegible]	[illegible]	[illegible]	[illegible]	[illegible]	[illegible]
July,	[illegible]	[illegible]	[illegible]	[illegible]	[illegible]	[illegible]	[illegible]	[illegible]	[illegible]	[illegible]	[illegible]	[illegible]	[illegible]	[illegible]
August,	[illegible]	[illegible]	[illegible]	[illegible]	[illegible]	[illegible]	[illegible]	[illegible]	[illegible]	[illegible]	[illegible]	[illegible]	[illegible]	[illegible]
September,	[illegible]	[illegible]	[illegible]	[illegible]	[illegible]	[illegible]	[illegible]	[illegible]	[illegible]	[illegible]	[illegible]	[illegible]	[illegible]	[illegible]
October,	[illegible]	[illegible]	[illegible]	[illegible]	[illegible]	[illegible]	[illegible]	[illegible]	[illegible]	[illegible]	[illegible]	[illegible]	[illegible]	[illegible]
November,	[illegible]	[illegible]	[illegible]	[illegible]	[illegible]	[illegible]	[illegible]	[illegible]	[illegible]	[illegible]	[illegible]	[illegible]	[illegible]	[illegible]
December,	[illegible]	[illegible]	[illegible]	[illegible]	[illegible]	[illegible]	[illegible]	[illegible]	[illegible]	[illegible]	[illegible]	[illegible]	[illegible]	[illegible]
Extremes, Totals, and Means.	[illegible]	[illegible]	[illegible]	[illegible]	[illegible]	[illegible]	[illegible]	[illegible]	[illegible]	[illegible]	[illegible]	[illegible]	[illegible]	[illegible]

Table showing the Temperature of the Air in Dublin in the Twenty-one Years 1877–1897, and the Average Temperature for the Twenty Years 1877 to 1896, inclusive, as recorded by Dr. J. W. Moore.

Years.	January.	February.	March.	April.	May.	June.	July.	August.	September.	October.	November.	December.	Year.
1877, . . .	[illegible]	[illegible]	[illegible]	[illegible]	[illegible]	[illegible]	[illegible]	[illegible]	[illegible]	[illegible]	[illegible]	[illegible]	[illegible]
1878, . . .	[illegible]	[illegible]	[illegible]	[illegible]	[illegible]	[illegible]	[illegible]	[illegible]	[illegible]	[illegible]	[illegible]	[illegible]	[illegible]
1879, . . .	[illegible]	[illegible]	[illegible]	[illegible]	[illegible]	[illegible]	[illegible]	[illegible]	[illegible]	[illegible]	[illegible]	[illegible]	[illegible]
1880, . . .	[illegible]	[illegible]	[illegible]	[illegible]	[illegible]	[illegible]	[illegible]	[illegible]	[illegible]	[illegible]	[illegible]	[illegible]	[illegible]
1881, . . .	[illegible]	[illegible]	[illegible]	[illegible]	[illegible]	[illegible]	[illegible]	[illegible]	[illegible]	[illegible]	[illegible]	[illegible]	[illegible]
1882, . . .	[illegible]	[illegible]	[illegible]	[illegible]	[illegible]	[illegible]	[illegible]	[illegible]	[illegible]	[illegible]	[illegible]	[illegible]	[illegible]
1883, . . .	[illegible]	[illegible]	[illegible]	[illegible]	[illegible]	[illegible]	[illegible]	[illegible]	[illegible]	[illegible]	[illegible]	[illegible]	[illegible]
1884, . . .	[illegible]	[illegible]	[illegible]	[illegible]	[illegible]	[illegible]	[illegible]	[illegible]	[illegible]	[illegible]	[illegible]	[illegible]	[illegible]
1885, . . .	[illegible]	[illegible]	[illegible]	[illegible]	[illegible]	[illegible]	[illegible]	[illegible]	[illegible]	[illegible]	[illegible]	[illegible]	[illegible]
1886, . . .	[illegible]	[illegible]	[illegible]	[illegible]	[illegible]	[illegible]	[illegible]	[illegible]	[illegible]	[illegible]	[illegible]	[illegible]	[illegible]
1887, . . .	[illegible]	[illegible]	[illegible]	[illegible]	[illegible]	[illegible]	[illegible]	[illegible]	[illegible]	[illegible]	[illegible]	[illegible]	[illegible]
1888, . . .	[illegible]	[illegible]	[illegible]	[illegible]	[illegible]	[illegible]	[illegible]	[illegible]	[illegible]	[illegible]	[illegible]	[illegible]	[illegible]
1889, . . .	[illegible]	[illegible]	[illegible]	[illegible]	[illegible]	[illegible]	[illegible]	[illegible]	[illegible]	[illegible]	[illegible]	[illegible]	[illegible]
1890, . . .	[illegible]	[illegible]	[illegible]	[illegible]	[illegible]	[illegible]	[illegible]	[illegible]	[illegible]	[illegible]	[illegible]	[illegible]	[illegible]
1891, . . .	[illegible]	[illegible]	[illegible]	[illegible]	[illegible]	[illegible]	[illegible]	[illegible]	[illegible]	[illegible]	[illegible]	[illegible]	[illegible]
1892, . . .	[illegible]	[illegible]	[illegible]	[illegible]	[illegible]	[illegible]	[illegible]	[illegible]	[illegible]	[illegible]	[illegible]	[illegible]	[illegible]
1893, . . .	[illegible]	[illegible]	[illegible]	[illegible]	[illegible]	[illegible]	[illegible]	[illegible]	[illegible]	[illegible]	[illegible]	[illegible]	[illegible]
1894, . . .	[illegible]	[illegible]	[illegible]	[illegible]	[illegible]	[illegible]	[illegible]	[illegible]	[illegible]	[illegible]	[illegible]	[illegible]	[illegible]
1895, . . .	[illegible]	[illegible]	[illegible]	[illegible]	[illegible]	[illegible]	[illegible]	[illegible]	[illegible]	[illegible]	[illegible]	[illegible]	[illegible]
1896, . . .	[illegible]	[illegible]	[illegible]	[illegible]	[illegible]	[illegible]	[illegible]	[illegible]	[illegible]	[illegible]	[illegible]	[illegible]	[illegible]
Average, .	[illegible]	[illegible]	[illegible]	[illegible]	[illegible]	[illegible]	[illegible]	[illegible]	[illegible]	[illegible]	[illegible]	[illegible]	[illegible]
1897, . . .	[illegible]	[illegible]	[illegible]	[illegible]	[illegible]	[illegible]	[illegible]	[illegible]	[illegible]	[illegible]	[illegible]	[illegible]	[illegible]

Dublin Castle,

20th May, 1898.

Sir,

I have to acknowledge the receipt of your Letter of the 19th instant, forwarding, for submission to His Excellency the Lord Lieutenant, the Agricultural Statistics of Ireland, with detailed Report on Agriculture for the year 1897.

I am,

Sir,

Your obedient Servant,

D. HARREL.

The Registrar-General,

Charlemont House,

Rutland Square.

www.ingramcontent.com/pod-product-compliance
Lightning Source LLC
Chambersburg PA
CBHW031440280326
41927CB00038B/1269
* 9 7 8 3 7 4 2 8 1 1 0 0 4 *